Camino Ignaciano

Walking the Ignatian Way in Northern Spain

The Bradt Trekking Guide

Murray Stewart

edition
1

First edition published January 2022
Bradt Guides Ltd
31a High Street, Chesham, Buckinghamshire, HP5 1BW, England
www.bradtguides.com
Print edition published in the USA by The Globe Pequot Press Inc,
PO Box 480, Guilford, Connecticut 06437-0480

Text copyright © 2022 Murray Stewart
Maps copyright © 2022 Bradt Guides Ltd; includes map data © OpenStreetMap contributors
Photographs copyright © 2022 Individual photographers (see below)
Project Manager: Laura Pidgley

The author and publisher have made every effort to ensure the accuracy of the information in this book at the time of going to press. However, they cannot accept any responsibility for any loss, injury or inconvenience resulting from the use of information contained in this guide. All rights reserved. No part of this publication may be reproduced, stored in a retrieval system, or transmitted in any form or by any means, electronic, mechanical, photocopying, recording or otherwise without the prior consent of the publisher.

ISBN: 9781784778125

British Library Cataloguing in Publication Data
A catalogue record for this book is available from the British Library

Photographs Basquetour (BT); Consell Comarcal del Bages: Carles Fortuny (CF/CCDB), Gerard Franquesa (GF/CCDB); Fresco Tours (FT); Jessica Johnson (JJ); Lleida Tourism: Iolanda Sebe (IS/LT); Manresa Turisme: Mercè Rial (MR/MT), Toni Galera (TG/MT); Shutterstock: aaltair (a/S), Arrietaphoto (A/S), ABB Photo (AP/S), Basotxerri (B/S), Cavan-images (C/S), David Marin Foto (DMF/S), ESCOCIA (E/S), Jorge Anastacio (JA/S), Joan Bautista (JB/S), Jesus Giraldo Gutierrez (JGG/S), maratr (m/S), Marcos Campos (MC/S), Myroslava Bozhko (MB/S), Matyas Rehak (MR/S), Miguel Angel Foto (MAF/S), nito (n/S), Oskar Calero (OC/S), Pascal De Munck (PDM/S), Santi Rodriguez (SR/S), thsulemani (t/S); Murray Stewart (MS); SuperStock (SS); Wikimedia Commons: Francis Raher (FR/WC)

Front cover Montserrat Monastery (MB/S)
Back cover Aizkorri-Aratz Natural Park (BT)
Title page Álava (BT); The Sanctuary of Loyola (BT); The jagged peaks of Montserrat (JJ)
Part openers Page 1: An information panel on Stage 4 (BT); Page 51: the Valle de Arana (BT)

Maps David McCutcheon FBCart.S

Typeset by Ian Spick, Bradt Guides
Production managed by Zenith Media; printed in the UK
Digital conversion by www.dataworks.co.in

AUTHOR

As well as being the award-winning author of Bradt's Basque Country and Navarre, **Murray Stewart** has impressive credentials as a long-distance walker. He has covered no fewer than four of the famous Camino de Santiago routes across France and Spain, as well as following the steps of fellow Scot Robert Louis Stevenson and completing the Chemin Stevenson trail in the Cevennes mountains in France. His wanderings have spawned publication of various magazine articles.

COVID-19

Please note that research for this guide was carried out during the Covid-19 pandemic. Because of the impact of the crisis on tourism, some businesses or services listed in the text may no longer operate. We will post any information we have about these on **w** bradtguides.com/updates. And we'd of course be grateful for any updates you can send us during your own travels, which we will add to that page for the benefit of future travellers.

ABOUT THIS GUIDE

MAPS You can walk the Camino Ignaciano using only the maps included. Extra maps are not required. The author has walked the entirety of the route, though there are a couple of variants which have not been walked – they are mentioned in the text, but not detailed on the maps as there is no particular reason to recommend them. The official route is currently being extended to reach Barcelona, but these two stages are not yet fully waymarked and thus not covered by this book.

Scale The scale of each map is 1:50,000.

Orientation All maps in this guide are oriented page north, ie: north is at the top of the page.

Symbols A key to the symbols used on the maps is on page vii. Symbols are given next to towns and villages marked, indicating the availability of transport, accommodation, restaurants, banks and pharmacies. City maps for Logroño, Zaragoza, Lleida and Manresa show more specifically where these facilities are found; in smaller towns and villages these facilities are easy to locate. Where symbols are next to those towns/villages which are *not* at the end of a day's stage, then those facilities are not described in the text.

HEIGHTS AND DISTANCES Elevations are given in metres (m) and distances in kilometres (km). Elevation profiles are given only for stages with significant ascent, descent or both.

TIMINGS The introduction to each stage gives the estimated walking hours required, assuming a walking speed of 4km/h. This does not include time for a meal or other stops.

GRADING Each stage is graded as easy/moderate/difficult, but this is not a hardcore hike and everything is relative. Any specific difficulties are highlighted in the stage's introduction.

TRUE RIGHT/LEFT All references to which side (bank) of a river you're on are given as true right/left, that is they refer to the right/left bank as seen **when facing downstream**.

LANDLINE AND MOBILE NUMBERS Landlines in Spain comprise a nine-digit number beginning with a 9. Mobile-phone numbers are also nine digits but begin with a 6. The international telephone code prefix for Spain is +34.

Acknowledgements

A few people have been instrumental in turning this book from an idea into a reality. As ever when my travel writing takes me to northern Spain, Itziar Herrán Ocharan is an indispensable 'Señora Fixit' when sorting out logistics and acting as the human catalyst who simply makes things happen that otherwise would not. A big thank you must also go to the tourist boards in the five Autonomous Communities through which the Camino Ignaciano passes: Euskadi (Basque Country), La Rioja, Navarre, Aragón and Catalonia. The support of all five was very welcome.

Special thanks must be given to individuals from those organisations who have been especially helpful: Iker Urcelay, Oihana Aranbarri Arrizabalaga, Anna Carrera Torner and Beatriz Nubiola de Palacio, Paula Carrión Jurado, José María Martinez Ruiz and Ana Beroiz Beorlegui. I am very grateful also to Carlos Zaldívar Ezquerro, who provided excellent contributions on fauna, and in particular to Padre Josep Lluis Iriberri, sj, who as a Jesuit and Director of the Camino Ignaciano Pilgrims' Office has kindly contributed text on the role of the Society of Jesus in the modern world. He has been the driving force in the development of the Camino Ignaciano, for which all those who walk this route should be eternally grateful. The timely encouragement of my dear friend, David Elexgaray, was instrumental in me initiating this project. Sadly, David passed away in 2021. Rest in peace.

A very heartfelt vote of gratitude has to go to Tati Gamboa and his two donkeys, Gaspar and Roque. Not only did these three hardy characters accompany me over the Basque Mountains for four of the stages – all of us being looked after by Zoilo the dog – but they captured the hearts of my friends and contacts. This allowed me to use the adventure to raise funds for The Royal Marsden Cancer Charity, a very worthy cause. Everyone, it seems, loves donkeys.

I must also wholeheartedly thank all at Bradt who, in difficult times, have shown great support for this project. Finally, as ever, a big hug to Sara, for her patience and encouragement.

Contents

Introduction ix

PART ONE: GENERAL INFORMATION 1
Chapter 1 Background Information 2
Geography 2
Geology..3
Climate 4
Flora and fauna 5
History of the Jesuits 12
Language.. 18

Chapter 2 Practical Information 19
The Camino Ignaciano – a summary.. 19
The five Autonomous Communities of the Camino Ignaciano 20
When to walk the Camino Ignaciano 27
Highlights 29
Tourist information and tour operators 31
Red tape 32
Getting there and away 34
Public transport 35
Accommodation 36
Eating and drinking 38
Money 40
Budgeting... 41
Communications.. 41
Public holidays and festivals 42
Travelling with kids.. 42
Maps and apps 42
Trail markings... 43
Packing light for the Camino Ignaciano... 44
Safety along the Camino Ignaciano 49

PART TWO: THE OFFICIAL STAGES OF THE CAMINO IGNACIANO ... 51

Gateway town: Loyola ... 53
Stage 1: Loyola–Zumarraga ... 58
Stage 2: Zumarraga–Arantzazu ... 65
Stage 3: Arantzazu–Araia ... 73
Stage 4: Araia–Alda ... 78
Stage 5: Alda–Genevilla ... 85
Stage 6: Genevilla–Laguardia ... 90
Stage 7: Laguardia–Navarrete ... 98
Stage 8: Navarrete–Logroño ... 105
Stage 9: Logroño–Alcanadre ... 113
Stage 10: Alcanadre–Calahorra ... 121
Stage 11: Calahorra–Alfaro ... 127
Stage 12: Alfaro–Tudela ... 135
Stage 13: Tudela–Gallur ... 143
Stage 14: Gallur–Alagón ... 153
Stage 15: Alagón–Zaragoza ... 160
Stage 16: Zaragoza–Fuentes de Ebro ... 171
Stage 17: Fuentes de Ebro–Venta de Santa Lucia ... 178
Stage 18: Venta de Santa Lucia–Bujaraloz ... 185
Stage 19: Bujaraloz–Candasnos ... 189
Stage 20: Candasnos–Fraga ... 194
Stage 21: Fraga–Lleida (Lerida) ... 200
Stage 22: Lleida–El Palau d'Anglesola ... 211
Stage 23: El Palau d'Anglesola–Verdú ... 217
Stage 24: Verdú–Cervera ... 224
Stage 25: Cervera–Igualada ... 229
Stage 26: Igualada–Montserrat ... 238
Stage 27: Montserrat–Manresa ... 246

Appendix 1 Language ... 259
Appendix 2 Further Information ... 268

Index ... 269

FEEDBACK REQUEST AND UPDATES WEBSITE

At Bradt Guides we're aware that guidebooks start to go out of date on the day they're published – and that you, our readers, are out there in the field doing research of your own. You'll find out before us when a fine new family-run hotel opens or a favourite restaurant changes hands and goes downhill. So why not write and tell us about your experiences? Contact us on ↘ 01753 893444 or **e** info@bradtguides.com. We will forward emails to the author who may post updates on the Bradt website at **w** bradtguides. com/updates. Alternatively, you can add a review of the book to **w** bradtguides.com or Amazon, or share your adventures with us on social media: @BradtGuides.

KEY TO SYMBOLS

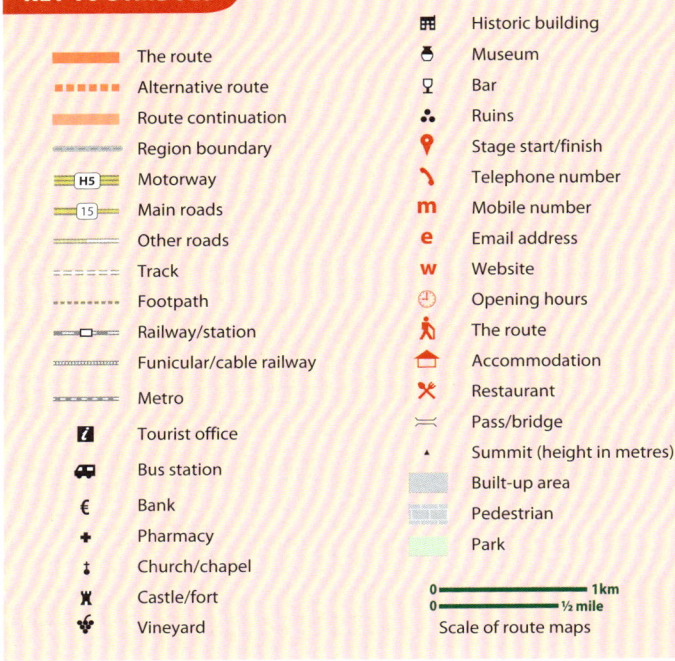

	The route
	Alternative route
	Route continuation
	Region boundary
H5	Motorway
15	Main roads
	Other roads
	Track
	Footpath
	Railway/station
	Funicular/cable railway
	Metro
i	Tourist office
🚌	Bus station
€	Bank
✚	Pharmacy
✝	Church/chapel
♕	Castle/fort
🍇	Vineyard
🏛	Historic building
	Museum
♀	Bar
∴	Ruins
📍	Stage start/finish
↘	Telephone number
m	Mobile number
e	Email address
w	Website
🕐	Opening hours
🚶	The route
🏠	Accommodation
✖	Restaurant
≍	Pass/bridge
▲	Summit (height in metres)
	Built-up area
	Pedestrian
	Park

```
0 ═══════════ 1km
0 ═══════════ ½ mile
```
Scale of route maps

Introduction

'The world reveals itself to those who travel on foot'

Werner Herzog

Celebrating a 500th anniversary is something very special, and that is exactly what this book does. In 1522, Ignatius of Loyola set out on foot from the Basque Country and made his way first south then eastwards to end up in Manresa in Catalonia. His intended destination was Jerusalem via Barcelona, but concerns that year about the plague meant he went into 'lockdown' (sound familiar?) without leaving Spanish shores. In Manresa, he lived in a cave for many months and wrote his *Spiritual Exercises*, before continuing his trip to Jerusalem in 1523. He returned to Spain to study, then a few years later, while studying in Paris, he and a few close companions communed together to deepen their faith. In 1539 they founded the Society of Jesus, which would soon become the Jesuits. To spread the word, Ignatius's companions were dispersed throughout Europe with his inspirational instruction: '*Ite, inflammate omnia*' or 'Go, set the world on fire'. In subsequent centuries, the Jesuit influence spread across the globe, and that original instruction remains current to this day.

While I am neither a Jesuit, nor religious, my previous wanderings on some of the more famous pilgrimage routes to Santiago de Compostela in northwest Spain, together with my many months spent in three of the provinces through which the Camino Ignaciano crosses, drew my curiosity to this relatively unwalked pilgrimage. I have a deep affection for Spain and each step of this 675km walk has increased my love for it.

In the strictest meaning of the word, this is certainly a pilgrimage for the Jesuits who choose to walk it. But for me, the Ignaciano offers the chance to get close to the parts of Spain that package holidays and city breaks never reach. No stuffed donkeys, flamenco dancers or sangria here, nor any Gaudi, *ramblas* or beach-filled *costas*; rather a slow crossing through rich landscapes and profound cultures. Spain is made up of many identities, which at times seem tied together by an increasingly fraying thread. Bookending this walk are two of the most strident of those identities, the Basque and the Catalan, while in between your footsteps will traverse the regions of La Rioja, Navarre and Aragón, less high-profile but with their own history, quirks and attractions. And identities, too, albeit less forcefully expressed.

These are beautiful and intriguing lands to visit by any means, but their rewards are surely best discovered on foot. Slow travel of this sort allows maximum interaction with local people, minimum adverse impact on the environment and endless freedom to liberate your headspace away from the pressures and humdrum of the everyday. When all you have to worry about is where to eat and spend the night, it is amazing how much time you find to contemplate the more profound, interesting and bizarre. There are few decisions to make when it comes to walking: you put one foot in front of the other, then repeat the sequence. No thought is required, so your brain can turn to more interesting matters.

Along the way, there are many tangible attractions. Your Ignatian walk will begin at the impressive sanctuary in Loyola and will then propel you up into the rugged Basque Mountains, down through rolling vineyards to handsome Laguardia, and on to wine-soaked La Rioja and lively Logroño with its bar-filled Calle del Laurel. From there, you will track eastwards following the flow of the mighty River Ebro, the Iberian Peninsula's second longest. This watery companion will stay with you into Aragón and beyond Zaragoza, the country's fifth-most-populous city with its incredible El Pilar Basilica. And then a huge contrast, as you depart the metropolis to traverse the desolate, barren desert of Los Monegros. Who knew that Spain possessed open spaces such as this?

Continuing east into Catalonia, the landscape changes once more as you can begin to focus on your final destination. After enjoying kilometres of traversing flatlands and following riverways, you will be challenged by slightly hillier terrain as you reach stunning Montserrat – the astonishing saw-toothed mountain – and its equally impressive monastery, before descending finally to the Ignatian city of Manresa and your journey's end. Unlike Ignatius, there's no need for you to spend any time in caves on arrival, or indeed in caves anywhere on your route. Municipal hostels and inexpensive hotels can accommodate you along the way.

Whether you are doing the route in a continuous, four-week stint, or picking a shorter section for a week or so, maybe intending to return at a later date to complete the route over several visits, the most important thing to remember is to enjoy your walk. Admire the scenery, embrace the cultures and bond with the welcoming peoples of Spain as you progress. By the time you reach Manresa, you will be physically fitter. Whether or not the walk also enriches you spiritually, it will surely do so culturally. It may change your perspective, or your life, or both or neither. But you'll never forget or regret that you've done it.

Part One

GENERAL INFORMATION

1

Background Information

GEOGRAPHY

At 676km, the Camino Ignaciano inevitably encounters a variety of terrains on its predominantly eastwards journey across northern Spain.

The route begins in the Basque Country's province of Gipuzkoa, at Loyola sanctuary in the valley of the Urola, one of several south–north-running rivers that characterise the rugged Basque interior. Rushing to eventually discharge themselves into the Cantabrian Sea, these fast-flowing waters explain why watermills have operated here for hundreds of years, and why industry is a perhaps somewhat surprising occupant of these otherwise rural landscapes. The Urola originates in the Aizkorri-Aratz massif which, at its highest point, stretches upwards to around 1,500m, forming part of the so-called Basque coastal ranges. Once across these mountains, walkers will find themselves on the flat but elevated Llanada Alavesa plain, which is also home to the Basque Country's administrative capital, the much-underrated city of Vitoria-Gasteiz.

Moving further south, the camino rises again to cross the Sierra Cantabria range towards its eastern end before descending into the rolling wine-growing country of Rioja Alavesa. As the route continues south, it has its first meeting with the Ebro, the longest river situated entirely in Spain, which neatly divides the Basque Country from La Rioja.

From this point onwards, the Cantabrian Sea is no longer relevant, as all the rivers you meet eventually find their exit in the distant Mediterranean Sea to the east. Having originated in Cantabria, hundreds of kilometres to the west of the Camino Ignaciano starting point, the Ebro gathers the waters of many, many lesser subsidiaries along the way, as they join both from the Pyrenees to the north and the Sistema Ibérico mountain ranges to the south. From cradle to grave, the Ebro is 930km in length and is a comforting companion for Ignatian walkers on over 220km of the journey, taking them through La Rioja, Navarre and into Aragón before departing just beyond the city of Zaragoza.

From the bustle of this large city to the solitude of the semi-desert – that of Los Monegros, the 'Black Mountains' – the landscape again changes rapidly and dramatically. Although the route spends only one day traversing its southern extremity, the desolate landscape of Los Monegros may leave a profound impression on those who pass through. From Aragón, the camino continues to Catalonia (Catalunya), where the landscape becomes more mountainous on its approach to Montserrat's incredible jagged peaks. From there, the final stage is predominantly characterised by a gentle descent to the city of Manresa.

GEOLOGY

When the then-island of Iberia collided heavily with mainland Europe around 15 billion years ago, the terrain crumpled, being forced upwards and creating not only the high Pyrenees but also the lower, craggy ranges which characterise a significant part of northern Spain. Among these is the massif of the Aizkorri-Aratz, near where the Camino Ignaciano begins its journey. This range is defined by its sharp limestone ridges, towering above the grassy valleys of the Urbia. The erosion of the limestone over the years has resulted in caves, ridges and other phenomena, among which the Arantzazu ravine and the tunnel of San Adrián are perhaps the most impressive.

To the south of these Basque Mountains lies the Llanada Alavesa, or plains of Álava, temporarily flatter lands that are again interrupted on the camino's southwards journey by the twin ranges of the Sierra Cantabria and Sierra de Toloño. These mountains form the eastern portion of a lengthy *cordillera* which begins way westwards in Cantabria itself. The route then encounters the wine-growing, largely calcareous clay lands of Rioja Alavesa, which stretch south to the River Ebro, and continue beyond into La Rioja itself. As the route then turns eastwards, the soil becomes silty and alluvial along the Ebro's banks.

Formed about the same time as the Pyrenees, the basin of the Ebro during the Paleogene period was connected to both the Mediterranean and the Bay of Biscay. Thus, it was a true marine basin, but in later times (Eocene period) none of its drainage reached either sea. With the arrival of the Ebro waters, much erosion of the basin fill took place, leaving spectacular oddities such as Montserrat (page 238). Despite the current agricultural activity along the Ebro Valley, the topsoils here are actually thin, with the subsoil being poor and sometimes calcareous. Sedimentary carbonate rocks are a feature. East of Zaragoza, the Los Monegros semi-desert is barren, though intrepid locals have in recent times made heavy inroads into it for cultivation. Often this terrain is referred to as 'badlands' and, while this might conjure up images of lawless cowboys in spaghetti westerns, in fact such a description refers to the dry terrain, with little vegetation, where soft, sedimentary rock and clay-rich soil have been largely swept away by the characteristic high winds and sporadic rainfall.

Once in Catalonia, the terrain again becomes more rugged. Montserrat is an impressive sight, a 10km-long, saw-toothed range of pinkish conglomerate and limestone, which has resisted erosion over the past 10 billion years much better than its now low-lying surroundings. Visitors can easily spot the distinctive sedimentary layers in these imposing mountains. Towards the end of the Mesozoic era, the area at the base of Monserrat was a huge river delta. The high presence of carbonate in the range is responsible for the many caves and karst towers that can be found here. Montserrat's isolation, together with the fact it rises directly from the River Llobregat, gives the impression that its peaks are much higher than they are: the loftiest summit, St Jerome (Sant Jeroni in Catalan) is in fact a fairly modest 1,236m.

CLIMATE

The **Basque** coastal areas are both cool and damp, with most months experiencing some rain. Strong winds encourage surfing, for which the Basque shores are renowned. Heading away from the coast, the land rises and the winter climate becomes colder up in the hills while inland summers are a bit warmer than the seaside towns and villages. Snow on the Basque Mountains is not unusual in the winter months at any time between November and April. In the southern Basque territories, the climate turns more continental and noticeably drier.

In the Ebro Valley, where the Basque Country meets **La Rioja**, the annual rainfall – at around 500mm – is half that experienced on the north coast. The presence of the Basque mountain ranges to the north prevents the Atlantic influence, so autumn and winter are drier. One of the meteorological features here, also affecting Navarre and Aragón, is the dry and sometimes cold El Cierzo wind that can blow at speeds of up to 100km/h. Temperatures in these wine-growing areas can be very hot in summer, with the mercury pushing over 30°C in July and August but plummeting to as low as 2°C in the winter months.

Next on the Ignatian route, **Navarre** is a region of climatic extremes, but the route passes through this Autonomous Community in its southernmost part, far distant from the high Pyrenees. Snow is never an issue for Ignatian pilgrims in Navarre. The Navarrese city of Tudela would expect only around 400mm of rain, and summer temperatures can often soar to 35°C.

For the most part, landlocked **Aragón** experiences a Mediterranean/continental climate: dry with infrequent rainfall. Again, the climatic consequences of the high Pyrenees in the region's northern extremity can be ignored by walkers on this route. The focus instead should be on the Ebro depression, through which the river of the same name flows for a significant part of the route. Surprisingly, perhaps, this is one of Spain's severest climates, with strong winds and temperature extremes.

Moving east into **Catalonia**, the climate of this final Autonomous Community is mainly Mediterranean: plenty of sunshine, hot summers and winters that are mild. But the plethora of mountain ranges and depressions can result in contrasting climatic conditions between neighbouring areas within Catalonia. For example, pre-coastal and coastal mountain ranges protect the region's interior to some extent from the Mediterranean's maritime influence.

For details on the best time of year to walk the Camino Ignaciano, see page 27.

FLORA AND FAUNA

Geographical diversity guarantees a diversity of flora and fauna. What the Camino Ignaciano can offer in this respect results from its route through those high Basque mountains, down to the banks of the River Ebro, to the semi-desert of Los Monegros and up again into the crags of Montserrat. Vigilant birdwatchers will be rewarded, although those preferring animals and reptiles will either be lucky or perhaps leave disappointed.

FLORA Where the Camino Ignaciano begins, at the gateway of the **Basque Country**'s Aizkorri-Aratz Natural Park, you can expect to encounter forests rich in beech and white oak. Pine has been planted for commercial usage and the region's year-round rain and high pasturelands always ensure a pleasantly green background for walkers.

La Rioja is of course bedecked in its glorious vineyards, but it is along the Ebro where we find its most distinctive natural vegetation. The Riojan *sotos del Ebro* (see box, page 134) are compact vestiges of what were previously much larger forest outcrops. Nowadays these small, dense, often isolated tree formations around the town of Alfaro, for example, are composed of species such as white willow (*Salíx alba*), black poplar (*Populus nigra*), white poplar (*Populus alba*) and narrow-leaved ash (*Fraxinus angustifolia*). Among these trees, shrubs can be found: roses (*Rosa* sp.), blackberries (*Rubus* sp.) or common hawthorn (*Crataegus monogyna*). Here too are climbers such as common ivy (*Hedera helix*)

BACKGROUND INFORMATION

▲ The River Ebro is known for its *sotos* MAF/S

and the delightfully named old man's beard (*Clematis vitalba*), but the density of the *sotos* prevents much light from entering and thus hinders grasses from growing. Similar *sotos* can be found as the River Ebro continues to accompany the route as it crosses southern **Navarre**.

The brief time in **Aragón**'s Los Monegros introduces walkers to a different type of landscape with its own distinctive flora. This semi-desert region is said to be home to over 1,000 plant species, despite it being predominantly flat in character and lacking in water. Its continental and arid climate, together with its limestone soils, present challenges to plant species that might otherwise grow here. Ephemeral plants, which can grow during the brief periods of water availability, are well adapted to Los Monegros's singular conditions; the rest of the time, they exist in seed form. Plants that can tolerate excessive salt in the soil are also adapted to this region, as the combination of geology and climate results in intense evaporation and thus significant salt residues.

Once upon a time, it is theorised that much of Los Monegros would have been forested, with Spanish juniper (*Juniperus thurifera*) being the dominant tree species. Humankind has changed that, this easy source of wood proving to be too tempting. Other changes over time have been the increasing cultivation of the area for corn, rice and latterly alfalfa, with water imported into many parts of the region through irrigation. Most of this development has occurred to the north of the Camino Ignaciano route and the introduction of water from outside has brought in uninvited 'non-native' plant species as well as allowing crop cultivation.

FLORA AND FAUNA

SPAIN'S QUICKFIRE MODERNISATION AND THE CONSERVATION FIGHTBACK

In places, Spain has been accelerated rather rudely into the industrial age. While the mountains of the Basque Country and Catalonia are undoubtedly beautiful, these two regions are the country's industrial engine rooms and the Camino Ignaciano cannot escape from some of the scars and ravages that have resulted from modernisation. Only a few decades ago, many Spaniards still lived in caves cut into the hills; now, the default dwelling for most is an apartment contained in a tower block. Many of these were hastily erected in the Franco years, when Spain was rapidly updated – for better or worse – and dragged from backwater into the modern, industrial age. Between 1960 and 1975, the percentage of GDP attributable to agriculture declined from 27% to only 9%; meanwhile steel production multiplied sixfold, cement production fivefold and there was a ninefold increase in export earnings.

That modernisation happened is unarguable, though the debate as to whether it would have happened without the dictator, or whether it might have happened faster, slower, at the same pace or in a different/better/worse fashion really belongs to a different forum than this one. The result is that while the centres of large towns and cities usually retain their sometimes quaint, medieval character, the outskirts of many can be quite abrasive to the eye of the visitor. As much of the Camino Ignaciano coincides with roads and railways, the industrial infrastructure that relies on such transport is never far away, nor is the residential infrastructure that houses those who rely on that industry for a livelihood.

Spain's admission to the European Union in 1986 ushered in flows of welcome funds for roadbuilding and other infrastructure projects. However, recent years have witnessed increased efforts towards conservation and 14% of Spain's landmass is now protected. In addition, the country has over 650 areas of Special Protection, among which are the Aizkorri-Aratz region in the Basque Country and various small pockets along the River Cinca in Aragón and the Segre in Catalonia.

Catalonia enjoys a Mediterranean climate and Montserrat in particular provides a focus for those interested in plant life. Oak is the dominant tree here, but there are claimed to be well over 1,000 plant species on this

BACKGROUND INFORMATION

mountain range alone. In the whole of Catalonia, over 200 tree species have been documented. The yellow weaver's broom (*Spartium junceum*) is loosely regarded as the most emblematic flower of the region, bursting into colour in late spring.

FAUNA *Carlos Zaldívar Ezquerro*

Birds Any avian journey along the Camino Ignaciano naturally begins in Gipuzkoa province in the Basque Country. Despite the ravages of heavy-duty industry wreaked over time on the River Urola and its environs, its waters are still capable of surprising and delighting keen birdwatchers with interesting discoveries. Look out in particular for the white-throated dipper (*Cinclus cinclus*) in the waters of this fast-flowing river as it heads towards the Bay of Biscay.

Once beyond Zumarraga, the route heads into the beautiful Aizkorri-Aratz Natural Park, where among its ancient woods and Atlantic meadows live many central European forest birds. But the park's imposing limestone rocks are where the true highlights lie; common sightings include griffon vultures (*Gyps fulvus*) and Egyptian vultures (*Neophron percnopterus*) [2], the latter also known endearingly as the 'pharoah's chicken' and curious in its habit of smashing opening open other birds' eggs with pebbles. Other interesting residents are the crow-like red-billed chough (*Pyrrhocorax pyrrhocorax*) and the Alpine or yellow-billed chough (*Pyrrhocorax graculus*).

Descending to the plains of Álava province, but still in the Basque Country, the mixed landscape of cultivated fields, woodlands and thorny scrublands is the ideal environment for species such as woodchat shrike (*Lanius senator*) and rock bunting (*Emberiza cia*).

The lagoons to the south of the town of Laguardia are an excellent place to spot a wide variety of aquatic migratory species and may also offer the chance to see a beautiful Western (or Eurasian) marsh harrier (*Circus aeruginosus*). Crossing the River Ebro to enter La Rioja, a prized sighting in the vineyards and rolling hills would be the rather rotund red-legged partridge (*Alectoris rufa*) [3]. Before reaching La Rioja's principal city of Logroño, La Grajera reservoir offers easy sightings of anatidae (ducks, geese and swans) as well as another wetland specialist, the orange-brown bearded reedling (*Panurus biarmicus*).

Beyond Logroño, the path follows the Ebro, with varieties of kite (*Milvus* sp.) and maybe even a booted eagle (*Hieraaetus pennatus*) hovering above. The call of the Eurasian penduline tit (*Remiz pendulinus*) will likely be heard in the river *sotos* (riverside wooded groves; see box, page 134), while the difficult-to-see zitting cisticola or streaked fan-tail warbler (*Cisticola juncidis*) and European bee-eater (*Merops apiaster*)

1 a/S

2 E/S

3 JGG/S

4 JGG/S

5 m/S

6 PDM/S

9

BACKGROUND INFORMATION

might be spotted in among the cultivated fields. The scrubland elements of the landscape provide cover for the Thekla's lark (*Galerida theklae*) and various warblers (*Sylvia* sp.), while the Eurasian crag martin (*Ptyonoprogne rupestris*) and blue rock thrush (*Monticola solitarius*) 4 are also visible here. Before departing La Rioja, Alfaro's San Miguel church is the reference point for the emblematic white stork (*Ciconia ciconia*); for more on these elegant birds, see the box on page 128.

Entering Navarre, the landscapes and avian life are similar to La Rioja as the route continues beside the Ebro. A mosaic of river *sotos*, wooded areas, fields, forests and *vegas* (grassy plains) give shelter to many common birds such as the spotless starling (*Sturnus unicolor*), rock sparrow (*Petronia petronia*), Alpine swift (*Tachymarptis melba*) and great spotted cuckoo (*Clamator glandarius*). Beyond Zaragoza, an obligatory stop (though slightly off-route) for avid bird lovers is the Sotos and Galachos del Ebro Natural Reserve to observe a host of migratory species as well as the colony of black-crowned night herons (*Nycticorax nycticorax*) 5.

Shortly after departing the town of Pina de Ebro, the route reaches Los Monegros, the barren 'steppe' with an ecosystem unique in Europe. Among its sparsely vegetated flatlands live great bustard (*Otis tarda*) 6, the little bustard (*Tetrax tetrax*), sandgrouse (*Pterocles* sp.), lesser kestrel (*Falco naumanni*), stone-curlew (*Burhinus oedicnemus*), short-toed snake eagle (*Circaetus gallicus*), red-necked nightjar (*Caprimulgus ruficollis*) and Dupont's lark (*Chersophilus duponti*).

Once in Catalonia, in the protected drylands area of Belianes-Preixana west of Verdú, you might spy the electric blue European roller (*Coracias garrulus*) 1, the only roller to breed in Europe. Also present here is the Calandra lark (*Melanocorypha calandra*).

Just past La Panadella, en route to Igualada, the route skirts the area of Carbasí, a favoured refuge of the northern goshawk (*Accipiter gentilis*). And finally, before reaching the end point in Manresa, the stunning landscape of Muntanya de Montserrat Natural Park gives opportunities – if you're lucky – to spot a tiny wallcreeper (*Tichodroma muraria*), identified by the red markings on its wings, or – at the other end of the size scale – a Bonelli's eagle (*Aquila fasciata*).

Mammals, amphibians and reptiles While many birds are easy to spot on the Camino Ignaciano, the resident **mammals** are, by contrast, more discreet and difficult to observe. Many are nocturnal in their habits and most – with the exception of the rabbit (*Oryctolagus cuniculus*) – will be detected not by actual sightings, but by their footprints, droppings and other traces.

FLORA AND FAUNA

An acorn, almond or gnawed pinecone usually signifies the presence of Eurasian red squirrel (*Sciurus vulgaris*), wood mouse (*Apodemus sylvaticus*), western Mediterranean short-tailed mouse (*Mus spretus*) or even garden dormouse (*Eliomys quercinus*). A trail of small bear-like footprints is normally an indication of a badger (*Meles meles*), while footprints that are elongated, medium-sized and more canine are those of a red fox (*Vulpes vulpes*), the largest of the fox family. Sheep-like footprints could well belong to the elusive wild boar (*Sus scrofa*) or even a roe deer (*Capreolus capreolus*). Forested terrains probably present the best opportunities to see any of these, but it may be a fleeting glimpse – and you will need some luck.

Other species are even harder to spot, due to their extreme scarcity. The European wild cat (*Felis silvestris*) is most likely to be found in forested areas, while the Eurasian beaver (*Castor fiber*) lives along the Ebro in Aragón. The now critically endangered European mink (*Mustela lutreola*) favours forest streams. Finally, although some subspecies of the Iberian ibex (*Capra pyrenaica*), also known as the Spanish wild goat, have become extinct in recent times, reintroductions of other subspecies such as the Gredos ibex have been made in the mountainous Montserrat region.

Easier to spot while walking are **amphibians**. These timid, silent creatures of habit are excitable only in the breeding seasons of spring and autumn, when the ponds and streams along the route provide opportunities to observe some of southwest Europe's endemic species. Among these are the Iberian frog (*Rana iberica*) in the Basque Country, the marbled newt (*Triturus marmoratus*) – which lives in woodlands and ponds – and Perez's frog (*Pelophylax perezi*), also called the Iberian green frog. The last can be seen on many of the stages, and its noisy song may also keep you company while you walk. More difficult to encounter is the Iberian spadefoot toad (*Pelobates cultripes*), which frequently buries itself in the sand for protection.

Reptiles are also quite common on sunny days, given that they bask in the sun to gather the energy before capturing their prey, though they'll likely scarper when they hear footsteps. The route runs through the territories of many species, some present in the rest of Europe but most of which are strictly Mediterranean. Walking through the Basque Country, the most visible reptiles are the common wall lizard (*Podarcis muralis*) and the western green lizard (*Lacerta bilineata*), while in the Ebro Valley wall lizard (*Podarcis liolepis*) or Algerian sand racer (*Psammodromus algirus*) are fairly common. You might also stumble across a non-venomous ladder snake (*Zamenis scalaris*) or a mildly venomous Montpellier snake (*Malpolon monspessulanus*): snakes often seek the warmth of tarmac, so road surfaces provide the best sightings.

BACKGROUND INFORMATION

On warm evenings, common wall gecko (*Tarentola mauritanica*) can be seen climbing on rocks. Finally, the enigmatic landscape of Los Monegros will certainly not disappoint: look for the vivid green of the ocellated (or jewelled) lizard (*Timon lepidus*) or perhaps the super-speedy spiny-footed lizard (*Acanthodactylus erythrurus*).

The biodiversity of the Camino Ignaciano is special and in the correct seasons we will be fascinated by summer flights of butterflies, dragonflies and endless invertebrates. While the highlights are described above, there are many more species to enjoy along the way.

HISTORY OF THE JESUITS

The Society of Jesus, more commonly referred to as the Jesuits, is a religious order which over five centuries has carried out some of the Roman Catholic Church's most effective missionary work. Since Pope Paul III gave them his approval in 1540, they have been hugely influential, particularly in the field of education, enjoying many high points as well as periods of ostracisation and suppression. Headquartered in Rome, they presently operate in over 110 countries.

IGNATIUS OF LOYOLA Ignatius of Loyola was born Iñigo López de Oñaz y Loyola (Ignazio Loiolakoa in the Basque language) in 1491. Although he took his name from a saint (Ennecus), Iñigo's early years were anything but saintly. By the age of 18, Ignatius had put himself into military service with a local duke and proceeded to prove his worth as a soldier by fighting bravely in numerous skirmishes. A swashbuckling dandy, popular with the ladies, his luck and his life would change dramatically in 1521, when a ricocheting cannonball shattered his leg as he fought to defend the city of Pamplona from French soldiers. It was game over for Ignatius's wild, hedonistic lifestyle, and he was carted back to Loyola to recuperate in his family tower-house (*casa-torre*; see box, page 55). Despite several rounds of

▼ Ignatius of Loyola SS

surgery – painful, as there were no anaesthetics in those days – he was left with one leg longer than the other, resulting in a lasting limp.

It was during his enforced stay back at Loyola that Ignatius was reluctantly introduced to religious texts, which replaced the dashing adventure stories he read with relish in his earlier years. The beginnings of a spiritual conversion ensued, his playboy tendencies now supplanted by devotion to God and a desire to follow in the footsteps of the Saints. To further his new-found faith, Ignatius resolved to undertake a pilgrimage to Jerusalem and, in 1522, set off on the first stage, but his trip came to a shuddering halt thanks to an outbreak of the plague in Barcelona, forcing him to hole-up in Manresa for 11 months. He spent much of his time there praying in a nearby cave, and submitting himself to such deprivations and austerities led him only into despair and depression. This formative, often unhappy, time in Manresa convinced him to turn away from the penances that were at that time being wholeheartedly prescribed by other religious orders; to reject the value attributed to monastic silence elsewhere and to instead give proper place to the development of conversations and interactions with others. His time spent in Manresa produced the *Spiritual Exercises*, a kind of 'user manual' for those seeking to get in touch with themselves and God. These writings would later become a cornerstone for the Jesuits, and retreat houses were specifically constructed for novices who spent a month in silence, undertaking the exercises.

It was only in the latter part of 1523 that Ignatius left Manresa and finally set sail for the Holy Land. Years later, in 1534 while studying in Paris, Ignatius and fellow students vowed to visit Jerusalem. Their plans were thwarted by political upheavals, but having reached Italy, they decided to seek papal approval for their proposed religious order: the Society of Jesus. Pope Paul III gave approval to the order in 1540, and a year later Ignatius was elected the first Superior General of the Society.

THE EARLY DAYS Much of the Jesuits' early influence can be attributed to their establishment of schools and indeed education remains central to their organisation today. Already by the time of Ignatius's death in 1556, they had established 30 schools across nearly every country in western Europe except Scandinavia and Britain. Dozens more operated overseas. Schools were for both clerical and lay students, with no levying of fees and thus in theory open to all. The subjects taught were not limited to clerical subjects such as theology and philosophy, but extended to history, drama and literature. The breadth of subjects taught, together with the mix of students, ensured that the Jesuits remained connected to the secular world, rather than separated from it. Another purpose, though not part of their founding constitution, was their opposition to the Reformation and Lutheranism, cemented by the rapid opening of schools in European countries where Protestantism had taken hold.

With their early success came some distrust and hostility. Some of this resulted from their inclusion of Jesus's name in their organisation's title, perceived by some fellow Catholics as arrogant and even blasphemous. The Jesuits' pastoral practices and lack of orthodoxy also attracted criticism from within the Catholic Church, but by 1640 – a century after their foundation – their influence had nevertheless reached its zenith with hundreds of schools established across the globe.

As well as their zeal for education, the Jesuits were equally committed to missionary work and India, Brazil, Japan and parts of Africa had all felt their influence by the time of Ignatius's death in 1556. After all, to 'travel at the drop of a hat' to spread the word was the 'fourth vow' of the Jesuit order – in addition to the three Catholic 'standard' vows of poverty, chastity and obedience. Indeed, the 'propagation of the faith' was one of their stated purposes and in essence this meant missionary work or taking the message right across the globe.

In the following decades, Jesuits extended their reach even further, establishing themselves in Spanish-controlled territories such as Peru and Mexico, and by the late 16th century they had entered China. The Jesuit infrastructure built overseas was impressive, with the costs of the schools in Latin America, for example, being funded by economic activities that stretched from mills, farms and plantations as well as potteries and fabric-making. Libraries, printing presses, hospitals and pharmacies were all part of the mix. Although there were failures as well, with the expulsion of missionaries by Japan in 1614 being a significant early reversal in fortune, this was an exception in the Jesuits' first 100 years of existence.

FLUCTUATING FORTUNES Having flourished initially, the following centuries brought setbacks for the Jesuits and, finally, disaster. Obviously, the Jesuits were opposed by those liberals promoting the Reformation. Being close to various warring 17th-century Catholic monarchs meant that they also fell foul of various ploys to undermine them. An attempt on the life of Henry IV, for example, was attributed to the Jesuits and they were expelled from Paris as a result (though they were soon readmitted); in England, the finger was pointed at Jesuits in connection with the Gunpowder Plot to assassinate James I in 1605.

The 1600s swept in the Age of Enlightenment with its challenges to the supremacy of the Catholic Church. The Jesuits became a target for the Enlightenment's most able spokesmen, with the anti-Catholic sentiment particularly strong in France. Voltaire summed up the mood, signing his letters '*écrasez l'infame*' or 'crush the loathsome thing', referring to the Catholic Church. But there were more problems to follow, as the Jesuits' tolerance of non-Catholic practices in China came under scrutiny amid criticism from Franciscans and others for this perceived 'tainting' of the religion. When the papacy eventually found against the Jesuits on this controversy, Rome's stance angered the Chinese and started a chain of events that eventually signalled the end of Christianity in the country. Meanwhile in South America, the Jesuit settlements known as 'reductions', which offered protection to natives from slave-traders, came under attack, both by way of criticism and actual assault. Their protection of the welfare of slaves was seen by many as a hindrance to colonial expansion and exploitation. Back in Europe, the Jesuits' perceived laxity and worldliness opened them up to vitriol from powerful opponents.

The 18th century brought further disasters as the Jesuits became caught up in the seismic European political upheavals of the time. First, in 1759, the Portuguese king ordered confiscation of Jesuit properties, followed by their expulsion after they were linked to his assassination attempt. Similarly, it was an attempt on the life of Louis XV of France, which began the downward spiral of the Jesuits there. The Society was outlawed in France in 1762 and suppressed by Royal Decree two years later. Then in 1769, Spain took action against them, confiscating their properties and expelling them. Sicily, Parma and then Rome moved against them, too, culminating in their abolition by Pope Clement XIV in 1773.

The results of this almost universal suppression were truly brutal, with 700 of the Jesuit schools forcibly closed or taken over to be converted into secular institutions. Documents were destroyed, books were pulped and artwork confiscated. In Poland and Russia, the esteem in which the Jesuits' schools were held led to them being treated more tolerantly by the respective rulers, but elsewhere it was carnage. Other religious orders suffered in the coming years, as a wider wave of anti-Christian sentiment washed over European cultures.

A NEW START But with turbulent times in Europe, including the pivotal French Revolution, nothing seemed destined for permanency. In 1814, Napoleon was defeated and the monarchy resumed in France. In the restored Europe, favourable once again to monarchies and set firmly – for a while – against republicanism, Pope Pius VII decreed the universal restoration of the Society of Jesus. With only around 600 Jesuits, properties confiscated and with much of their documentation destroyed, they were starting out again from virtually nothing.

BACKGROUND INFORMATION

The 19th century was a period of persistent rebuilding, re-establishing the reputation of their schools, regaining some – but by no means all – of their properties and increasing their numbers. By 1900, this stood at around 15,000. But the century was a game of snakes and ladders, with the volatile political situation resulting in another wave of expulsions by France, Spain and Germany as well as many Latin American countries. On the positive side, the order returned to China in 1842, and many of the Jesuits expelled by this second wave became missionaries instead in Africa and Asia. The United States were also fertile ground in this century, as was the Middle East and Australia.

A PILGRIMAGE FOR THE MODERN AGE

Many dictionaries understandably still centre the definition of 'pilgrimage' firmly around religion. And why not? After all, most major faiths include pilgrimage as an important element. In Islam, the Hajj is one of the five pillars of the religion, an obligation to pilgrimage to Mecca during the devotee's lifetime. In Christianity, the names of pilgrim sites – past and present – are known to all, and still much-visited: Jerusalem, Rome, Canterbury, Lourdes, Santiago de Compostela. For Hindus, sacred books document pilgrimage as far back as 1500BC. But the role of formal religion in many countries has experienced a gradual decline in recent decades. So, is there a place for pilgrimage in the modern, secular Western world, and if so, what does it mean?

An expanded definition might capture 'pilgrimage' as a journey which seeks a new insight about oneself, or about something higher. An element of personal transformation on our journey to Manresa is at least a possibility for us all, and it certainly was for Ignatius way back in 1522. Having walked various camino routes in Spain myself, it seems to me that many fellow walkers are looking for something that is missing in their lives, and there is not necessarily a need to know exactly what is missing when you set out. When I walked from Le Puy-en-Velay to Santiago de Compostela a few years ago, my nine weeks on the road afforded me the headspace to reassess my life. Though not immediate, the consequence of this rare and precious thinking time was my decision to quit a well-paid career and set out into the unknown world of self-employment without any track record in travel writing.

For others I met on that walk, the missing pieces of the jigsaw of life fell more quickly and tangibly into place. An affable Australian I encountered on my journey relocated himself to Germany soon

THE JESUITS TODAY The two World Wars, the post-war dismantling of the previous colonial world structure and the rise of communism all raised important questions for the Jesuit order in the 1900s as to their proper role in the world. Much soul-searching around questions of how to contribute to the alleviation of poverty and hunger took place, though to some this new focus on human rights and justice were viewed as a straying into the political realm and as being too closely aligned with Marxism. One tangible result of the self-review was the creation of the Jesuit Refugee Service in 1980, an organisation that advocates rights for people seeking asylum. Another was the creation of the Cristo Rey

---

afterwards to marry a lady with whom he had shared his route to Santiago. A happy ending, indeed. Others become serial pilgrims, returning year after year to walk the same route, or to choose a different one, perhaps never finding the piece missing from the puzzle of life.

In medieval times, pilgrims were afforded respect for the sacrifice they made in leaving home for what might be months on end. Respected by those they met on the route and respected when they eventually returned home. Part of the joy of being a modern pilgrim remains the experience of being well received by your temporary hosts. In today's Spain, some hotels acknowledge the 'obligation' of hospitality by offering a discount on accommodation, and some pilgrim hostels are on a *donativo* basis, which means you pay what you want – including nothing at all if you genuinely cannot afford it. A Spanish town hall (*ayuntamiento*) will try and find a pilgrim a bed for the night, though it might only be provision of a gym mat in the local sports hall. Restaurants might provide a cut-price pilgrim menu. Taking care of travellers (especially pilgrims) and offering them hospitality as they pass through is also a well-observed tradition in Muslim countries and one that I experienced myself when I visited Syria at the turn of the millennium. I will never forget how Hassan, a complete stranger, spent the whole day showing me his home city of Damascus and how shocked he was when I suggested he might want payment for his day's work.

So following in the 500-year-old footsteps of Ignatius is perhaps an opportunity to achieve something more than just completing a long-distance walk. It's an opportunity to feel special, to embrace the sentiment of being a pilgrim and to enjoy the privileges that come with it. Yes, there is a place for a pilgrimage in the modern world, even for those who are not religious. And it's largely up to you to define what it might mean.

BACKGROUND INFORMATION

network of schools in the United States, focused on education for the economically disadvantaged. From its foundation in 1996, this network now comprises 38 schools. Thirdly, founded in Venezuela and now operational in 21 mainly Latin American countries, the international federation Fe y Alegría promotes a more just world through education, serving 1.5 million students.

Although the number of Jesuits has fallen in recent decades (see box, page 226), the number of Jesuit universities, secondary schools and the 2013 election of a Jesuit as Pope demonstrate that the at-times-difficult historical relationship with the Catholic Church is now in calmer waters. Whatever your view, it is undeniable that the Jesuit flame of influence still burns bright in the 21st century.

LANGUAGE

You may encounter at least three native languages in the course of your walk, if you choose to cover the whole route from Loyola to Manresa. The first six-and-a-half stages traverse the Basque Country, but the chances of meeting anyone who speaks *only* Basque are very slim. Perhaps that is just as well, as Basque is a language that is unrelatable to any others. Even in the region itself, only just over a quarter of the inhabitants actually speak it.

From then on, at least until you get close to Lleida on Stage 21, most of the natives will speak Spanish (Castilian); after that, you will be in Catalonia (Catalonia), but again you are unlikely to encounter anyone who speaks Catalan and nothing else. Both the Basques and Catalans protect their languages fiercely, but they will certainly not expect you to speak to them in their own language. What can be frustrating is that information panels at tourist sites can sometimes be expensively manufactured with only Basque or Catalan text, preventing any visitors – including many Spaniards – from benefiting from their wisdom (see box, page 236).

In the cities along the route, finding an English speaker is never too difficult, especially among young natives. Once you are out in the smaller towns, villages and rural areas, however, you should not expect to be understood if you speak only English. Some knowledge of Spanish is very helpful, therefore, as visitor footfall can be minimal. For a list of Spanish phrases that a walker will require to enable eating, sleeping and dealing with emergencies, see page 259. If you want to endear yourself to the Basques or Catalans, you can learn a few of the greetings given in the boxes on pages 23 and 27, respectively. It is best to consider the Camino Ignaciano as an adventure, and to view the linguistic challenges as part of it.

2

Practical Information

THE CAMINO IGNACIANO – A SUMMARY

Running from the Basque Country to Catalonia, and crossing La Rioja, Navarre and Aragón, the Camino Ignaciano might be justifiably nicknamed the 'Quiet Camino'. Its route traces the journey made in 1522 by Ignatius of Loyola, but to date few have followed in his footsteps. For those who have walked the most overtrodden branches of the much more renowned Camino de Santiago, and perhaps become tired of their near-processional nature, the comparative solitude of the Ignaciano may seem more welcome and more comparable in spirit to a medieval pilgrimage. Of course, things may change, but any increase in the number of walkers is likely to be gradual.

Over mountains, through vineyards, along the banks of the Ebro, across the desert landscape of Los Monegros, in the shadow of the towering crags of Montserrat and finally into the Ignatian city of Manresa, here the pilgrim, the distance walker or the curious Hispanophile will all find attractions and distractions at a pace and with the space to appreciate them.

The route is split into 27 stages, varying from 13km to 40km, and combines rugged rural mountain scenery and manicured vineyards with visits to lesser-frequented cities such as Logroño, Zaragoza, Lleida and finally Manresa. Everyday Spain will accompany you along the way: the Spain of the shepherd, the winemaker, the small-time farmer, the immigrant worker, the lorry driver and the city dweller. You will nod greetings to them and rub shoulders with them over your morning coffee and at mealtimes.

This is not a walk for hardcore hikers, adrenalin junkies or mountaineers, but rather is an adventure accessible to all who enjoy a reasonable level of physical fitness. As a young, lesser-developed camino, the infrastructure here is, at times, thin on the ground. To guarantee a bed for the night, the Ignaciano also demands a bit of careful planning – a

PRACTICAL INFORMATION

> ### TOURING THE CAMINO IGNACIANO BY CAR
>
> If you don't have endless time or energy to spare to walk the Camino Ignaciano, you could simply select some highlights and spend a week enjoying a road trip between Loyola and Manresa. With a car, the distance is under 600km and non-stop the journey would take around 6 hours to cover. Of course, driving it in such a short time would be missing the point, so here's a selection of the attractions you might visit in a week's holiday by car.
>
> An overnight stay in **Loyola** would allow you to visit the sanctuary and birthplace and to absorb as much of the Ignatian story as you like. And if you have time to spare, next-door **Azpeitia** has an excellent railway museum, the Museo Vasco del Ferrocarril (page 57) with plenty of British-built locomotives and the opportunity for a heritage train trip.
>
> **Arantzazu** should be your next stop to visit its imposing sanctuary, of great significance to Basque culture. A half-day there should be enough, then you can retrace your route slightly to loop south and cross the Sierra Cantabria to make **Laguardia** your second overnight stay. Leave yourself the best part of a day to wander the narrow streets of this beautiful, elevated settlement, longer perhaps if you want to enjoy one or more of the several world-class wineries in and around town or take a stroll to the bird-rich lagoons just south of town.
>
> Next, drive south and overnight in **Logroño** city for an evening along its renowned bar street, the Calle del Laurel. Once the head is clear, hit

love of logistics can be a useful quality to possess. Consideration should be given to dividing a few of the official stages, perhaps taking an extra day to complete the longer ones if time allows and suggestions as to how this might be done are provided in the stage descriptions. Building in a few rest days into a four-week schedule is also recommended, allowing you time to enjoy some of the route's highlights in more depth than a single overnight stay might permit (page 29). At the time of writing, two new stages are under development, extending the Camino Ignaciano through to Barcelona.

THE FIVE AUTONOMOUS COMMUNITIES OF THE CAMINO IGNACIANO

PAIS VASCO (THE BASQUE COUNTRY OR EUSKADI IN BASQUE)
Capital city Vitoria-Gasteiz
Population 2.2 million

THE FIVE AUTONOMOUS COMMUNITIES OF THE CAMINO IGNACIANO

the road the following day, heading eastwards for Zaragoza with a lunch stop-off in **Alfaro** to see its famous storks. When in **Zaragoza**, the venue for your fourth night's stay, take time to visit the mighty **El Pilar** basilica and the city's other attractions.

Walkers will be moved by their day trekking across the **Los Monegros** semi-desert, but if you have a car then you can get even more out of a visit to this unusual, desolate landscape by deviating slightly from the Ignatian route and heading north to the **Laguna Sariñena**, rich in birdlife and home to an observatory from which to observe the lake waters. Those seeking a city experience might choose **Lleida** for the next night's stay, while those who prefer small-town Catalonia should push on a bit further to **Verdú** or **Cervera**.

Your penultimate visit should be to spectacular **Montserrat**, an absolute 'must see' and definitely a whole-day affair, maybe with an overnight stay depending on your level of interest in what is one of northern Spain's biggest visitor attractions. **Manresa** is only a half-hour drive away, so you can spend longer at Montserrat before setting off or leave early to make the most of your time in this Ignatian city. There are plenty of sights to see which tell the tale of Ignatius's time spent there, but you don't need to be a Jesuit to absorb the city's history; its Modernist buildings are an unexpected attraction, too.

Languages Basque, Spanish
Area 7,234km^2
Main Camino Ignaciano towns Azpeitia, Laguardia
Highest points on the route Puerto de Biozkorna (Stage 2, 1,274m); Urbia (Stage 3, 1,215m)
Length of Camino Ignaciano 140km
Points of interest Sanctuary of Loyola, Sanctuary of Arantzazu, Laguardia (medieval town, wineries)

What does the Basque Country mean to foreign visitors? Maybe their sole reference point is Bilbao's glistening Guggenheim Museum, or the golden crescent of sand that is San Sebastián's La Concha beach. Or perhaps, the only connotation will be one that now lies firmly in the past, in a time when Basque nationalism expressed itself distastefully through violence rather than the ballot box. But the Basque Country, profound and intriguing, cannot be accounted for by simply joining a few prominent dots. With its own language, history, traditions and a people proudly and noticeably different from Castilian Spaniards, this is a complex culture that is never easy to pin down in a few sentences. Rewarding yourself with a Basque coastal trip could prove a fascinating prefix or suffix to your Camino Ignaciano walk, but the Ignatian route itself begins instead deep in the interior of economically powerful Euskadi, as the locals call their territory. And from there, it penetrates even further inland.

Loyola is the start point for the walk, being the birthplace of Ignatius. The Basque Country of this route is initially one of well-weathered, craggy mountains, then one of mellow vineyards, rather than one of golden beaches or vibrant cities. It is well worth spending half a day in Loyola itself to visit the tower-house museum and to absorb the backstory of the man whose footsteps you will shortly follow. While these mountains are hardly Pyrenean in either height or aspect, nevertheless they are to be respected and anyone walking in winter would need to be experienced and well prepared. Beyond these mountains lie yet more, specifically the eastern end of the long *sierra* that begins way west in Cantabria and thus bears its name. Here the range separates the rugged terrain to the north from the gentler wine-growing region of Rioja Álavesa, which is still very much Basque though with a softer landscape and a slightly diluted Basque identity.

While you begin the walk in Gipuzkoa province, most of your camino time in the Basque Country will be in neighbouring Álava, which some might describe as being 'Basque-lite'. The climate and outlook here are more Mediterranean – indeed, the river waters of Álava flow into the Ebro and end up in the Mediterranean, not the Bay of Biscay/Cantabrian Sea to the north.

Basque cuisine is well renowned and if you get a chance to gorge on a *chuleton* (beef chop) or some *kokotxas de merluza* (hake cheeks) to fuel

A WORD ON PLACE NAMES

Thanks to the co-existence of two languages in this region – Spanish and Basque (Euskera) – place names in the Basque Country can cause a bit of confusion, though perhaps less so for those towns visited on the Camino Ignaciano. Often the difference is just a letter or two. Bilbao becomes 'Bilbo' in Basque, while for Loyola you could substitute 'Loiola'. Away from the walking route, matters become a little more difficult, as San Sebastián is 'Donostia' and the Basque Country itself ('Pais Vasco' in Spanish) becomes 'Euskadi' in the Basque language.

THE FIVE AUTONOMOUS COMMUNITIES OF THE CAMINO IGNACIANO

you up, then do so. There's no need to speak any Basque here, though a few words of greeting and gratitude never go amiss in getting closer to the natives (see box, right). Despite a fiercely protected identity and, at times, fanatical pride in their territory,

> **A FEW WORDS OF BASQUE**
>
> Hello – *kaixo*
> Thank you – *eskerrik asko*
> Please – *mezedez*
> Goodbye – *agur*

the Basques have always been an outward-looking people, enjoying flourishing trade with England and Flanders, as well as whaling off Newfoundland. All these are testament to their historic internationalism. Even now, some Basques would rather speak English to you than Spanish, and the relationship with Madrid and the Spanish State remains at times uneasy. A week's walk here will hopefully give you an appetite to return and explore further this rich and enigmatic region, its glorious cuisine and its deep-rooted, complex and profound culture.

Trail information The route through the Basque Country is the most challenging, most mountainous and most scenic part of the Camino Ignaciano. Together with Manresa, it is also the section that connects most closely with Ignatius. The ever-pragmatic, industrious Basques have invested in good signposting for their part of the trail and are keen to promote the route originally taken by one of their most famous landsmen. Trail markings, signposts and information boards are among the best you will find along the route.

LA RIOJA
Capital city Logroño
Population 315,000
Language Spanish
Area 5,045km^2
Main Camino Ignaciano towns Logroño, Calahorra, Navarrete, Alfaro
Highest point on the route No significant climbs
Length of Camino Ignaciano 105km
Points of interest Logroño's Calle del Laurel, La Rioja wines, Alfaro (stork nesting)

By population, La Rioja is the smallest of Spain's 17 Autonomous Communities; by area, it is the second smallest. Wine is what gives this compact region a powerful presence on the global stage, and its reds find their way on to top restaurant menus across the world. Perhaps like Champagne, more people drink the region's product than ever actually visit the region itself, which is a shame. For wine connoisseurs, there would be nothing better than to enjoy an extended tour of some of La Rioja's excellent wineries.

Although grapes have been cultivated here for many, many centuries, it is only in much more recent times that they have been developed and turned into a high-quality, lucrative commodity. Logroño is by far and away the biggest Riojan conurbation, but the more than 500 *bodegas* and vineyards are spread right across the region. As well as the export value of the wine itself, wine tourism is also an important engine for the economy here, with many wineries opening their doors to visitors. But if as a pilgrim you don't have time to loiter and visit any *bodegas* or bathe yourself in a wine spa, you will at least have time to sample the rich, warming liquid product of the terrain in the bars and restaurants at the end of a day's walk. In Logroño the best place to do so is the Calle del Laurel, a street overflowing with bars whose counters simply groan with delicious tapas. And you will be rubbing shoulders with exuberant Spaniards doing what they do best: enjoying wine, enjoying food, enjoying each other's company and – most of all – enjoying life.

Trail information The waymarking in La Rioja is certainly sufficient to guide you through the region in straightforward fashion. The trail here coincides with two of the more popular Camino de Santiago routes (Camino Frances and the Camino del Ebro), which of course head westwards, but whose excellent waymarking assists Ignatian pilgrims as they travel east. Additionally, the presence of the River Ebro and the general flatness of the landscape make your passage through La Rioja fairly unproblematic.

NAVARRE
Capital city Pamplona
Population 650,000
Language Spanish, Basque (in the north)
Area 10,930km^2
Main Camino Ignaciano towns Tudela
Highest point on the route No significant climbs
Length of Camino Ignaciano 46km
Points of interest Tudela, Navarre's second-biggest city, with a rich, multi-religious heritage

With only a brief visit into Navarre, the Camino Ignaciano barely allows the determined pilgrim much time to get properly acquainted with this large, sparsely populated region. Navarre was once a kingdom and its complex history is beyond the scope of this book. Like its neighbour La Rioja, Navarre produces excellent wines, but its world renown depends largely on its capital, Pamplona, and in particular that city's annual San Fermín festival, with its raucous bull-running and past connections with Ernest Hemingway. The American writer was a frequent visitor to the city, a venue for his hard partying. The Ignatian route is far removed from Pamplona and even further removed from Navarre's northern, Pyrenean border with France and the Basque-speaking valleys.

Instead, the camino cuts across Navarre's southern terrain, where the Ebro flows and the attendant Mediterranean-influenced climate is ideal for vegetable cultivation. Your Navarrese camino stretch will barely serve as a taster, but if you ever get a chance to return to the region for a car tour, you are guaranteed to have a rewarding time. Navarrese lands stretch from those high Pyrenees down to the Ebro, with a multitude of geographical features along the way. Those lands are strewn with imposing, ruined castles, intact monasteries, Roman remains, wineries and the fascinating, bleak, semi-desert of the Bardenas Reales. Proud of its past, Navarre still retains plenty of attractions to justifiably fuel much pride in its present.

Trail information The Camino Ignaciano cuts through the southern part of Navarre in a gentle southeasterly direction, taking walkers (officially) only two days. At nearly 40km, the second of the recognised stages, from Tudela to Gallur (in Aragón), is the longest on the camino. Although midway accommodation options are admittedly few on that lengthy stretch, thought should be given to splitting it in two, adding in an additional day if possible. A combination of the Ebro and the railways assist with direction finding, so it is difficult to take a wrong turn despite the waymarking being occasionally deficient.

ARAGÓN
Capital city Zaragoza
Population 1.3 million
Language Spanish
Area 47,719km^2
Main Camino Ignaciano towns Zaragoza, Fraga
Highest point on the route No significant climbs
Length of Camino Ignaciano trail 206km
Points of interest Zaragoza's El Pilar Basilica, *mudejar* architecture, Los Monegros semi-desert

To the outsider or the history student, Arágon has a profile that was perhaps higher in the past than it is in the present (see box, page 150).

PRACTICAL INFORMATION

Despite a varied landscape and, mainly in the north, its own linguistic characteristics, its identity to the outside world is much less prominent than some of its neighbours.

Zaragoza is, by a stretch, the largest conurbation you will pass through in your month or so of walking. Indeed, nearly three-quarters of Aragón's population live in the regional capital, Spain's fifth-largest city. Perhaps it has little profile outside of Spain, certainly less than other Spanish cities, such as Madrid, Barcelona or Seville, but it would certainly not disappoint anyone visiting for a weekend break. Its showstopping must-see is the El Pilar Basilica (page 169): it is easy to be impressed by the sheer size of many a church, but this one really is huge by any comparison. If you choose Zaragoza as the location for a break in your walk, the city has enough museums and points of interest to fill a couple of days, as well as sufficient restaurants and nightlife to make memorable your evenings.

From the big city to the desert: two days beyond Zaragoza, you will find yourself in a whole different Aragonese world, almost alien. Baking hot in summer, freezing in winter and always exposed to strong winds, the Los Monegros ('Black Mountains') are a desolate space that occupy a good half-day of walking. Most likely you will be alone with your thoughts here, as despite some low-level cultivation, attempts to develop it into something truly monstrous have thankfully failed (see box, page 179). It remains a soulful environment.

Trail information The camino continues its southeasterly direction to cross the mid-section of Aragón. The terrain poses no great challenges, with little elevation to worry about. Although the waymarking is not always at its finest, there is permanent navigational help from the parallel running of the Ebro and the proximity of the railtrack. Even crossing Zaragoza itself is easy, as there is no need to deviate far from the south bank of the Ebro as the river and the camino meander in tandem through the city.

CATALONIA (CATALUNYA)
Capital city Barcelona
Population 7.7 million
Language Catalan, Spanish
Area 32,115km^2
Main Camino Ignaciano towns Lleida, Igualada, Manresa
Highest point on the route Castellferran (Stage 26, 790m)
Length of Camino Ignaciano 180km
Points of interest Lleida, Verdú, Cervera, Montserrat, Manresa

Catalonia is the second-most-populous of Spain's Autonomous Communities after Andalucía. With its own language and a good deal of lead in its economic pencil, this is a seat of a super-strong regional identity which for some is not sufficiently reflected in the amount of autonomy it currently enjoys.

> **A FEW WORDS OF CATALAN**
>
> Hello – *hola*
> Thank you – *gràcies*
> Please – *si us plau*
> Goodbye – *adéu*

On the Camino Ignaciano, Lleida is a city of some 140,000 people, with some very worthwhile sights. Montserrat and Manresa may not *quite* compete with Barcelona just down the road, but they are nevertheless hugely important to Catalonia's tourist economy, especially for those visiting from within Catalonia itself. Montserrat is truly iconic, while Manresa is the global reference point for Jesuits and merits a prolonged stay for anyone wanting to learn more about Ignatius.

Away from the camino, Catalonia could provide a lifetime of holidays. Mountains, dozens of sandy beaches, protected reserves, the sheer energy of Barcelona – the region is fully geared to welcome visitors. Add in tasty cuisine, a rich viniculture (and we're not just talking about Cava) and the renowned cultural icons of Salvador Dalí and Antoni Gaudí, and your Catalan tick-list starts to become endless.

Trail information The camino stops any southbound tendency as it traverses Catalonia, proceeding almost perfectly eastwards until it reaches Montserrat. There, it changes tack and heads directly north to its end point, Manresa. Given that many people walk only the stage between Montserrat and Manresa, rather than the full route, it is no surprise that the signposting in Catalonia is among the best encountered along the entire route. You will mostly be able to rely on fixed signs, rather than the odd orange-painted arrow randomly splashed on a lamppost or boulder.

WHEN TO WALK THE CAMINO IGNACIANO

As the Ignaciano begins in the Basque Mountains, yet in the later stages passes through the Los Monegros desert, careful planning is required if you are intending to walk the entire route in one visit. Those Basque Mountains may not be the Pyrenees, but they still attract snow every year; and that Monegros desert might not be the Sahara, but it can be dangerously hot in high summer. Avoiding the two climatic extremes presented by those very different geographical features is the key to a safe and enjoyable walk.

PRACTICAL INFORMATION

▲ Autumn is a great season for walking the camino *BT*

Planning is much easier if you are intending to walk just a short section of the route, or if you plan to walk the whole route but spread across several visits. In those cases, you can simply pick the best time of the year for each section.

WINTER Snow is a common visitor to the Basque Mountains at any time between November and March, and so beginning your walk in these months would be ill-advised. For the inexperienced, it could be downright dangerous and winter fatalities are not unknown. In general, walking any part of the camino in the winter months is not recommended, and not just in terms of climate. Many of the pilgrim hostels close over winter, and even some hotels take a break. Los Monegros is another part of the route that is inhospitable in winter, experiencing extreme cold and with nothing by way of shelter if things get really adverse.

SPRING Whether you are setting off from Loyola to complete the whole route or undertaking any part of it, spring is a good time to start. Rain is a probability in the mountains of the Basque Country in most months, so even an April or May departure will require waterproofs. Temperatures will generally be pleasant, without being too oppressive at either end of the mercury.

SUMMER July–August is high season for almost everything in Spain and because of this (and the high temperatures) these months are not recommended for this walk. Struggling in the heat with a backpack gets you no extra 'pilgrim points' and crossing Los Monegros could be fatal. August is also Spain's own holiday month, so there can be extra pressure on accommodation at this time.

AUTUMN A great season for undertaking the walk. Come September, Spain returns to work and school so there is much less demand for accommodation, unless there is a local festival. Temperatures are thankfully on the slide, making a daily dose of 30km of walking much more pleasurable, although even in early September it can be too hot for some.

HIGHLIGHTS

On a walk such as this, sightseeing is probably not high on the priority list. Walk, eat, sleep, repeat is the basic routine. But to make the whole experience more enjoyable, a few well-chosen days off are recommended – not only to give you some rest and a chance to wash some clothes, but also to give you some time to visit the route's highlights. The suggested attractions detailed here are listed in the order in which you will encounter them along the way.

SANCTUARY OF LOYOLA It would seem a bit remiss not to visit the sanctuary and 15th-century tower-house where Ignatius was born, and absorb some of the history that resulted in him setting off to Manresa some 500 years ago. Allow a half-day if possible. Page 54.

ARANTZAZU Austere and severe, the bold, Basque architectural style of this sanctuary will nevertheless leave an impression on all who see it. Although the current basilica was only constructed from 1950 onwards, this is a place steeped in over 500 years of history. A 'who's who' of creative Basques has contributed to the styling and décor of the modern building. Page 70.

LAGUARDIA The Basque Country's only member of the official 'Most Beautiful Towns of Spain,' and a well-deserved listing. Narrow streets, wine cellars, characterful old-world hotels and good restaurants all combine to create a truly memorable place. Page 96.

LOGROÑO For one night, dump any pretensions at being a pious pilgrim, unleash your inner party animal and bar-crawl your way down the effervescent Calle del Laurel and – energy permitting – back up again. Page 108.

PRACTICAL INFORMATION

▲ The Sanctuary of Arantzazu, Stage 2 *A/S*

ALFARO La Rioja is all about wine… and storks. The wine you can enjoy in any of the towns and villages, but Alfaro is the self-styled 'storks' paradise' and these quirky birds favour the town for nesting and chick-rearing, as well as happily posing for photos. They arrive from December and depart for Africa around the end of August. Page 130.

ZARAGOZA The country's fifth-largest city is off the radar for many visitors heading for Spain. And although it cannot truly compete for the tourist dollar with Barcelona or Madrid, the Camino Ignaciano not only passes right through it, but also runs straight by its showpiece attraction, the giant Basilica de Nuestra Señora del Pilar. Marvel at the Baroque cupolas, one decorated by no lesser figure than Goya. Page 164.

LOS MONEGROS Spain has only a few deserts and Los Monegros in Aragón is one of them, perhaps more semi-desert than 'full Sahara' but nevertheless a bleak, soulful landscape prone to droughts, extreme temperatures and occasionally battered by the dry, cold wind known as El Cierzo. Page 182.

LLEIDA The camino takes you to parts of Spain you might otherwise never set foot in, but Lleida has been the site of human settlement since the Bronze Age, was a major city in Roman times, fell under Moorish rule for 400 years before being liberated, suffered invasion by the French, bombardment during the Spanish Civil War and is now an unassuming, multi-cultural conurbation getting on with its everyday existence. Spain, in a nutshell. Loads of history, worth a visit. Page 206.

MONTSERRAT Surely the Camino Ignaciano's natural highlight, the intimidating, jagged peaks of Montserrat thrust into the sky, defying you not to take photo after photo. Luckily, you don't have to climb them. A visit to the monastery is a must, as this is one of Catalonia's top visitor attractions. Page 243.

MANRESA Being your journey's end is enough on its own to justify celebrating this city, but there are other reasons to dwell here a while. Revered among Jesuits due to the months Ignatius spent here, there is also some engaging and accessible Modernist architecture to admire. Page 264.

TOURIST INFORMATION AND TOUR OPERATORS

Each of the five Autonomous Communities has its own tourism board and comprehensive websites (page 268). Individual tourist offices are detailed in the text for each stage.

At present, the most convincing proof that the Camino Ignaciano is still off the beaten track is that there very few operators offering organised

> **LIGHTEN THE LOAD WITH A BEAST OF BURDEN**
>
> Five hundred years ago, Ignatius set out from Loyola with a mule, both to accompany him and to carry some of his luggage. Even now, in the age of the motorised vehicle, a four-legged friend is an option to bring a smile to your face and ease the strain of hiking the Basque Mountains with a heavy backpack.
>
> **Burros Trekking** (**m** 609 22 80 95; **e** info@burrostrekking.com; **w** burros-trekking.com) is a small, friendly company based south of Arantzazu which can hire you a donkey – accompanied or not – and which covers any or all of the stages between Arantzazu and Laguardia. It's important to point out that the donkey will carry your backpack, not you, though it can transport a child of up to 40kg in weight. You can rent for one stage or more and hire more than one donkey if you are in a group. As the charismatic owner, Tati, speaks little English, enquiries are best made by email. The *burros* are loveable, occasionally stubborn, but provide a fantastic experience to the start of your Camino Ignaciano. Your furry friend will be uplifted by vehicle once he (they are all male) has completed the stage(s) of his hire and transported back to base while you continue on your way towards Manresa on foot.

trips. And while the route is easily walked on your own, the advantage of a trip with an operator is that you don't need to worry about the weight of your backpack – they carry it for you – or the logistics. Walking stages on organised trips also tend to be shorter, as these operators perhaps cater to a slightly older clientele.

Fresco Tours   Colón de Larreategui, 48009 Bilbao; 001 888 246 6089 (toll free, North America); 944 248 989; e info@frescotours.com; w frescotours.com. Enthusiastic & professional Bilbao-based company with 20 years' experience of organising guided & self-guided tours on Spain's caminos, particularly the Camino de Santiago but now also including the Ignaciano.

Marly Camino   Calle Lopez de Hoyos, 28002 Madrid; 917 864 636; e info@marlycamino.com; w marlycamino.com. Organises a number of guided trips along many of Spain's pilgrimages, including some stages of the Camino Ignaciano.

RED TAPE

Citizens of the Republic of Ireland and other EU countries do not need a visa to visit Spain at the time of writing. A valid passport or national identity card is sufficient. There is no 90-day limit on the length of stay, though there are certain limitations imposed on citizens of some of the countries that have most recently joined the EU.

The best advice for UK citizens is to check the Spain country-specific foreign travel advice section of the UK government website (w gov.uk/foreign-travel-advice/spain) as rules and regulations do change. At the time of writing, UK citizens can travel to countries in the Schengen area (which includes Spain) for up to 90 days in any 180-day period without the need for a visa. On entry, you may be asked to show that you have enough funds for your trip and also be asked to show a return ticket. You should also ensure that you have at least six months' validity left on your passport. Citizens of the US, Canada, Australia or New Zealand are subject to the same rules as UK citizens and no visa is required. Further information may be found on the Spanish government website (w exteriores.gob.es), including a full list of countries whose citizens do require a visa to enter.

All of the above information presupposes that your trip is for tourist purposes. Different rules apply if your trip is for work, study or other purposes. To keep up to date with entry requirements, check the Spanish government website.

THE PILGRIM'S PASSPORT   Unashamedly copying the Camino de Santiago, those behind the creation of the Camino Ignaciano issue their own *credenciál* (pilgrim's passport) for walkers who want a memento of their

RED TAPE

▲ The pilgrims' passport (*credenciál*) is an excellent memento from the walk *BT*

achievement. Don't worry, it is not obligatory to possess this document to walk the Camino Ignaciano, but you will need one if you are intending to stay in any of the municipal pilgrims' *albergues* (hostels) along the way. You will also need one if you want to get the certificate of completion from the Pilgrims' Office in Manresa. If nothing else, these two documents are attractive when framed and put on your wall when you're back home.

The idea of the passport is to get it stamped and dated at least once a day during your walk and this can be done at most accommodations, tourist offices, *ayuntamientos* (town halls) and even bars and restaurants on the route. The *credenciál* costs a modest €0.50 and is obtainable from the places listed. The certificate is obtained in Manresa and costs a similar fee. To be entitled to the certificate of completion, you need to have walked at least 100km of the route.

Loyola (Basque Country) Santuario de Loyola; ✆943 02 50 00; ⏰ 08.00–14.00 & 16.00–19.00 daily

Logroño (La Rioja) Parroquia de San Ignacio, Calle Huesca; ✆941 20 35 04; ⏰ 10.00–13.00 & 17.00–20.00 daily

Tudela (Navarre) Oficina de Turismo (tourist office), Pl de los Fueros 5; ✆948 84 80 58; ⏰ mid-Mar–mid-Oct 10.00–14.00 & 16.00–19.00 Mon–Sat, 10.00–14.00 Sun, mid-Oct–mid-Mar 10.00–17.00 Mon–Sat, 10.00–14.00 Sun

Zaragoza (Aragón) Centro Pignatelli, Paseo de la Constitución 6; ✆976 21 72 17; ⏰ 09.00–14.00 & 16.00–20.00 Mon–Fri

Lleida (Catalonia) Parroquia de Sant Ignasi, Pl de España 4; ✆973 27 10 99; ⏰ 17.00–19.00 Mon–Fri

Barcelona (Catalonia) Curia de los Jesuitas, Carrer de Roger de Llúria 13; ✆933 01 23 50; ⏰ 09.00–21.00 Mon–Fri

PRACTICAL INFORMATION

GETTING THERE AND AWAY

BY AIR Where you fly to will of course depend on whether you are intending to walk the whole route or just a section of it and, if the latter, *which* section. If you want to start at Loyola, and you are coming from the UK, your best bet is to fly to Bilbao and then take a bus from there. Several airlines service Bilbao directly, though in recent times many of these have been suspended, or reduced their frequency, due to the pandemic. Airlines that have offered direct services to Bilbao in the past, and may do so again, include British Airways, easyJet, Iberia, Ryanair and Vueling. Biarritz Airport is another option.

Bilbao Airport has a swift, cheap, regular bus service into the city and its main bus station, from where you can get a bus to Loyola (Azpeitia), taking around 2 hours. This may involve a bus change at either Zarautz or San Sebastián. Buses to Loyola from the latter are frequent and you can connect without leaving its bus station. Check **w** lurraldebus.eus for times and prices.

If you want to start your walk a bit further along the camino, Ryanair fly from London to Zaragoza. And if you just want to walk the last few stages, sufficient to get your pilgrim's certificate, you could fly to Barcelona – served by the airlines listed above from London and many other UK and international destinations – and take the bus or train back to, for example, Lleida.

BY SEA Even without a vehicle, you can take the ferry to Spain from Portsmouth or Plymouth with Brittany Ferries (**w** brittanyferries.com). Foot-passenger tickets are available to Santander, but not Bilbao – you need to have a car for that route. For onward travel, Santander's bus station is only a short walk from the ferry terminal, with frequent connections to Bilbao (90mins; check **w** alsa.es for times and prices).

BY RAIL Travelling to Spain from the UK by rail is entirely possible, but is inconvenient, time-consuming, expensive and really only for those who are avid train fans. There are few practical plus-points for preferring it to air travel and you will have to factor in some changes of train to get to either Bilbao or Barcelona, and then get the bus or a further train to your chosen starting point. You can grapple with all the complexities with the help of The Man in Seat 61 (**w** seat61.com/Spain). You should certainly reserve tickets well in advance to minimise costs.

BY BUS Reaching Spain by bus faces most of the same challenges as reaching it by rail, but it can be much cheaper. London to Barcelona is a route operated by ouibus/BlaBlaBus (**w** ouibus.com) for example, but there are currently no direct buses from London to Bilbao.

BY CAR If you are taking a vehicle to Spain from the UK, you have options to hop across the Channel on a short ferry crossing or use the Eurotunnel and then drive down from one of the French ports, or else take the much longer car ferry from either Portsmouth or Plymouth to Bilbao or Santander. In good weather, the long ferry journey is a pleasant one and the standards on board are high, though the voyage is not cheap. To make a proper comparison between the two possibilities, you need to factor in the additional petrol, motorway tolls and an overnight stay in France if choosing the first option. And if you are then going to walk some or all of the Camino Ignaciano, you will need to leave your car somewhere safe while doing so. If you decide that you are not ready to walk the Camino Ignaciano, but feel inspired to visit some of its highlights by car, you can take some ideas from the box on page 20.

PUBLIC TRANSPORT

Public transport in Spain is generally reliable, comfortable, reasonably priced and runs to time. What can let it down is the quality and user-friendliness of what might be called the 'information infrastructure', namely the operators' websites, out-of-date timetables displayed in train stations and so on. The advice has to be to check, check and check again.

If starting from Loyola (Azpeitia) or anywhere else, you will have to use public transport to get there. I have also made suggestions in the descriptions of some of the longer stages so that you can use public transport to split these lengthy sections into two and use the bus or train again the next day to return to where you left off. Some people are simply not capable or desirous of walking nearly 40km in one day, and no medals are awarded for doing so.

BUS Buses are the mainstay of the Spanish public transport network and are not only cheaper and usually more frequent than trains, but are also surprisingly quicker on some routes. Tickets can often be bought online, if the relevant bus operator has a website, or in larger towns can be bought in advance at the bus station. You can also buy tickets from the driver on shorter routes, though not always on longer intercity ones. You may need to enter your passport details when buying tickets online in advance or show the passport at the ticket office. The relevant websites for transport options are given in each stage, as appropriate.

PRACTICAL INFORMATION

RAIL Trains are comfortable and reliable, making them a useful alternative for intercity travel and on some shorter routes of the Camino Ignaciano. But although many of the smaller towns along the way do have stations, the frequency of services is low and not all trains stop at every station. Tickets can be bought in advance online, in person at the larger stations or on the train itself, but it is not unusual for ticket machines to be 'out of order' or for the station ticket booth to be closed. When buying tickets at the station, you might be asked for your passport; when buying from some ticket machines, you might be asked for a mobile phone number which frustratingly needs to be formatted for Spain (ie: it is impossible to input a UK or other foreign number). I must confess, I have occasionally made one up in frustration.

TAXI These are usually cheaper in Spain than in the UK, and there may be occasions when you need to summon one to complete a stage, perhaps due to adverse weather or fatigue. Taxi numbers are given in each stage description, and you can use the phrases on page 262 to (hopefully!) make yourself understood, as not many small town or rural taxi drivers will speak English.

ACCOMMODATION

Choosing your style of accommodation along the route is a huge factor in determining how much you will enjoy your experience. Purist, pious pilgrims sometimes argue that staying in the municipal pilgrims' refuges/hostels is the only 'correct' choice and might try to infer that staying in hotels or elsewhere is, in some way, cheating. Nonsense. A good night's sleep is essential if you are walking long distances on consecutive days, so choose what you are most comfortable with and what suits your budget. Note that on some stages ending in villages or smaller towns the choice will be very limited – especially if you are seeking luxury. Pre-booking gives peace of mind and is advisable especially in summer. One last thing to consider is that some places will offer a discount for pilgrims who can present their pilgrim's passport (page 32), so it is always worth asking if you are booking direct with the accommodation.

Any accommodation prices quoted in this book exclude the cost of breakfast, unless otherwise stated.

CAMPING This is an option for some, of course, whether it is in official campsites or 'wild'. If you are an experienced long-distance walker *and* camper, you will scoff at any suggestion that you need four walls and a roof over your head each night. But if you are not both of these, you

ACCOMMODATION

might want to consider the wisdom of carrying a tent and cooking equipment over long distances only to succumb to the temptations of a hotel or hostel after a hard day's trek. Although Spain's coastline is well provided for with official campsites, the less-visited interior is not and thus they are not numerous on the Ignaciano. There are not organised campsites at the end of each stage and there are no convenient campsites at all during the camino's first six stages.

Wild camping is tolerated in some parts of Spain more so than in many other countries, but the situation is complicated by the fact that the 17 Autonomous Communities all have different rules. In Navarre and Aragón, wild camping is totally prohibited, and campers can, in theory at least, be fined quite heavily. Outside those two regions, wild camping is tolerated in the Basque Country and Catalonia and in rural areas elsewhere. Lighting a fire anywhere would be extremely foolish and, of course, all litter should be taken away.

PILGRIMS' HOSTELS Known as *albergues*, these are run by municipalities, religious organisations or private enterprises. The advantage of staying in them is mainly one of cost, which is anywhere between €5 and €20 per person per night. Some are even *donativo*, which means you pay what you choose, including nothing at all. However, this is not to be abused. For most of them, you will have to show your pilgrim's passport (page 32) to prove yourself as a genuine pilgrim. The downside is that you will usually be in a dormitory, often mixed gender, with bunk beds and shared bathrooms. Ear plugs are recommended, as snorers are common!

Some hostels provide breakfasts, sheets, blankets or towels, but you should pack a sheet sleeping-bag, travel towel and probably also a warmer sleeping bag unless you are walking in the height of summer. Some establishments will have cooking facilities, usually a shared kitchen, so you can bring your own food and prepare meals. Some allow reservations, whereas others do not.

If a municipality does not have a pilgrims' hostel/shelter/refuge, then it will sometimes make a basic alternative available if you enquire. This might be no more than a mat in a sports hall, for example.

Individual hostels are listed in each stage, and to contact a municipality, you could simply present yourself at the *ayuntamiento* (town hall) in the relevant town, although these are open only in normal office hours, Monday to Friday.

HOSTALES AND PENSIONES Confusingly, perhaps, a *hostal* in Spain refers to a guesthouse style of establishment and *not* a pilgrims' hostel. A *pension* is similar, sometimes more basic than a *hostal*, and both are

PRACTICAL INFORMATION

usually more rudimentary and hence cheaper than a hotel. A single room in either costs €20–35 for one night, a double €30–60. Some rooms share bathrooms and breakfast is not normally included in the rate. It is sometimes difficult to discern the difference between staying here and staying in a cheap hotel, which means that it probably does not matter.

HOTELS In Spain, these cover the whole spectrum from basic one-star facilities to five-star chain hotels and *paradores* (state-run, though often privately managed, accommodation sometimes fashioned from historic buildings such as castles and convents). Single rooms in basic hotels cost from around €35 and doubles from €45: the sky's the limit for the maximum. Breakfast is usually not included in the quoted rate, though there are exceptions.

EATING AND DRINKING

REGIONAL SPECIALITIES For anyone used to walking long distances, the joy of a hearty meal in the evening needs no explanation. Some regional specialities found along the way are highlighted in the relevant stages of the walk, but for an overview, read on.

Many Spaniards will admit that **Basque** cuisine is the finest in Spain and anyone who has gorged on *pintxos* (Basque for *tapas*) in the bars of Bilbao or San Sebastián will surely agree. But even outside the cities, food is taken seriously. Fish may be a bit scarcer in inland areas, but hake (*merluza*) is a Basque speciality, so try it if you have the chance. For meat lovers, the beef chop (*chuletón*) is a much-revered dish, usually served pink in the middle. Basque ewes' milk cheeses such as Idiazabal (see box, page 59) are another must-eat.

La Rioja is synonymous with wine, but there is excellent food to accompany it, too. White asparagus, artichokes and the small, sweet piquillo peppers are all local delicacies. *Chuletillas al sarmiento* (lamb chops barbecued over vine roots) are a restaurant favourite, and beef or pork cheeks in a red wine sauce is also recommended. Chorizo, although not unique to La Rioja, does serve to spice up its bean stew (*caparonnes*), which is another local dish. And then, there is all that silky wine…

Your stay in **Navarre** will be short, so make the most of your few evenings here by enjoying the cuisine. In truth, Navarre's deep south shares culinary choices with its Riojan and Aragonese neighbours: the common link is the River Ebro, so asparagus, artichokes and peppers are excellent. Roncal cheese, unpasteurised and truly delicious, comes from the northern valley of that name, but can easily be found here in the south. And after your meal, try the fruity local *pacharán* spirit, which is a true

▲ The Catalan town of Lleida is known for its snails (see box, page 207) IS/LT

Navarrese delicacy. Although produced commercially, it is also made by many at home by soaking sloe berries in an anise-flavoured spirit.

In **Aragón**, you might scan the restaurant menu for *ternasco* – suckling lamb that can take 10 hours to slow-cook. That makes pre-ordering a must! For the sweet of tooth, get hold of *guirlache*, a delicious peanut-brittle-style confectionery made from almonds, sugar and lemon juice.

Start your days in **Catalonia** with *pan con tomate* (or *pa amb tomàquet* in Catalan). Smearing bread with tomato, garlic and olive oil may sound simple – and it is – but it makes for a delicious breakfast. Other highlights along the Catalan route are the *cassoles de tros*, hearty stews which combine Lleida's snails with pork, spinach and potatoes. Another typical dish is *escudella*, a predominantly winter favourite based on chicken, ham, chickpeas and pasta. Drinks-wise, almost everyone has heard of the region's cava sparkling wine, but don't ignore up-and-coming alternatives, like the powerful red Priorat.

EATING OUT For anyone who has not visited Spain before, you need to know that **breakfast** is not a huge event on the Iberian Peninsula. If it is not included in your accommodation price, and its extra cost seems excessive, the solution in towns or cities is to find a café nearby. In larger

PRACTICAL INFORMATION

places, you can often find one open from 07.00 where €4 will get you a coffee, a croissant or *bocadillo* (sandwich) plus one of the joys of Spain: a genuine freshly squeezed orange juice. By contrast, **lunch** *is* a big deal here and many Spaniards take advantage of the competitive prices offered by restaurants keen for custom. (Many pilgrims will prefer to settle for a picnic at lunchtime.) A midday restaurant meal or *menú del día* can cost as little as €10 for three courses, and sometimes includes bread and wine. If that is too much food when you have significant after-lunch walking to do, many places offer a one-course *plato del día*, which is the equivalent of a main dish of the day for €6 or €7. Where there is significant 'pilgrim traffic', for example in Navarrete on Stage 7, you can find a 'pilgrim's menu' in the evening for a similarly or even lower-priced **dinner**. For this low cost, you will get something filling, though largely unsophisticated. Note that most Spanish restaurants will only offer dinner from 20.00 onwards.

If you are a foodie, take advantage of your evenings spent in the cities such as Logroño, Zaragoza, Lleida and Manresa, where you will find a great choice of restaurants at every price range.

DRINKS **Coffee** is the staple morning drink, sipped in café-bars as there is no real coffeeshop culture, unlike in the UK or US. If you are a **tea** addict, getting a breakfast-style tea can be almost impossible: expect instead to be offered all sorts of exotic infusions, none of which might be what you want. Finding space in your backpack for a few teabags is recommended. When it's time to relax, **wine** is cheap, and in many bars or cafés a mere euro will get you a basic glass of the local product. This is often very good, unsurprisingly given that vines are plentiful in all five Autonomous Communities you pass through on your camino. **Beer** costs not much more than wine, and for those who want something other than the mass-produced pilsner-styles of San Miguel, Damm or Mahou, the good news is that the craft beer revolution is now well under way in Spain. All sorts of pale ales are now frequently seen, with Zaragoza-based Ambar being one of several artisan beers readily available. The Basque Country also has a number of specialist breweries, and Zaragoza even has a few brew pubs.

MONEY

The euro is the currency in Spain. ATMs are everywhere and, despite some consolidation after the 2008 economic crisis, the Spanish banking sector remains bloated, meaning that even a small town will usually have more than one bank with an ATM. Note that the fee for withdrawing cash varies quite considerably from bank to bank, and you should also note the exchange rate being offered as it's a bit of a minefield. Most places accept Visa or Mastercard, though in the more rural areas you should try to have a bit of cash at all times for your accommodation, cafés and restaurants. American Express is often a no-no.

BUDGETING

Although Spain is definitely a good-value destination (though not 'cheap'), four weeks on the road will still incur significant expenditure. But besides your travel costs in getting to your starting point, most likely by plane, most other expenses are controllable. Accommodation costs can be minimised by staying in the pilgrim hostels or wild camping. Even if a dislike of dormitories or tents drives you into staying in hotels, these can be fairly inexpensive, especially if you are sharing a room each night with a companion. Breakfasting in a bar or simply enjoying coffee, accompanied by a pastry from the local *panadería* (bakery) is a cheap way to start the day. Most walkers will choose to make do with a sandwich or picnic at midday, though the inexpensive restaurant menus can be tempting. One main meal, taken in the evening, is usually enough each day. A couple of beers or glasses of wine alongside does not really blow the budget, and if you need to resort to public transport, you will usually discover that it is good value. For an idea of costs of accommodation and food, see pages 37 and 39 respectively.

COMMUNICATIONS

INTERNATIONAL AND LOCAL AREA CODES The dialling code relevant to the Camino Ignaciano is +34 (the international code for Spain). The emergency phone number to access fire, ambulance, mountain rescue or police is 112; calls are free of charge and operators should speak local languages and English.

MOBILE PHONES Mobile coverage is good for most of the trail, but it may occasionally be hard to find a signal in remote areas. Spanish mobile numbers start with a 6.

INTERNET Most accommodation has free Wi-Fi, including many pilgrims' hostels. You will also find that many cafés offer Wi-Fi and a few municipalities also provide free access, usually in the main square and a few other public places. Accommodations listed in this guide all have free Wi-Fi, unless otherwise stated. Apart from on a few isolated places in the mountains, there is good 4G signal along the whole route.

PRACTICAL INFORMATION

PUBLIC HOLIDAYS AND FESTIVALS

Date	English name	Spanish name
1 January	New Year's Day	Año Nuevo
6 January	Epiphany	Día de Reyes
19 March	St Joseph's Day	San José (not in the Basque Country)
March/April	Maundy Thursday	Jueves Santo
March/April	Good Friday	Viernes Santo
March/April	Easter Monday	Lunes de Pascua
1 May	Labour Day	Día del Trabajador
15 August	Assumption	Asunción
12 October	National Day	Fiesta Nacional de España
1 November	All Saints' Day	Día de Todos los Santos
6 December	Constitution Day	Día de la Constitución
8 December	Immaculate Conception	Inmaculada Concepción
25 December	Christmas Day	Navidad

As it is impossible to list all festivals and events taking place annually, the best advice is to use the tourist office websites in advance of your stay or visit the offices in person. A website with an English-language option that can prove useful is **w** fiestas.net, which allows you to search 'what's on' by town and province. In high season, you will almost certainly find something being celebrated in the vicinity. Note that restaurants are closed on Christmas Day and New Year's Day, and booking meals on Christmas Eve or 6 January can also be difficult.

TRAVELLING WITH KIDS

If your children are avid walkers and happy with the outdoors, there are no real obstacles to them walking the Camino Ignaciano. Having said that, there is nothing particularly child-friendly about the route and no great child-orientated attractions. A few stages with a donkey (see box, page 31) could prove unforgettable, though!

MAPS AND APPS

There is no necessity to buy any additional maps for the Camino Ignaciano, but of course some people prefer to arm themselves with more detail than is provided by this guidebook. The waymarking on the route, while not perfect, is an enormous help in your orientation.

Maps at a scale of 1:25,000 are published by Spain's Centro Nacional de Información Geográfica (**w** www.cnig.es) and can be ordered through Stanfords (**w** stanfords.co.uk). It might take several weeks for them to arrive, as they are not stock items, and check the date of publication as some are a few years old.

The Institut Cartogràfic de Catalunya (**w** icgc.cat) also publishes a good series of 1:25,000 maps covering all parts of Catalonia, though you would need four of their maps just to cover the Catalan section. Finally, useful links to online maps and GPS can be found on the official Camino Ignaciano website (**w** caminoignaciano.org/en).

TRAIL MARKINGS

Trail markings are very variable along the way, reflecting the relative investment of each of the five Autonomous Communities through which it passes and the extent to which the route has been identified as a 'tourist product'. An orange painted arrow is the basic marking and this can often be found on gateposts, lampposts, the sides of buildings and random rocks. In certain sections, the markings are much more formal than a hand-painted arrow, sometimes being expensively manufactured signposts with a 'sun' symbol and the name Camino Ignaciano. In many places the route shares its space with other local or national paths, often with some of the GR (Gran Recorrido)/Grande Randonnée) network of long-distance paths – this has good red-and-white waymarking, which is

▼ Trail markings along the camino vary from sun symbols to hand-painted arrows *GF/CCDB & MS*

useful to Ignaciano walkers. Where you coincide with these, it is noted in the text. For many stages after Navarrete, the Camino Ignaciano runs on the same path as the Camino de Santiago, but in the opposite direction; this can be helpful, as the yellow arrows and markings of the popular Santiago-bound routes can be used to sense-check your progress.

As you approach Catalonia, you will observe that considerable investment has been made in trail markings and Montserrat and Manresa are particularly well signposted. It is only in a few places where the painted arrows have faded that you might encounter difficulties. Bear in mind that many locals may never have heard of the Camino Ignaciano, so if you do get lost you are probably better asking for directions to your next known destination town, rather than referring to the name of the route itself. Some of the waymarking and signs you will encounter can be seen on page 43.

PACKING LIGHT FOR THE CAMINO IGNACIANO

If you have not walked long distances before, then perhaps the most useful single piece of advice is to pack light. If you are intending to camp, then you will obviously need to follow a different set of rules, but otherwise you should aim for a backpack that weighs around no more than 10% of your bodyweight. If you are of particularly large or small build, you may have to vary this rule-of-thumb. Otherwise, be ruthless in sticking to this when stuffing your backpack and don't be tempted to add a few extra kilos with 'just in case' items. A couple of times on pilgrimages I have found myself at a post office after only a few days' walking, queuing up to send stuff home. Remember that those extra kilos will put strain on your knees, back and feet.

As a pilgrim/long-distance walker, nobody expects you to look like a fashion model in the evenings, so designer threads can remain at home. And remember that in addition to what you pack, you may need to carry at least a litre of water every day. That in itself weighs around 1kg, and you will also want to carry a bit of food as well. Remember: you can always buy items that you chose *not* to pack and later decide that you can't do without.

For clothing, much will depend on when you choose to walk, but for any season choosing layers (rather than, for example, a heavy fleece) is advisable. Part of the pilgrim routine is to wash clothes every night, so quick-drying garments are a must. Another tip for novices is to try out your backpack, fully laden, on a number of practice walks of decent length before you leave home.

Outdoor specialists are common on the high street and online, but what is sold by some of these is of dubious quality and is really leisurewear with

▲ Packing light is essential on a walk such as this *BT*

a few pretensions. In truth, for a four-week walk of this sort, medium-quality clothing and equipment is sufficient. If you are more serious and want to get proper, ultralight specialist gear then maybe try a seller such as Backpacking Light (**w** backpackinglight.co.uk) or Ultralight Outdoor (**w** ultralightoutdoorgear.co.uk).

BACKPACK If you follow the advice on maximum weight (see above), then a backpack with a capacity of around 35–50l should be sufficient. (Intending campers may need something larger.) Your backpack, like your walking boots/shoes, should not be brand new, or at least should have been tried, tested and worn in by you before departure.

A pack with a few easily accessible pockets as well as a main compartment can save a lot of faffing about to find something small and vital halfway through a day's stage. Most people will select a pack with an internal frame, on grounds of comfort. Do some research, and don't buy solely on price as you don't want something that leaks or with straps or zips that give up. An additional waterproof cover for your pack is well worthwhile, as are waterproof wallets for keeping paperwork dry. Check that the pack has a good padded belt, as the cheaper ones without can result in you rubbing away the skin around your midriff.

HIKING BOOTS/SHOES Footwear is a matter of personal choice, but getting it right is very important. A pair of shoes or boots that are genuinely waterproof is highly recommended (avoid any that are

PRACTICAL INFORMATION

> ### DON'T FORGET TO PACK SOME *TAPONES*
>
> Weekend, urban Spain goes to bed late and wakes late, but pilgrims generally go to bed early and wake early. At times, particularly when your stage ends in a city, this incompatibility of schedules can cause problems, which is why a pair or two of *tapones* (earplugs) are essential for pilgrims. As you try and get some shuteye at 22.00, the incessant street noise of Spaniards still enjoying themselves will do everything it can to stop you.
>
> And just when they finish the party, maybe at 03.00, typically an army of dustcarts and their hi-vis-clad operatives invade the town centre to commendably clear up the mess and empty the bins. If you are puzzled by the wet pavements when you emerge from your hostel or hotel, it probably has nothing to do with rain, more with the hosing down that has been administered by these municipal workers.
>
> So, pack some *tapones* – you will be grateful that you did. They are also indispensable to shut out the inevitable snoring if you choose to stay in dormitory-style accommodation.

described as just 'water-resistant'). The choice is then between heavier hiking boots, which support the ankles, or lighter walking shoes. Again, the time of year you choose to walk will be a factor in which you prefer. And again, research pays off, as does a visit to a good outdoors retailer whose staff should be able to advise on weight and waterproofness. Wear in any new footwear before you go.

EVENING FOOTWEAR There is something deeply satisfying about taking off your walking footwear, and something equally demoralising about having to put them on again after you have showered at the end of the day's walk when you are ready to go out and dine. A very lightweight pair of sandals, boat shoes or espadrilles is recommended, bearing in mind your need to pack light.

RAINPROOF JACKET A waterproof jacket is essential at any time of year, at least if you are walking the whole route. Again, ensure you get water*proof*, not merely water-resistant. Focus on a lightweight, foldable option when choosing a jacket, as you will (hopefully!) not need it every day. Breathable fabric has to be the choice, with Gore-Tex perhaps the best-known and easiest to find. An alternative – or additional item – could be a decent cape/poncho, which covers you and your backpack.

SOFTSHELL JACKET Warm, preferably windproof softshell to keep out any chills. Lightweight and not too bulky.

LIGHTWEIGHT BASE LAYERS Take a couple of long-sleeved tops with good wicking properties. One to wear, one spare and a third just in case.

HIKING TROUSERS Two pairs of lightweight, quick-drying trousers, preferably with zips to convert them to shorts. Again, what you choose will depend on the season and which part of the route you are walking.

WALKING SOCKS Socks are important, but the choice is personal. Some long-distance walkers swear by wearing two pairs at a time; others make do with one. It is certainly worth spending a bit of money and visiting a decent outdoors shop. Cushioned socks help prevent blisters, but blister plasters should form part of your first-aid kit (page 48).

TREKKING POLES Again, this is a matter of personal choice. Most research shows that using these eases knee-strain and they can be useful to steady yourself on downhill stretches. Make sure they comply with your airline's baggage restrictions.

WATER BOTTLE A properly insulated water bottle will keep your liquids cool. Environmentally, using one reduces the number of disposable plastic bottles bought in Spain. Some backpacks are designed to carry two bottles in easily accessible pockets. A popular alternative to bottles is a Camelbak system (**w** camelbak.co.uk). Note that tap water is safe to drink in Spain, though many Spaniards prefer bottled water simply because it tastes better. If you want to cut down on plastic bottle usage, you might choose to bring a bottle with a filter. You will find that many towns and villages on the camino have a water fountain or tap; a sign declaring *agua potable* means that the water is drinkable.

COMPASS You may handily have a compass on your mobile phone, but there are only a few stages on which it might be necessary (mainly the Basque Mountains). Perhaps it's not essential to have a standalone compass, but if you take one, make sure you know how to use it.

TORCH/HEADLAMP Very useful if you are camping or staying in the dormitory-style accommodation of the pilgrims' hostels. Otherwise, this is not really an essential item. The few tunnels you will encounter on the camino (Stages 1 and 26) are easily navigable without artificial illumination and walking at night is certainly not recommended.

▲ The town of Laguardia is a highlight on Stage 6 *BT*

SUN PROTECTION AND SUNGLASSES A proper sunhat which protects your neck is advisable, rather than just a peaked baseball-style cap. Choose an easily foldable one for when you're not using it. Suncream is also essential even if walking in early spring or late autumn (SPF 20+ is advisable). As most people do most of their walking in the morning, and much of the Ignaciano's direction is eastwards, good-quality sunglasses are also a necessity.

TOWEL A small, quick-drying travel towel is essential if you are staying in the pilgrims' hostels, as most will not provide these.

SLEEPING BAG AND SLEEPING-BAG LINER A sheet sleeping bag is essential if you are staying at the pilgrims' hostels. Silk versions are considerably lighter and a bit warmer than the cotton ones. Outside summer, those using the pilgrims' hostels may also prefer a proper sleeping bag in lieu of the blankets that are sometimes provided.

FIRST-AID KIT This is essential, although you will see from the stage maps that Spain's towns and villages are very well endowed with pharmacies. Suggested items are: blister plasters (these are super-adhesive and will remain in place all day); fabric plaster strip for any general cuts and wounds; non-stick bandages; alcohol wipes; hand gel; face coverings (subject to the pandemic situation); paracetamol and ibuprofen. A good foot cream is also recommended for anyone prone to dry or cracked feet (I favour the Swedish brand, CCS). A multi-functional knife is a must.

OTHER ITEMS For those intending to sleep in dormitory accommodation, earplugs (see box, page 46) are recommended. To keep any rain off your footwear, a pair of gaiters is useful and spare boot/shoelaces take up little space. As for other clothing, three sets of underwear should be enough and three (or six, if doubling up) pairs of socks. Some favour a lightweight fleece for the evenings. If you intend to ritually wash your 'smalls' every night like a good pilgrim, you will need some washing liquid, but given airline restrictions on liquids, this might be better bought in Spain.

Don't forget all the necessary phone/camera/laptop/shaver chargers you need and remember that all of them will be useless if you forget your two-pin adaptor to plug them in. Spain's electricity supply is 220V.

SAFETY ALONG THE CAMINO IGNACIANO

It is only in the Basque Mountains on the first few stages where you might encounter difficulties, and even this is unlikely unless you injure yourself. Winter walking, times of fog or electrical storms are other risky conditions which could spell danger for the inexperienced. Being rescued from the mountains in Spain involves accessing the 112 general emergency phoneline. Mountain rescue services are free of charge, though a recent change in the high Pyrenees to charge those who have been negligent (ie: setting out when adverse weather has been forecast) might be introduced to other areas of Spain in the future.

Unwanted insects might join you for a nibble on a couple of the stages, so a good insect repellent is a valuable addition to your packing list.

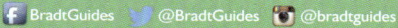

Part Two

THE OFFICIAL STAGES OF THE CAMINO IGNACIANO

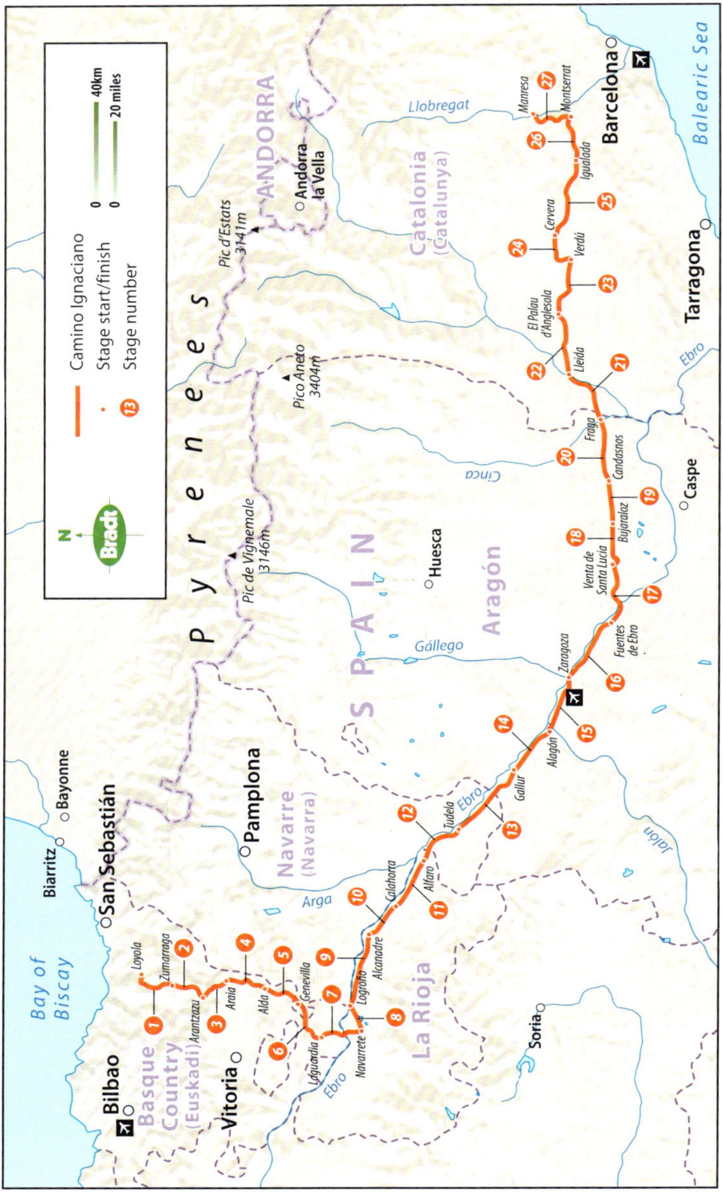
Camino Ignaciano
Stage start/finish
Stage number
13
N
Bradt
0 40km
0 20 miles
Bay of Biscay
Bilbao
Basque Country (Euskadi)
Vitoria
Biarritz
Bayonne
San Sebastián
Pamplona
Navarre (Navarra)
La Rioja
Soria
P y r e n e e s
ANDORRA
Andorra la Vella
Pic d'Estats 3141m
Pico Aneto 3404m
Pic de Vignemale 3146m
SPAIN
Huesca
Aragón
Catalonia (Catalunya)
Barcelona
Tarragona
Caspe
Balearic Sea
Llobregat
Cinca
Gállego
Arga
Ebro
Jalón
Loyola
Zumarraga
Arantzazu
Araia
Alda
Genevilla
Laguardia
Navarrete
Logroño
Alcanadre
Calahorra
Alfaro
Tudela
Gallur
Alagón
Zaragoza
Fuentes de Ebro
Venta de Santa Lucia
Bujaraloz
Candasnos
Fraga
Lleida
El Palau d'Anglesola
Verdú
Cervera
Igualada
Manresa
Montserrat
1
2
3
4
5
6
7
8
9
10
11
12
13
14
15
16
17
18
19
20
21
22
23
24
25
26
27

GATEWAY TOWN: LOYOLA

Where it all began, and where it all begins.

Everyone on a long-distance walk wants their destination to be special, and Manresa in Catalonia, a distant 675km away from where your walk begins, is certainly that. But as a pilgrim or simply as a long-distance walker, you will surely treasure the excitement of your departure just as much as the thrill of your arrival. On the Camino Ignaciano, the start and end points are separated by at least four weeks of walking. And the Sanctuary of Loyola complex will instill a feeling of excitement among those ready to follow in the footsteps of Ignatius, 500 years after the future saint set out on his own adventure.

If religion holds no interest for you, time spent here will nevertheless reward the curiosity which at some point along the route – if not now – will inevitably prompt you to ask questions about Ignatius, his life, the Jesuits and their far-reaching influence. And maybe to ask some questions about yourself. When your pilgrim passport receives its first stamp in Loyola, prior to your departure, you will feel the sensation of becoming part of something. A pilgrimage, whether religiously motivated or not, encompasses a sense of purpose. If you want to experience some solemnity before your departure, there is a short mass held at Loyola every morning at 08.30. Just present yourself at the reception to the *casa-torre* a few minutes beforehand and you will be led to the small chapel where mass is conducted in Spanish. Other masses are held later in the day, in the basilica itself. Take a moment to reflect on your imminent journey. Welcome to the pilgrims' world.

WHERE TO STAY AND EAT Two nights spent at Loyola or in nearby Azpeitia or Azkoitia are advisable if you can manage it, giving a relaxed start to your walk and lots of time to visit the *casa-torre*, the basilica and to generally absorb the ambience. If you arrive in time to visit these on your first day, then one night will be enough. The Hotel Loiola restaurant is highly rated, the Uranga is acceptable: for more choices, the old town of Azpeitia beckons, and Azkoitia's Isidro Erretegia restaurant is recommended.

Albergue Jesús-María (56 beds in unisex dorms & 2 rooms) Avda de Loyola 24, Azpeitia; 943 81 10 34; **e** casajesusmaria@gmail.com; **w** jesus-maria.org/loyola. Close to the sanctuary. All meals can be ordered. Communal spaces & garden, kitchen facilities. Sheets & towels for hire, extra cost. *€16/20/36/40 dorm bed/room/dorm HB/room HB*

⌂ **Baiolei** (4 rooms) Izarraitz Auzoa 16, Azpeitia; **m** 620 11 78 54. Welcoming place, within walking distance to the sanctuary. *€60 sgl/dbl*

⌂ **Balentziaga** (5 rooms) Santa Kutz Auzoa s/n; **m** 688 60 21 20; **e** info@balentziaga.eus; **w** balentziaga.eus. A delightful, very chic place, set less than 1km from the path but worth the detour. Good b/fast, large, brightly decorated rooms. To find it, turn right off the camino at a metal water fountain, crossing on a concrete bridge road between houses, to reach the main road. The casa is in front of you: access it via the roundabout to your right. *€50 sgl/dbl*

⌂ **Casa Rural Txanpardin** (4 rooms) Avda de Loyola, Carretera Txote, Azpeitia; **m** 658 73 81 53; **w** txanpardin.com. Lovely traditional-style Basque house, walkable from the sanctuary though uphill. Great views, outdoor space, but a bit pricey. *€85 sgl/dbl*

⌂ **Centro Arrupe** (50 rooms) Located on the sanctuary site; ☏ 943 02 50 26; **e** cel@loyola.global. In the building to your left as you face the basilica main entrance. This was a hotel until recently & now caters mainly for Jesuits attending meetings, etc, but welcomes those setting out on the Ignaciano. Rooms have TV & bathroom. Meals available on prior request. *€28 pp*

⌂ **Hotel Larramendi Torrea** (11 rooms) San Juan Auzoa 6, Azkoitia; ☏ 943 85 76 66; **w** larramenditorrea.com. A tasteful hotel located within a beautifully renovated 15th-century tower-house, with snacks/tapas available. Situated 5km from the sanctuary. *€60/67 sgl/dbl*

⌂ **Hotel Loiola** (35 rooms) Loiolako Inazio Hiribidea, Azpeitia; ☏ 943 15 16 16; **e** loiola@hotelloiola.com; **w** hotelloiola.com. A comparatively modern construction, very close to the sanctuary, with bright, spacious rooms & a good restaurant. *€60/85 sgl/dbl*

✕ **Isidro Erretegia** Aingeru Kalea 16, Azkoitia; ☏ 943 85 20 03. A small, unassuming place but with an authentic ambience & excellent *chuletón* (beef chop) at a good price. A good place to try this hearty Basque favourite. *€20*

✕ **Uranga** Loiola Auzoa 7, Loyola; ☏ 943 14 23 87; ⏱ 10.00–20.00 daily. On-site dining at the sanctuary, with outdoor tables & the pleasant sound of a burbling stream to soothe any pre-walk nerves. Although it does not get rave reviews, the lunchtime menu is daylight robbery (you are the robber), very acceptable at €11 for 3 courses, wine, bread & coffee.

TOURIST INFORMATION

Tourist office Located opposite the sanctuary entrance; ☏ 943 15 18 78; **e** i-loiola@urolaturismo.net; **w** urolaturismo.eus; ⏱ Sep–Jun 10.00–14.00 & 15.30–18.30 Mon–Sat, 10.00–14.00 Sun, Jul–Aug 10.00–14.00 & 15.00–19.00 daily. Helpful, multi-lingual staff. Worth a visit to get extra information about the basilica, tower-house, Azpeitia & Azkoitia.

WHAT TO SEE For those who have never visited the Basque Country, the sudden sight of the **Sanctuary of Loyola complex** (reception ⏱ 08.00–14.00 & 15.30–19.00 daily), which includes the basilica and the thick-set tower-house where Ignatius was born, may come as a bit of a shock. Big and

THE *CASA NATAL* OR *CASA-TORRE*: THE BIRTHPLACE OF IGNATIUS OF LOYOLA

Even before you enter the *casa natal*, you will be struck by the sheer muscularity of this building where Ignatius was born. Medieval Spain was a bit of a roughhouse, which explains why a noble family would choose to live in a *casa-torre* (tower-house) such as this one in Loyola that played such an important part in Ignatius's life. The lower part of the building is constructed of stone, its 2m of width signalling a necessary defence against unruly neighbours, which was very much a key consideration back in the day. The upper part is in brick, *mudéjar*-style, following a 15th-century reconstruction.

In medieval times, the isolated northern Basque valleys were each ruled by a chief, not unlike the head of a Scottish clan, and similarly supported by a number of loyal kinsmen. Each chief would build a *casa-torre* for himself and his not-so-merry band, and they would spend their time in fiercely fought feuds and brutal battles with the neighbouring chiefs and their bands. Orgies of throat-slitting and house-burning (with the inhabitants still inside, of course) were commonplace. Fed up with the senseless killing and destruction, those who were not members of these bands eventually joined together and formed self-defence organisations known as *hermandades*. For even more protection, this 'safety in numbers' principle eventually drew people together to create and live together in *villas* (towns) and also to seek military help from the Castilian monarchy.

In the mid 15th century, the power of the bands waned and many of the tower-houses were demolished, though some were adapted into homes for the nobility. It was into one of these rather palatial buildings that Ignatius was born.

imposing, set at the foot of the Basque Mountains and with the waters of the River Urola alongside, the huge building looks a little bit out of context. But there is something about the Basques, their buildings, their sculptures and even their language that conspire to challenge you. Everything here is different from the rest of Spain. Different, but for those who stay long enough to savour it, delightfully and intriguingly profound.

For anyone setting out on the Camino Ignaciano, a visit to the **tower-house** (⊕ 10.00–13.00 & 15.30–19.00 daily; €4/free adult/under 13s; see box, above) is strongly recommended. At the time of writing, the interior

The Sanctuary of Loyola's impressive dome *MS*

had just undergone a major makeover. But even before this most recent update, the house itself was hugely impressive and well restored, and these days it serves as a very worthwhile museum. It was here that Ignatius was born; it was here that he was brought after he had been injured at Pamplona; it was here that he began his religious conversion, leaving behind his previous life as a soldier and his 'jack-the-lad' reputation. And it was from here that he set out on the route you are about to follow, 500 years later. A visit will certainly help put his walk in its spiritual and historical context, and will add extra colour and purpose to your own journey. It's also the place to go to buy your *credenciál* (pilgrim's passport) and get it stamped; the reception desk opens at 08.30 each day.

Construction of the **basilica** (free), with its design inspired by Italian churches, began in the 17th century to satisfy the expressed desire of Mariana, the Spanish Queen Mother, that a basilica and school should be constructed next to Ignatius's birthplace. Using massive limestone blocks sourced from nearby Izarraitz mountain, the construction was completed in the 19th century. Particularly impressive is the dome, which stretches to 65m in height.

In Azpeitia, the **Museo Vasco del Ferrocarril** (Julián Elorza 8; ↘943 15 06 77; w bemfundazioa.org; ⏱ 10.00–13.30 & 15.00–18.30 Tue–Fri, 10.30–14.00 & 16.00–19.30 Sat, 10.30–14.00 Sun; €2/free adult/under 16s) is unmissable for rail enthusiasts, with several British-built locos and a marvellous display of clocks. Occasional steam train trips on Saturdays add to the experience.

TRANSPORT See page 34 on how to get here from Bilbao via San Sebastiàn.

Taxis

🚕 **Taxi Beatriz Mendizabal** (Azpeitia) ↘943 81 20 01

🚕 **Taxi Roberto Jauristi** (Azkoitia) ↘943 85 05 59

🚕 **Vallina Taxis** (Azpeitia) ↘943 39 38 48

1 LOYOLA–ZUMARRAGA

A pleasant, unchallenging opening to your camino adventure. One of the route's shorter stages, allowing plenty of time to visit Loyola's fascinating basilica and imposing tower-house. The walk largely tracks the course of the Urola River, which flows in the opposite direction. The path is good, and after Azkoitia it follows the route of a disused railway, criss-crossing the river and road while plunging in and out of numerous illuminated tunnels, which makes route-finding almost foolproof. Arm yourself in advance with a map of Azkoitia from the Loyola Tourist Office, as this will help you negotiate the town. While the route does climb, the incline is only gentle: you can comfort yourself that 300m of ascent today is 300m fewer tomorrow.

Start Sanctuary of Loyola, Loyola
Coordinates 43.17454, -2.28221
Finish Zumarraga
Difficulty Easy
Distance 18.2km
Duration 4hrs 30mins

THE ROUTE Go down the right-hand side of the massive basilica on a cobbled road. Proceed through the car park, with the River Urola and road parallel to your right. Red-and-white waymarkers guide you on this tarmac path, which is shared with a cycle lane. Basques are keen, occasionally daredevil cyclists, so stay alert. This riverside path will take you the 3km to Azkoitia. (If staying at the Balentziaga, look out for the turn-off to the right – see page 54.) After just over 1km, a signboard notes the former site of a spa (*balneario*), which closed in the 1950s. There's virtually nothing to see now, but in its heyday it welcomed famous names such as the former Empress of the Austro-Hungarian Empire.

The riverside path ends at a road, with a bridge and main street to your right. Turn left on to the latter (Julio Urkijo Etorbidea), continuing to the end and crossing the river to then turn left on to the Kale Nagusia to pass **Azkoitia**'s shops, bars, church and Baroque town hall. English-language panels offer insight into the numerous tower-houses and palaces here too. Unless diverting to see the Frontón Jorge Oteiza (see box, page 63), at the end of the long street, take a 90-degree right, cross the road and take the first bridge across the river. Straight in front of you, beyond the San Francisco hermitage and barely 100m away, are the

SAY CHEESE, BASQUE STYLE

Few things are more important to the Basques than their food and near the top of their list of favourites is cheese. The Basque Country and neighbouring Navarre are proud of their Idiazabal, a hard, sheep's cheese whose name may be totally unfamiliar to those from outside Spain. Each year in the small Basque town of Ordizia, the winning entry in the Concurso de Quesos de Oveja (Sheep's Cheese Competition) can fetch over €12,000 at auction! Though, in truth, local companies bid over the odds and then donate all the money to charity.

Time spent in the region would be incomplete without tasting Idiazabal. The milk – always unpasteurised – only comes from the Latxa breed of sheep, or very occasionally from Carranzana. Strict regulations govern the production process and the name carries a fiercely protected DO (Denomination of Origin). Frequently this nutty, spicy cheese will be offered on restaurant menus accompanied by *membrillo* (quince jelly) and the two are a delicious combination, particularly when washed down with a local red or another Basque speciality, cider.

▼ The small Basque town of Ordizia is known for its cheese *MS*

STAGE 1

sturdy wooden fence posts that mark the start of the *via verde* ('green way') disused railway. Turn briefly left to access it.

The clanking and whirring of heavy industrial machinery as you exit town on this path, set beneath a bucolic surround of tree-clad mountains, captures the twin characteristics of these Basque valleys. Pass under a bridge and almost at once, with the Ibarmia factory ahead, the path veers left and begins to rise slightly. It is immediately obvious that you are now on a former railtrack. Ignore any deviations from this straight path. Soon you will cross the river and the GI-631 road, the first of many such crossings as you climb towards your stage end. Soon in your sights is the first of many, many tunnels through which you must pass. The motion-activated overhead lights are sufficient to get you through, though carrying a small torch to alert oncoming cyclists is a good idea.

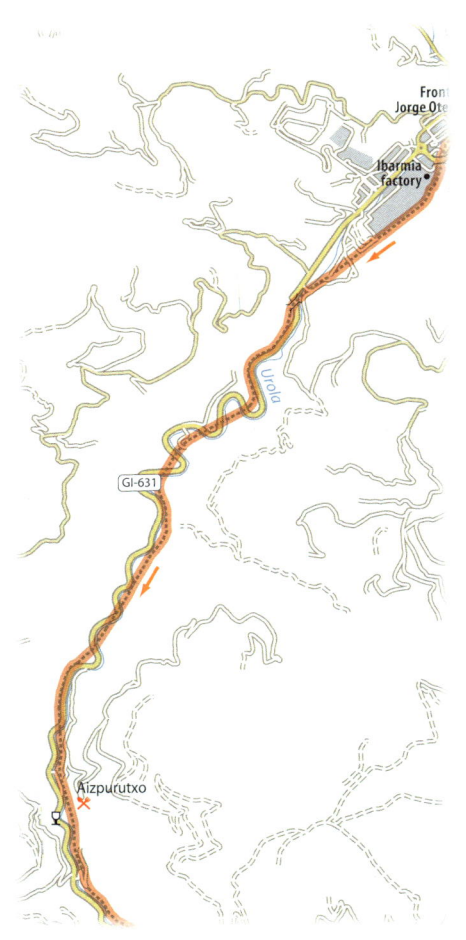

Around 7km after leaving Azkoitia, you pass the abandoned and graffiti-clad station of **Aizpurutxo**. A sign here promising Zumarraga in 5km is sadly about 2.5km over-optimistic, but down on the main road beneath there is a good local restaurant (page 61) and a few hundred metres beyond the **San Agustin bar** (signposted off the path), should you need a break. Your path continues as before, at times high above road and river, with a wall of ferns, mosses, beech trees and – higher up – the darker tones of evergreens. Rain has its visible benefits. After 2km, an active quarry can be seen to your right. Eventually, the path reaches a small picnic area next to the road and then runs parallel to the tarmac to lead you towards **Zumarraga**. Tucked behind the first tall apartment blocks is the Etxeberri (see below), but if not staying there continue down the same path as it descends past the disused train station and into the twin towns of Zumarraga and Urretxu.

WHERE TO STAY AND EAT With its sizeable population, Zumarraga offers more options than some stage ends on the Ignaciano. For dining, the **Etxeberri** (see below) and the **Kabia** (Legazpi Kalea 5; 943 72 62 74) are the classiest places in town, though either will blow a tight budget.

Hotel Etxeberri (16 rooms) B Etxeberri s/n; 943 72 12 11; e hoteletxeberri@etxeberri.com; w etxeberri.com. Well before you reach the town centre, so although you shorten this stage, you lengthen the next. A smart, well-cared-for place with lush gardens in which to relax. Excellent family-run restaurant on site. Free b/fast for pilgrims if you book direct & ask for it. *€65/79 sgl/dbl*

Pensión Balentiña (11 rooms) Urola Kalea 6; 943 72 50 41; e balantinapensioa@gmail.com. Central place with restaurant. *€35/50 sgl/dbl*

Pensión Zelai (6 rooms) Legazpi Kalea 5; m 670 26 49 22; e urretxu@etxarre.com; w zelai.org. Directly on the route & 200m beyond the town hall. Simple rooms have fridge & microwave. *€33/49 sgl/dbl*

✕ **Itziar** Aizpurutxo; 943 85 26 30; ⏰ lunchtimes Mon–Sat. A good lunch choice around the halfway point of your first stage, but booking is *essential*. Their hearty *menu del diá* will fuel you for the remaining kilometres. *€11*

✕ **Saski Taberna** Piedad 4; 943 22 92 60; ⏰ Wed–Sun. Open early for b/fasts, plus lunches, dinners & tapas. Price/quality ratio is perhaps the best in town. *€10*

STAGE 1

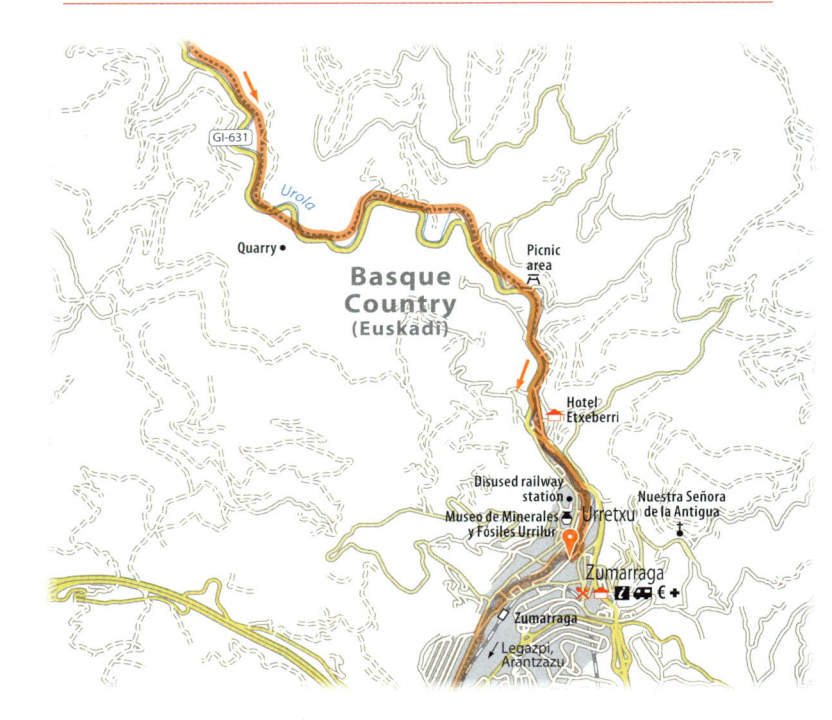

TOURIST INFORMATION
Tourist office Av de Beloki; 943 72 20 42; **w** urolagaraia.com; usually lunchtime Tue–Sat

WHAT TO SEE Given it's such a short stage, you have time to spare at the Sanctuary of Loyola (page 54) before you set off, but if you managed to visit it the day before then there are some attractions at the other end. Among these is the mineral and fossil museum, **Museo de Minerales y Fósiles Urrilur** (Jauregi Kalea 19; 943 03 80 88; closed Aug) at Urretxu, which displays 1,000 pieces in its private collection. Otherwise, a stiff 2km hike (or taxi) from Zumarraga town centre takes you to the **Nuestra Señora de la Antigua church**, often commended for its simple, beautiful interior. Its wooden-beamed ceiling, fully restored in 1976, resembles an upturned ship. Details of other points of interest in the river valley can be found at **w** urolagaraia.com.

> ### PELOTA
>
> Having just started your walk you are probably in no great hurry to linger, and luckily much of what Azkoitia has to offer is encountered without even deviating from your route. But one curiosity does require a very slight deviation: the **Frontón Jorge Oteiza**. Pelota is a very Basque sport and Azkoitia has produced many champions of what is said to be the fastest ball game on the planet. The *avant-garde* structure bearing the name of Oteiza, one of the Basque Country's most famous sculptors, comprises no fewer than seven *frontones* (courts on which it is played) and can be found just before leaving town. Each of the seven represents one of the claimed Basque provinces: four in Spain, three in France. As for the sport itself, there are over 20 variants and this is a town where its roots are deep.

For those just passing through, however, Zumarraga's star attraction is probably the **Plaza Euskadi**, a truly handsome square with lovely stone porticos and a 19th-century Neoclassical town hall. Centre stage is the statue in honour of the *conquistador*, Miguel López de Legazpi (1502–72), born here before moving first to Mexico and then becoming conqueror and governor of the Philippines. Of course, a small-town hero instrumental in empire-building may be viewed very differently these days, but the Philippines remained a Spanish colony until 1898 when it was ceded to the United States. The Treaty of Spain signed in that year marked the end of the Spanish Empire. Zumarraga's modern history mirrors that of many Basque towns in the river valleys, with the acceleration of heavy, metal-based industries after the Civil War and a consequent influx of workers from elsewhere in Spain to labour in them.

TRANSPORT Zumarraga is served by both bus and train, with the respective stations next to each other in the southwest of town. The D003 bus line runs once daily directly to Bilbao, otherwise you will have to connect in Bergara or elsewhere (**w** lurraldebus.eus). Trains run to Irun in the north and southwards to Madrid (**w** renfe.com).

Taxis

Taxi Ivan Molina (Zumarraga)
m 620 51 15 33
Taxi Javi Gaztañaga (Zumarraga)
m 679 44 34 83

Vallina Taxis (Azpeitia) 943 39 38 48

PILGRIMAGE ROUTES

WE OFFER YOU THREE ROUTES THAT, IN ADDITION TO TAKING YOU THROUGH THE MOST BEAUTIFUL PARTS OF THE BASQUE COUNTRY, WILL STAY WITH YOU FOREVER.

ST. JAMES'S WAY COASTAL ROUTE

DISCOVER THE VERY BEST OF THE BASQUE COASTLINE ALONG THIS ANCESTRAL ROUTE.

THE IGNATIAN WAY

RECREATE THE JOURNEY THAT IGNACIO DE LOIOLA MADE FROM HIS HOMETOWN IN 1522.

ST. JAMES'S WAY INTERIOR ROUTE

GET TO KNOW THE VARIED LANDSCAPE AND CULTURE OF THE BASQUE COUNTRY IN SEVEN DAYS.

PLAN YOUR ROUTE BY VISITING:
tourism.euskadi.eus/en/

BASQUE COUNTRY

2 ZUMARRAGA–ARANTZAZU

Today is without doubt the hardest of all the Ignaciano stages, and the one with the biggest ascent – which will be challenging, whatever the weather. But it's worth the effort as the views are truly stunning: layer upon layer of Basque Mountains stretching away into the distance. At the stage end you can look forward to both the Sanctuary of Arantzazu and the spectacular ravine which it overlooks. At the start of the day, you have to escape from the rather ragged industrial environment of Zumarraga and Legazpi, before negotiating the very significant climb over the 1,274m Biozkorna mountain pass to reach Arantzazu. If the weather is good, the rewards are phenomenal and the vistas from the pass truly photogenic. But you must exercise caution: checking the forecast carefully before departing as there is a propensity for fog here, which can make wayfinding difficult, and rain can be torrential in any month. There is no opportunity for refreshment between Legazpi and Arantzazu, so beware. Note that Arantzazu is a sanctuary, not a town, with hotels and restaurants, but no food shops or pharmacies.

Start Railway station, Zumarraga
Coordinates 43.08749, -2.31989
Finish Sanctuary of Arantzazu
Difficulty Hard
Distance 21.5km
Duration 7hrs
Ascent 900m
Descent 550m

THE ROUTE From your accommodation, find your way to the train station (the active one, not the disused one that once marked the end of the track you followed from Azkoitia yesterday). Facing the front of the station, follow the road to your right, the GI-2630, and use the path that runs parallel to it. This will take you in the direction of Legazpi, with the railway also running parallel. Without deviation, continue for 3km through this rather industrial wasteland until a short descent on your right leads you through a factory yard to connect again with the aforementioned GI-2630. Turn left on to it, alongside the massive CIE Automotive parts factory. At its height, this multi-national employed 4,000 locals in this small town and its predecessor company was owned by the Basque Country's richest man at the time, Patricio Echeverria. The town still has healthy heavy industry (CIE have factories in many continents), but it

STAGE 2

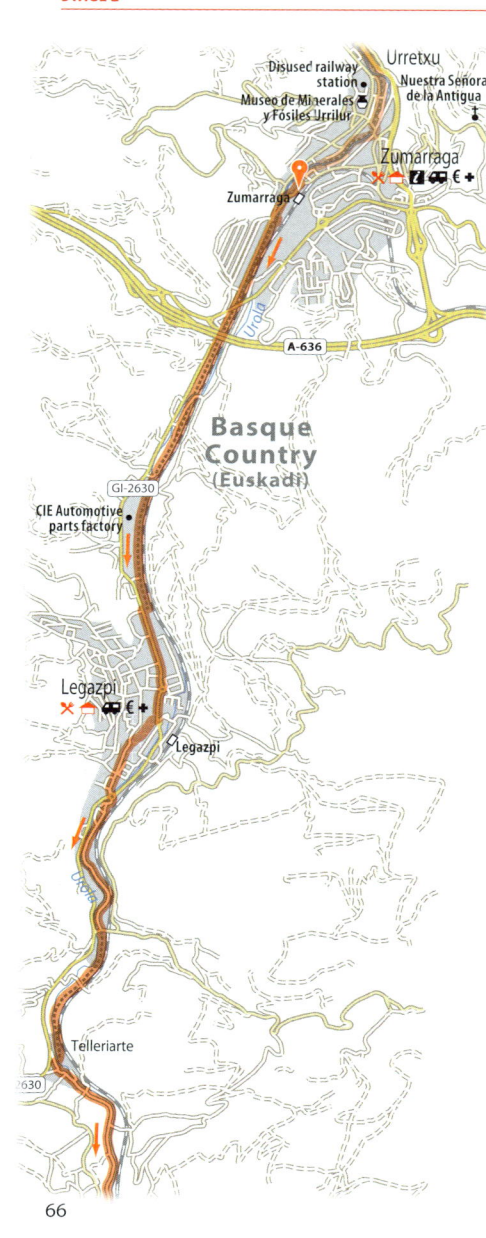

also shows the scars of abandoned factories whose days are now long gone.

Four hundred metres past the factory, you reach a roundabout with the **Legazpi** name proudly manufactured in iron, an industry that has been central to the town and valley's history. Continue straight ahead, passing on your right the former house of Echeverria which today serves as a music school. A few metres further on, veer right down the semi-pedestrianised Kale Nagusia, which leads down to the parish church and main square (home to an authentic farmers' market on Fridays). Continue down the same street as it becomes Aizkorri Kalea until it reaches a further roundabout. Take the quiet street straight in front of you, with the river now to your right and with both the orange arrows and red-and-white GR markings on lampposts to assist you.

Soon a cobbled path leads to the right, closer to the river. Continue

▲ The Brinkola Valley *OC/S*

in the same direction as the path crosses a road and continues towards Brinkola, 2.6km away. The path curves right and circumnavigates a building to proceed in the same direction with a pelota court on your left. Keep following the Telleriarte/Brinkola signs as the path leads up to the left. The first sign for Arantzazu, now 12km away, also appears, while the train track is above to your left. On reaching a renovated stone house, turn right to cross the river on a stone bridge and then immediately left on to the tarmac, which takes you through **Telleriarte** village with the river now immediately on your left. Shortly after, pass the Ferreria de Olarreggi ironworks; a sign explains that these date back to 1384!

The path now runs under a beautiful stone viaduct, the site of an old cement factory – some old millstones are on display – before entering sleepy **Brinkola** with its train station up to the left. Continue straight through on the same road until you reach a three-way junction, at which you pick up the sign – to the right – for Arantzazu and **Barrendiola reservoir**. Follow the tarmac road to reach the dam on your right; cross it and turn left at the end to continue with the reservoir on your left. Soon the path splits; choose the right-hand fork, which rises through trees. The climb has begun!

At the top of the first ascent, you enter **Aizkorri-Aratz Natural Park,** a popular hiking venue brimming with lofty limestone crags and rich

STAGE 2

beech forests. The path reaches a clearing with a junction; follow round to the left to re-enter the forest. Climb steeply through majestic pines and, at the next junction, keep right, following the GR signs. At a three-way junction, continue up through the woods on this GR-283/GR-286 with Arantzazu now 6.7km away. At the next fork, take the left, with both red-and-white markings and an Ignatian orange arrow, and then a sharp left at the following junction. At a junction a few hundred metres further, and with some derelict buildings behind you, follow the curve round to the right. You reach a ridge where some more abandoned buildings appear off to your right. (Astonishing, but the end of the 19th century witnessed mining for both zinc and lead here, despite the altitude being in excess of 1,000m.) Ignore the path that leads to them, instead taking the path that continues to climb, with the buildings now below you, and zig-zags upwards. After 5 minutes of zig-zag, the path climbs diagonally left and upwards across the scree, with just a single marker post to guide you. At the end of the scree, the route traverses a rocky section before reaching a grassy plateau. This is **Biozkorna**, representing the highest point of the day – a great place for a rest, and well deserved. Feast your eyes on the seemingly endless mountains stretching away in front of you.

To continue, note the marker post in the centre of the plateau and follow the direction for Arantzazu, now 4.2km away. A line of stones initially shows the direction – helpful in fog – and the route descends with a little pond appearing on your left. Shortly after is a small copse of trees, providing shade to the horses that live here. Immediately past the copse, look for a badly marked path which rises diagonally to your left. (If you miss this path, then after 400m of rocky descent you will in any event arrive at a dirt road and some stone houses: going left along this road for 500m will connect with the correct route.) A line of wind turbines becomes visible ahead in the distance. Your path is now the lower of two narrow dirt tracks, running parallel with the dirt road below and soon angling down to meet the road at a metal shelter, where you follow the sign to Arantzazu – all downhill from here.

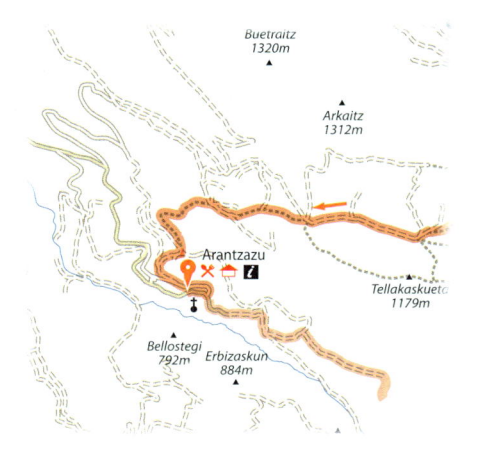

Ignore two paths that leave to the right. Where the wide dirt road turns sharply right, leave it in favour of a grassy path descending straight ahead towards woods. When the path reaches the line of trees, keep them initially to your left. Now you have a steep descent on what can be a muddy path strewn with tree roots (slippery in times of rain). Reaching a small stone cottage on your right, continue down through the trees on a better-quality path. At a group of stone houses, the route veers sharply right and you meet a road and turn right. Reaching a further group of

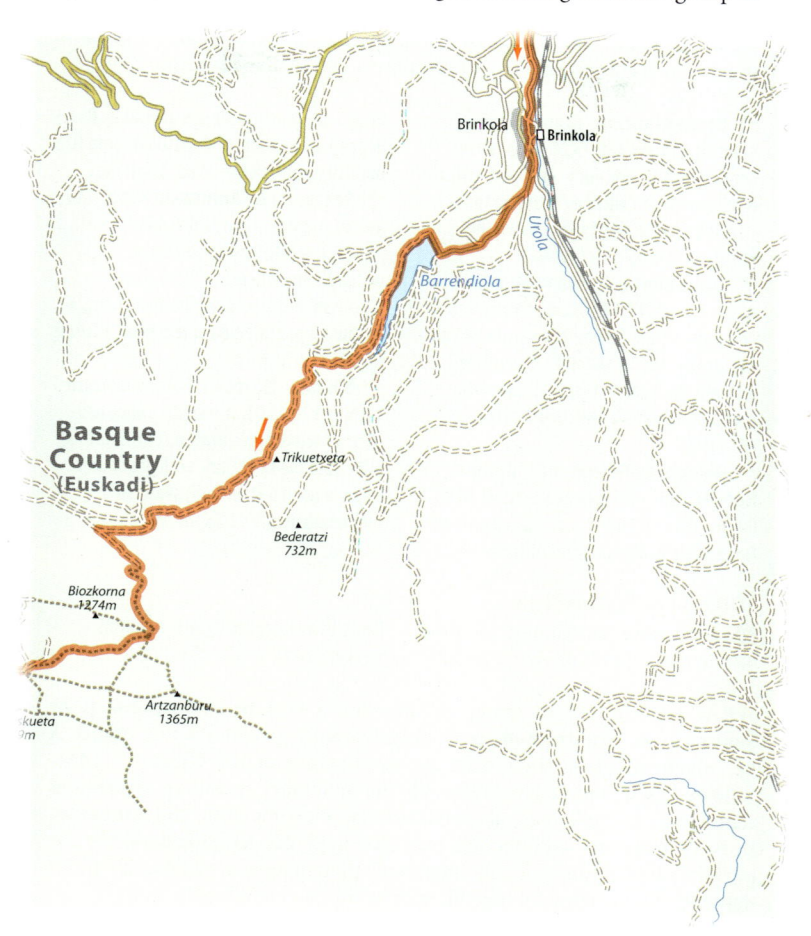

STAGE 2

houses, look for the grassy path on the left (Arantzazu, 1.6km) and leave the road to descend on a rocky steep section, tough on tired knees, but with welcome shade. Soon you reach a triangular clearing, where you turn right and cross a cattle-grid. (The alternative route signed to the left is longer, with no compensating advantage.) After a few hundred metres, the first buildings of **Arantzazu** appear, the very first one being the pilgrim shelter. The sanctuary is just beyond.

WHERE TO STAY AND EAT All of the following are within a short distance of the Sanctuary of Arantzazu at the stage end. Most walkers will eat at their own accommodation – there are no separate restaurants.

Borda Aranzazu (2 apts) Barrio Arantzazu 11; m 628 13 24 12; w www.bordaaranzazu.com. Fully equipped, stylish apartments with kitchen & outdoor terrace, sleeping up to 4. Great views down the valley. *€100–140 (whole apt)*

Goiko Benta (10 rooms) Arantzazu Auzoa 12; 943 78 13 05; e goikobenta@goikobenta.com. Stunning views down into the canyon, from a tasteful & beautifully restored 500-year-old establishment that pre-dates Ignatius's visit. Good restaurant. *€65 sgl/dbl*

Refugio de Peregrinos (Pilgrims' Hostel) (56 beds) Altamira 5; 943 78 05 00; m 656 74 31 48; e arantzazu@ateri.net. No cooking facilities, except microwaves. Reservations are possible & advisable. Prices depend on your age, the season & room size but costs approx €14–24 pp, b/fast inc.

Santuario de Arantzazu Hotel (46 rooms) Arantzazu Auzoa 8; 943 78 13 13; e info@hsarantzazu.com; w hotelsantuariodearantzazu.com; closed mid-Dec–Feb. Spacious rooms & restaurant featuring Basque cuisine. *€50/60 sgl/dbl*

Sindika (35 rooms) Barrio Arantzazu 11; 943 78 13 03; e h.sindika@hotmail.com; w www.hotel-sindika.com. Short walk from the sanctuary, with panoramic views, a good restaurant & seasonal swimming pool. *€42/55 sgl/dbl*

TOURIST INFORMATION

Tourist office Located at the side of the main car park; 943 71 89 11; Jun–end Sep & Easter week daily, other months weekends only

WHAT TO SEE Try to arrive in time for a visit to the sanctuary, or **Santuario de Nuestra Señora de Arantzazu** to give it its full name. A hermitage was built here after the appearance of the Virgin in 1468, followed by a sanctuary. Although the sanctuary is rather severe and dark inside, its style is a collaboration between some of the biggest names in Basque art and architecture (see box, page 72). On Sundays, the car park fills with visitors, while important pilgrimages on 28 March and 9 September underline the significance of this special place.

▲ The striking exterior of the Sanctuary of Arantzazu AP/S

Arantzazu lies within Aizkorri-Aratz Natural Park, which the camino crosses on the next beautiful, hilly stage, and the **Aizkorri-Aratz Interpretation Centre** (⏲ weekends & holidays), with interactive displays spread over three floors, is just up above the sanctuary's car park. Arantzazu also holds a special place in Basque hearts, as it was here that their language was 'rationalised' in the 20th century (see box, page 72).

TRANSPORT Arantzazu is fairly isolated and buses to the town of Oñati, a 10km drive north and which has onward connections to Bilbao, run only on Sundays and during festivals. The only alternative is to scrounge a lift from a visitor – or pay for an expensive taxi.

ARANTZAZU: A PLACE OF SPECIAL BASQUE SIGNIFICANCE

'Don't judge a book by its cover' might be a suitable piece of advice to absorb as you stand before the huge, abrasive hulk of the Santuario de Nuestra Señora de Arantzazu. Should a holy place really look like this? On a rainy day (and there are plenty of those in the Basque Mountains) it can be a hard-sell if you're trying to attract visitors here based purely on its aesthetics. But to really appreciate this imposing edifice, you need to take a crash-course in Basque art, architecture, history and even the development of the Basque language. Ready?

First, history. The original sanctuary was built on the site of a hawthorn bush in which a local shepherd discovered an image of the Virgin Mary in 1468. To this day, Arantzazu remains a popular pilgrimage for Basques, though the original building and many of its successors were destroyed by fires, both accidental and intentional, across the intervening centuries – most recently torched by the military in 1834. The construction of the current basilica began as recently as 1950 but contains elements which seem destined to hold significance for many years to come.

Many of the biggest hitters in the world of Basque art were involved and were granted enormous freedom as to the design of their artistic contributions. Sculptors Eduardo Chillida and Jorge Oteiza designed and made the iron doors and the apostles above the entrance respectively. The latter work holds particular interest, given that there are 14 of them and no single explanation for this surplus of holy figures has been proffered! The funky paintings in the crypt are by Nestor Basterretxea, another Basque cultural giant.

But perhaps Arantzazu's most lasting significance will be as the place where the disparate strands of the Basque language, which suffered from existential threats under Franco, were brought together and standardised. This work was completed as recently as the 1960s. Prior to this project, natives of each of the isolated, north-to-south Basque valleys sometimes struggled to converse with each other, as their dialects were so diverse.

Taxis
- **Ana Orueta** (Oñati) 943 53 40 82
- **José Luis Rabanete** (Oñati)
943 71 65 34; **m** 658 73 27 09

3 ARANTZAZU–ARAIA

With both a significant climb and descent, this is a moderately challenging stage that continues through the stunning Aizkorri-Aratz Natural Park – but the good news is that the climb is not nearly as hard as the previous stage. The high Urbia pastures and surrounding mountains are stunning and tranquil but, given the imperfect waymarking, a weather check is advisable, as fog and low cloud can be encountered on the route, which meanders gently through high pasture below peaks that represent the high points between the Bay of Biscay and the distant Mediterranean. Setting off in good time will reward you with a timely arrival in Araia, where you may wish to shop for provisions for the next stage. Note that Araia has no accommodation, so after a pause you will have to walk for a further 40 minutes to reach the two overnight options just west of San Román de Millán.

Start Sanctuary of Arantzazu
Coordinates 42.97914, -2.39854
Finish Araia (accommodation at San Román de Millán)
Difficulty Moderate/hard
Distance 18km (plus 4.4km to reach San Román's accommodations)
Duration 5hrs (Araia), 6hrs (Hotel Andamur/Pension El Ventorro in San Román de Millán)
Ascent 650m
Descent 745m

THE ROUTE From the sanctuary, continue to ascend the road to pass the Sindika hotel on the right. Where the path divides take the wider, rising, stony path to reach a walkers' car park, from where you turn left through metal gates to continue your ascent on a wide track signposted for Urbia. On weekends this route is very popular, perhaps partially due to the bar at the summit of the Urbia pass, 4km away. After around 3km, the path reaches a small clearing in the beech trees where you take the left fork to continue your ascent. Red, white, yellow and orange waymarkers guide you, meaning it is almost impossible to get lost. Less than 1km further, the path reaches a high-altitude meadow; at 1,100m, most of today's ascending is done.

Continue on the path, avoiding the temptation to follow any walkers heading higher up as they follow the line of stones planted in the grass

STAGE 3

off to your right. In front of you, the full beauty of the Aizkorri mountain range is apparent. Staying on your same path, there is now a short descent to the Ermita de Urbia hermitage – which can provide shelter in stormy weather – and then between lines of trees to **Urbiako Fonda** (🕒 Jun–Oct Wed–Sun), a patriotically Basque bar/restaurant serving meals and selling sandwiches. There are often herds of horses present in this gorgeous valley, their clanking bells providing a mellow sonic backdrop. Try to roll your tongue around some of the mountain names here – there is a helpful information board identifying them: Arbelaitz, Aketegi, Aizkorri... the highest of these, Aitzuri, is 1,551m, but fortunately we don't have to climb any of them.

After a well-earned rest at the bar, follow the wide path as it sweeps around to the right, passing the turn-off to Aizkorri and then a modest **dolmen**, or strike out diagonally across the grass, crossing a stream to follow a line of 'planted' vertical stones. The two paths both run parallel to the craggy mountain range off to your left and join together after a short distance, just before reaching a group of shepherds' dwellings. One of these buildings houses the **Aizbea Ttontor quesería** (cheese factory). From this tiny unit, some 1,200kg of tasty Idiazabal (see box, page 59) are produced in only two months, before the 500 sheep are driven to lower pastures to provide milk for a further 5,500kg made in a nearby village. The higher and lower pasture grasses result in significantly different tasting cheeses.

Just 150m beyond the shepherds' houses, either follow the road (advisable in poor weather) or set off at a shallow angle to the right, through woods. After 2km the routes converge, and from here continue to follow the road, ignoring a path that deviates to the left. Soon after, the woods open up to give incredible views off to the right, down to the open plains of the Llanada Alavesa, to the mountains of Vitoria and then to the higher Sierra Cantabria beyond. Away to your right, the city of Vitoria-Gasteiz – the Basque Country's administrative capital – may also be visible on a clear day.

Just 100m beyond this viewpoint, look out for the red-and-white markings on the left and leave the road to follow a narrower path skirting some woods on your left. This path carries waymarking on the trees and is prettier as well as shorter, but in bad weather it is better to stay on the road, as although it takes an hour longer it is easier to follow in poor conditions. If you choose the path rather than the road, it starts to descend on a rough, stony section through the trees. It can occasionally be indistinct, muddy after rain, but the waymarked trees are enough to guide the vigilant walker. After 1km, you reach a clearing where there are red-and-white waymarkings on a path that leads *upwards* to your left. Ignore this! Instead, look for the *yellow* (and occasional orange) arrows leading downwards. You are now on a Camino de Santiago route and, rarely for once, you are heading in the *same* direction (in later stages, the Ignaciano heads east as the Santiago goes west). Part of this path

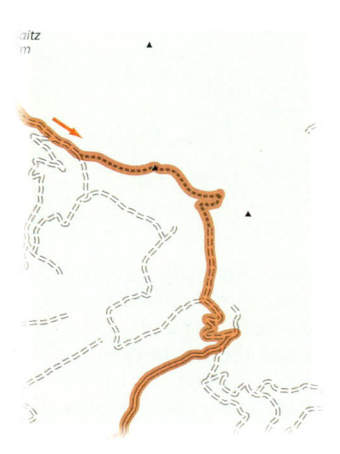

STAGE 3

is an old Roman *calzada* or cobbled road, with its stones visible beneath your feet.

Soon you reach a wider path which descends, again following yellow arrows, to a T-junction with another path where you follow the sign that tells you it is now 6.3km to Araia. After less than 1km, the road joins another and you are 'yellow-arrowed' to the right, still descending. Be aware: always stay on this road and ignore any signs off to the left for Araia as these will take you back up the mountain! Also ignore a sign to your right leading through the woods, visible just before the road crosses a concrete bridge. Eventually the descending road ends at another T-junction and here you turn left for **Araia**, now 2.2km away, as the Camino de Santiago path departs to the right, on its way to Zalduondo village. The road passes a seasonal bar with tempting swimming pool before arriving in town, with the church on your right. Opposite it is **Café Kuttuna** (Elizalde Kalea 5), which has a stamp for your *credenciál*. Araia is the official stage end, and there is little to see in town, but make sure you arrive in time to stock up here or visit the late-night shop at the Hotel Andamur, as tomorrow's stage has no shops or restaurants. For somewhere to stay tonight you will need to follow the

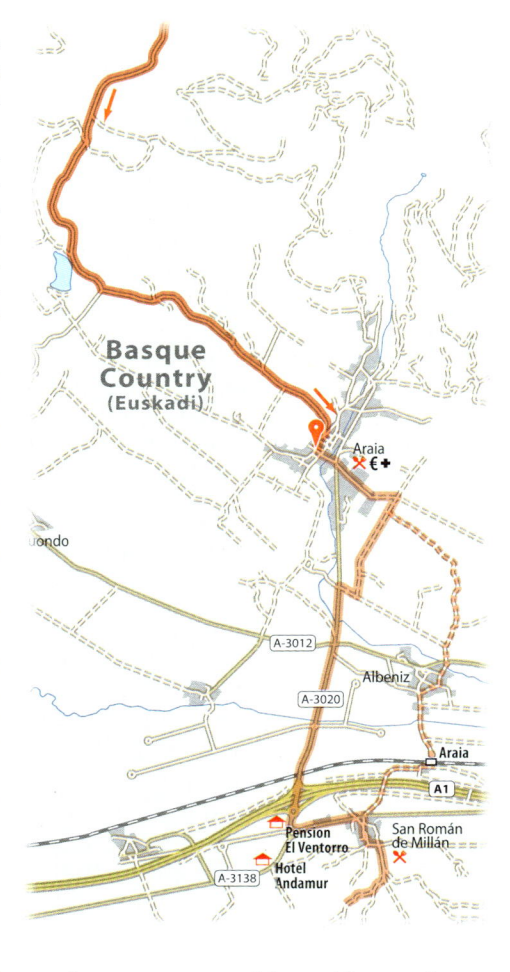

▲ High pastureland characterises Stage 3 *BT*

instructions for the beginning of the next stage to arrive at the two San Román accommodations listed below.

WHERE TO STAY AND EAT Pre-booking is definitely advisable on this stage as options are limited. A pilgrims' hostel has been constructed in Araia but was not in operation at the time of writing. You could contact the *ayuntamiento* (city hall; 945 30 40 06) to see if the situation has changed.

Hotel Andamur (45 rooms) Poligono Otikurri, San Román de Millán, just off the A1/N-1 main road; 945 31 47 83; **e** hotelsanroman@andamur.com; **w** andamurhotel.com. Located 4km beyond Araia, so on the next day's stage, a pilgrim-friendly, efficient, clean & spacious truck-stop hotel with good standards. All-day restaurant & bar on site, & a good place to stock up on supplies for the next stage. *€35/49 sgl/dbl (inc pilgrim discount)*

Pension El Ventorro (6 rooms) Media Legua 1, San Román de Millán; 945 30 43 72; **e** marisolselva@gmail.com. Also beyond today's stage end, this motorway service station full of hungry truck drivers on the south side of the A1/N-1 highway has a few rooms (some with shared bathrooms). Bar & good-value restaurant. *€20/35 sgl/dbl*

✕ **Umandi** Andoni Urrestarazu 4, Araia; 945 31 46 15; daily, closes Mon–Wed at 17.00. Good daily menus, plenty of hearty Basque tapas. Probably the best in town. *€12*

TRANSPORT Araia has a train station with services to Zaragoza, Madrid and Pamplona. There are also trains to Miranda de Ebro, for connections back to Bilbao. See **w** renfe.com for times and prices.

Taxis
Javier Elizondo Irabarren (Agurain) **m** 608 87 18 20

Taxi Berasategui (Araia) **m** 699 44 54 03

4 ARAIA–ALDA

Unless you slept out in the open, or the hostel in Araia has opened, it is likely that your starting point today will be San Román rather than Araia. This lessens the walk by about an hour, which is welcome as you have a significant, 700m climb in the morning and a descent at the end of the stage. The challenge today is both physical and logistical, as there are no opportunities for refreshment after you leave San Román and only one place to stay and eat in Alda. If that is full, then you will have to extend the day to reach San Vicente de Arana, an extra 3km but with additional accommodation and dining options.

It's a world away from the busy A1 road you met this morning to the craggy Sierra de Entzia or the ultra-sleepy Valle de Arana you will encounter this afternoon. Descending into that beautiful valley is like entering a land that time truly forgot, with the few inhabitants going about their business as if their environment had been severed from the outside world. While there are no great sights to marvel at, the contrast with chaotic worlds elsewhere will surely leave you pondering. At one time, potatoes were the great crop here, but these have been replaced by wheat and other cereals. But with only around 200 people resident in the whole valley – nearly half over 65 years in age – there is not a great demand for employment here.

Start Cooperitiva (supermarket), Presalde Kalea, Araia (or from San Román accommodations)
Coordinates 42.88950, -2.31656
Finish Alda
Difficulty Moderate/hard
Distance 22km (18km if starting from San Román)
Duration 6hrs (5hrs if starting from San Román)
Ascent 725m
Descent 510m

THE ROUTE In Araia, make sure you get your *credenciál* stamped in Café Kuttuna, next to the church, before departing, though the Hotel Andamur in San Román will also oblige. With the church on your right and Kuttuna on your left, leave Araia on the continuation of the road on which you arrived. Pass a small park on your left – where there is a Camino Ignaciano info panel – and turn right and then immediately left to pick up signs for Albeniz and Alda, 21.2km away. After 200m, follow the sign to the right for Albeniz. Very shortly, the official route is signposted off to your left but this will eventually take you to the rail tracks, where there is no safe crossing – you would literally have to jump down on to the tracks – and is (in the author's view) downright dangerous. Ignore this sign, therefore, and instead continue on the dirt road straight ahead for 300m and turn right to reach the main road (A-3020), at which you turn left. Continue by the side of this road to cross first the railway then the motorway, with the twin accommodations of Ventorro and Andamur (page 77) visible off to your right. Cross the first roundabout and, at the second, turn left towards **San Román de Millán**. Pass the rather severe-looking church on the right after a few hundred metres, turning immediately right after it to reach a square with a bright mural. (This is a protest against a planned high-speed railway, which might resonate with British readers.) Circumnavigate a large stone house and at a T-junction with a road, look for the narrow path straight ahead. After 100m, this path joins a road and the familiar red-and-white markings are again visible.

Cross a cattle-grid to find a sign for Alda, now 16km away. Take the right fork as the wide path begins to ascend; the sheer rock faces of the **Sierra de Entzia** tower high above to your left. Head left

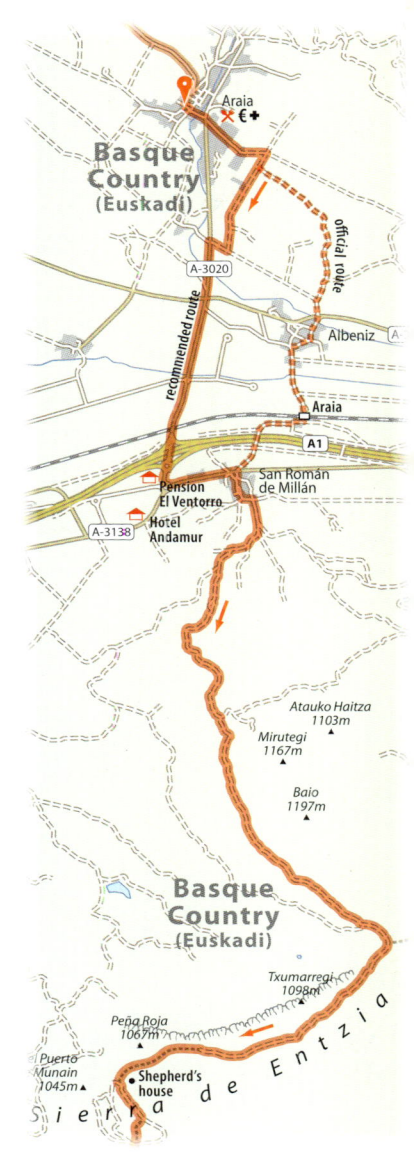

STAGE 4

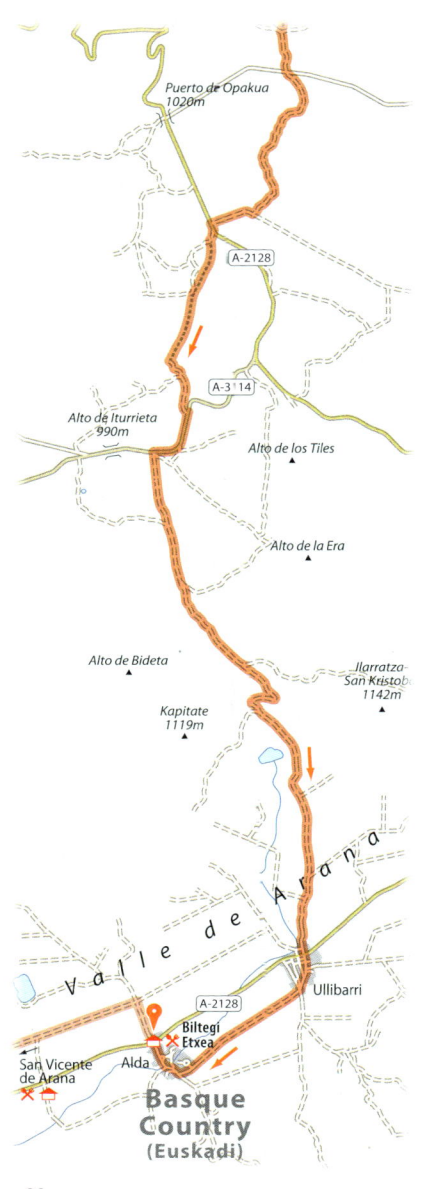

at the next fork, guided by orange Ignatian arrows and occasional signposting for Alda. Soon you will see the odd tree with tree-hut and a ladder, used by hunters in autumn to shoot pigeons – you might see them if here on a Thursday or at the weekend. (In other parts of the Basque Country, hunting is by net.) After more climbing, you reach a fork at which you take the right. The mountain up behind you with the metal cross on the summit is **Mirutegi** (1,167m). The next stretch of path can be very muddy, even in the summer months. Eventually you arrive at a T-junction where you turn right, signposted for Alda and San Vicente de Arana. The journey will be mainly flat or downhill from this, the highpoint of the stage.

Pass through a gate (there is a break in the chain), but be vigilant: once through, veer fairly sharply right to quickly pick up signs to confirm you are still on the GR-120. Take care, especially in times of fog, though there are clear red-and-white markings on the trees to guide you. After 200m, the path emerges from the woods to give great views down over the Alavan plains and to the mountains beyond. Beware that there are very steep drop-offs here –

▲ Looking down over the plains of Álava *BT*

don't get too close – and as it continues along this balcony, the path gets extremely close to the edge at times. At the end of a small open meadow, look carefully for the path that leaves up to your left, waymarked on a tree. Our path continues along the balcony: sometimes through woods, sometimes through grassy areas, and the red-and-white markings can be difficult to see in the shade of the trees. The steeper slope/drop-off is never more than 20m off to the right.

Eventually, the path leads out of the woods and you descend by marker poles, passing between a sculpture on your left and a memorial on your right. On reaching an open area with a renovated stone **shepherd's house** and a corrugated shed on your left, take a 90-degree left, looking for a couple of red-and-white waymarked posts to your left and passing with the corrugated shed close by also on your left. At the end of the shed's enclosure, veer right following the red-and-white marks on a tree. After 300m on this wide path, you reach another building with a signpost illustrating that you're still on the GR-120 and Alda is 10.2km away. Cross the wide meadow, following the short line of posts, and the grassy path turns slightly right. You now head for the road, which becomes visible 200m in front.

Joining this rough road, it leads down to a car park at a tarmac road which you cross, and you pass between two wooden corrals. Crossing a small river on a bridge, continue on a beautiful, level grassy path and,

▲ The beautiful Valle de Arana *BT*

after 1km of rising through grassy pasture, turn right on to a slightly elevated road that leads to a tarmac one. This is close to the **Puerto de Opakua pass**, at 1,020m. Turn left on to the A-2128 road and after only 50m turn right through a metal gate to join a wide dirt path heading for trees; when the path splits, take the left-hand fork. Pay attention to the waymarking on this section, as the path now enters a wood and soon you leave the main path, to head right on another narrow path that rises gently. The path then descends to a metal gate and cattle-grid by the A-3114, on to which you turn right.

At the sign for the **Alto de Iturrieta** (990m), take a 90-degree left on to a wide but uneven road. Follow this for 1km until it begins to curve left, at which point you leave the road and take a narrow path straight ahead, leading down through a gate and into woods. Some of the beech trees here are an incredible 50m high. Directly ahead is the beautiful, sparsely populated **Valle de Arana**. Rather oddly, '*valle*' in Spanish means 'valley', while '*arana*' in Basque means… valley! The village you will soon see ahead is **Ullibarri** while off to the right is **Alda**. On a clear day, you will also see through the trees the Sierra Cantabria off to the right, with the distinctive shape of the appropriately named 'Sleeping Lion' mountain, correctly titled La Pena de Población. The road leads down to a junction with the A-2128; cross it to enter Ullibarri and find the village's San Juan church and *fronton* (the court for the Basque sport of *pelota*) on your right and the unnamed village bar – occasionally open – off to your left. There is also a seasonal swimming pool here. At a round tower, look out for the sign to Alda, now just over 1km away. Follow this road between fields to reach the stage end. The road continues and then curves right to cross a bridge and arrive at the main road: the Biltegi Etxea (see below) is straight in front of you.

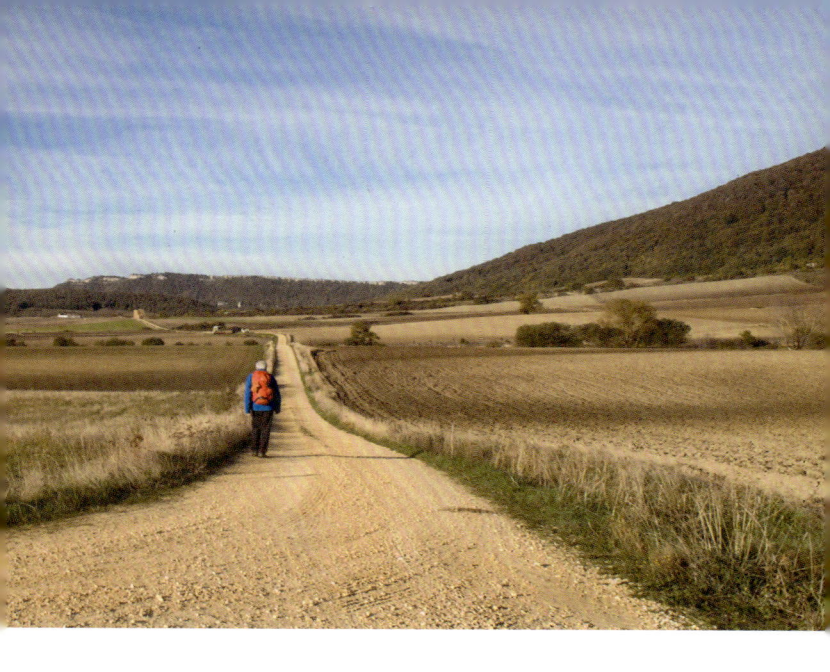

WHERE TO STAY AND EAT The population of Alda has halved in 15 years, yet the decline can hardly be called dramatic: it has fallen from around 60 inhabitants to fewer than 30, certainly not enough to sustain a hotel or restaurant, just a solitary guesthouse. Consequently, you will need to pre-book your accommodation in advance and also ensure that evening meals are being served at the Biltegi Etxea. Your other option is to walk the additional 3km southwest to San Vicente de Arana (page 85).

Biltegi Etxea (8 rooms) Carretera 3, Alda; 945 40 60 42; **m** 656 76 27 93; **e** marisolgarciadeazilu@yahoo.es. Beautifully converted potato warehouse, a traditional Basque establishment. Heating & great views. Will provide good-value, simple meals. *€36 sgl/dbl*

🏠 **Refugio de Peregrinos (Pilgrims' Hostel)** (10 beds) Sar Vicente de Arana; 945 40 61 23 or 945 40 60 06. Bookable through the Obenkun restaurant or *ayuntamiento* (town hall) whose numbers are given. No cooking facilities. Advanced booking advisable. *€10 pp*

✖ **Obenkun** Pl Juegabolos 2, San Vicente de Arana; 945 40 61 23; ⏰ lunchtime Mon–Sat. Meaty cuisine straight from the farm, & they make their own nutty Idiazabal cheese in a tiny production unit on site. Limited options for vegetarians. *€15*

TRANSPORT Given its diminutive size, it should be no shock to learn that Alda has no public transport connections, nor do any of the nearby villages. A 19km taxi ride from Alda to Salvatierra-Agurain will hook you up to trains heading westwards for Vitoria-Gasteiz, the Basque Country's administrative capital, or to Zaragoza to the east.

Taxis

🚕 **Juan Francisco Gonzalez** (Salvatierra-Agurain) 945 30 11 13

🚕 **Juan Pérez** (San Vicente de Arana) 945 40 60 64; m 659 64 11 83

5 ALDA–GENEVILLA

A medium-length stage, this section has only half the number of the up-and-down undulations you have experienced over the past four days and they are all fairly gentle. The route described here is the shorter of two variants and reaches Genevilla via the village of Orbiso, joining up with the longer route (via Oteo and Antoñana, 6km longer and not described here) at Santa Cruz de Campezo. Today the Camino Ignaciano leaves the Basque Country and passes into Navarre for one night before returning again on the next stage. Largely traffic-free, today's walk passes through sleepy villages and tranquil countryside. Around the pretty town of Genevilla, the locals make a living from small-scale cultivation of beans, potatoes and, formerly, tobacco.

> **Start** Biltegi Etxea, Alda
> **Coordinates** 42.75435, -2.33215
> **Finish** Genevilla
> **Difficulty** Easy
> **Distance** 19km (via Orbiso)
> **Duration** 5hrs (via Orbiso)

THE ROUTE Facing the front of the Biltegi Etxea, take the dirt road to its left, leaving the accommodation to your right. At the first junction, turn left, signposted to **San Vicente de Arana**. After 2.5km, you reach a junction with a road where you turn left into San Vicente. Just past the church in the centre, turn right on to Calle Uriondo to pick up signs. (Just before the church, you can turn right to find a bar/shop and the Obenkun restaurant at which you collect the keys if you are staying in the *refugio*; page 84.) After the last of San Vicente's buildings on Calle Uriondo, a sign for Oteo points up into fields on your right – this is the longer variant, which we do not follow. Instead, after a few hundred metres, turn right at a T-junction.

The tarmac road peters out and changes to a rougher surface. After 200m on this uneven road, turn left following the orange arrow as the path climbs slightly uphill. You will notice how the beech trees of earlier stages have been replaced by oak and holm oak, as the climate is now Mediterranean. The path soon turns right and you negotiate a gate, continuing straight ahead with a field flanking to your right, before trees take over on both sides and you pass through another gate. After 1km or so, the path splits and you follow up to the left, guided by orange as well as red-and-white markings. When the path splits again, follow the

STAGE 5

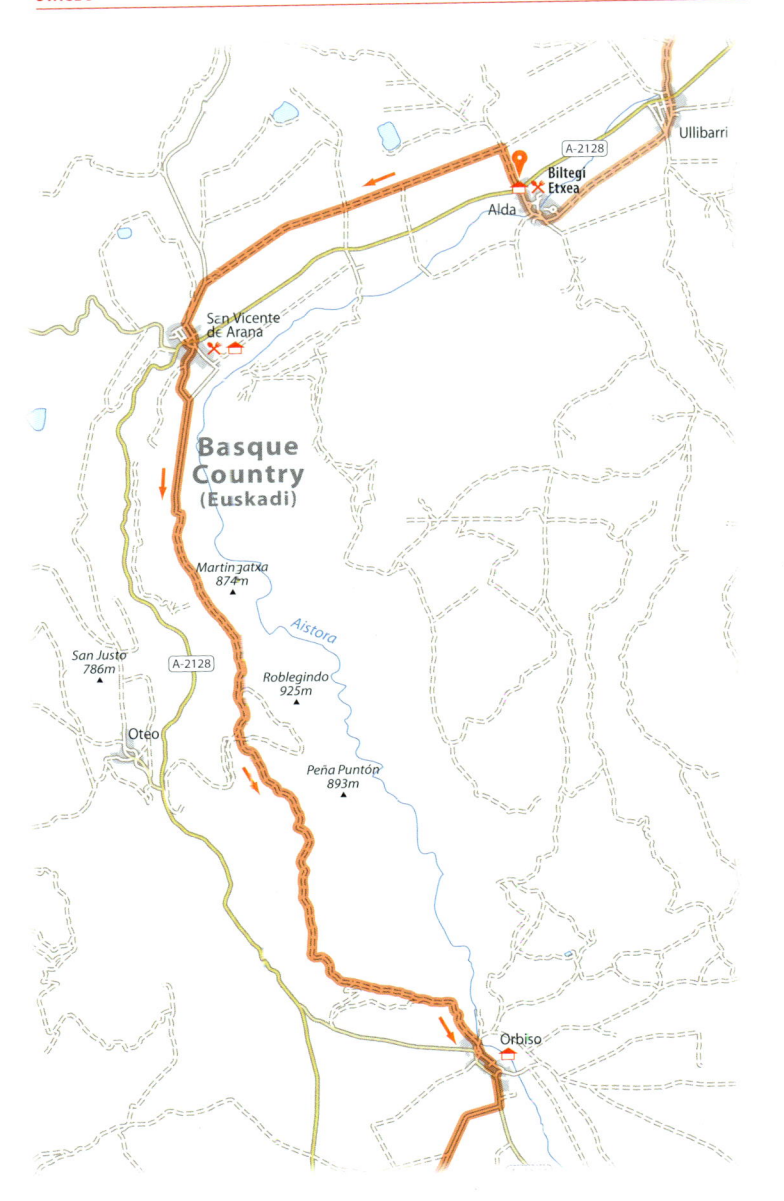

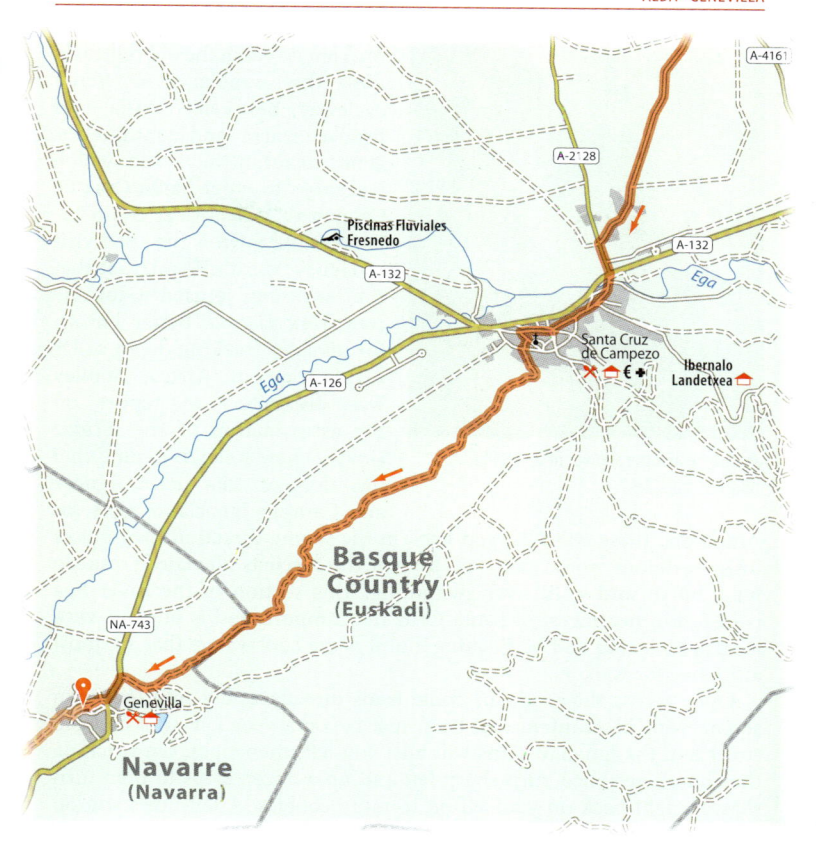

waymarked path as it gently descends until it reaches a T-junction with a road. Turn right past a water fountain to enter the centre of **Orbiso** village.

Continue down into the church square and veer diagonally right to pick up the new-style Ignaciano signs which have appeared. (At the far end of the village there is a community bar (a *txoko*), open weekends only. There's also a basic hostel if you are in need of accommodation (page 89).) After a short descent on this narrow street, look for a 'Stop' sign on your right and, at this junction, turn left on to the tarmac. Eighty metres after passing the Orbiso town sign, turn right on to more tarmac with fields on either side. In front of you, 2km away and off the route, is the **Ibernalo Landetxea** (page 89). When the road ends after around 2km,

STAGE 5

▲ The freshwater shower in Genevilla's 'pilgrims' park' MS

turn left crossing the old railtrack, now the popular Via Verde cycleway between Vitoria and Estella-Lizarra, and continue for 200m to reach the A-132, which you cross to enter **Santa Cruz de Campezo**. A historical claim-to-fame of the town is the 1869 visit of Henry Morton Stanley, at that time a young journalist for the *New York Herald*. Better known for his later tracking down of Dr Livingstone in Africa, Stanley was dispatched to report on the assassination of the *alcalde* (mayor) here following some civil disorder. At this point, ignore any Camino Ignaciano signs for Antoñana: these will take you back in the wrong direction! Just out of town, a detour would take you to visit the **Piscinas Fluviales Fresnedo** for a bit of mid-walk river swimming. This section of the River Ega is just 1km northwest of Santa Cruz de Campezo and is popular with locals picnicking and barbecuing, but it is the cool waters that are most attractive for walkers.

Once across the road, the route leads directly uphill into the main square with its fountain and bars. Just beyond, veer left up a cobbled street and the Ignatian signs will take you left, then right. On reaching the church entrance, turn sharp left and up a dozen steps to then turn sharply right back on yourself on to more cobbles. A left takes you on to the Plaza del Castillo, then take a right following the 'Continuacion del Camino' signs. Cross a cobbled street to join a dirt path descending between buildings. On reaching tarmac, turn right for only 20m later and you see the sign for Genevilla, now 4.7km away.

The signs soon take you to the right and the path rises slightly to give views to the 'Sleeping Lion' before leading into more shady surrounds, welcome on a hot day. From here, the path is waymarked through the woods, at one point turning sharp left then right before continuing. Signs will soon take you on to a wide, stony path through more trees. This path ends at a main road, the NA-743, where you turn left before veering right after a few hundred metres down a smooth concrete road to enter **Genevilla**, with its church ahead of you. The 'NA-' road prefix signifies that you have passed into Navarre. Both accommodation options are easy to find, directly on this road and within 200m of each other. If you need drinkable water, be sure to use the fountain attached to the church.

🏠 **WHERE TO STAY AND EAT** Careful planning and pre-booking are once again advisable to ensure that you have a bed for the night. Note that not all options listed are exactly on the Ignatian route. Genevilla has no restaurants, though both the El Encinedo and the Usategieta can organise evening meals with advance notification. Failing that, bring your own food or stay the night in Santa Cruz de Campezo, which has four dining options, but ending your stage here, or at the hostel in Orbiso, will make for a *very* tough next stage.

🏠 **Casa Rural El Encinedo** (3 rooms) Calle Norte 2, Genevilla; 948 44 40 16; m 616 28 95 03; e reservas@elencinedo.com; w elencinedo.com. Family-run & friendly, though no English spoken. Large rooms, full of character. All meals available. *€45 sgl/dbl*

🏠 **Casa Rural Usategieta** (3 rooms) Mediodia 2, Genevilla; m 649 85 16 02; w casa-usategieta.com. Lovely, quirky place with pleasant outdoor space. The name translates as 'the pigeon house' &, according to the website, 'all travelling pigeons & lovebirds are welcome'. Also welcome are pilgrims, who may get a discount. Hearty b/fast inc. If you want a rest day, they can offer mountain bikes & organise winery visits. *€55/68 sgl/dbl*

🏠 **Hostel Marivi** (6 rooms) Herreria 7, Orbiso; 945 41 50 30. Basic accommodation, shared bathrooms. B/fast & dinner available. *€45 sgl or dbl*

🏠 **Ibernalo Landetxea** (8 rooms) Carretera Ibernalo 30, Santa Cruz de Campezo; 945 10 22 71; m 647 91 14 84; e biharra@gmail.com. A couple of kilometres (30mins' walk) out of the village. Check in advance if their restaurant is open. *€45/65 sgl/dbl*

WHAT TO SEE Genevilla has a population of 46, with many abandoned houses, but has created a '**pilgrims' park**', just 100m past the Iglesia de San Esteban church, with an impressive freshwater shower (see photo, opposite). A chance to refresh yourself, but only if you're feeling brave – the water is cold!

TRANSPORT At the time of writing there were no buses serving San Vicente de Arana, Santa Cruz de Campezo or Genevilla, so your only option is a taxi.

Taxis

🚕 **Juan Pérez** (San Vicente de Arana) 945 40 60 64; m 659 64 11 83

🚕 **Taxi** (Genevilla) 931 78 00 30; m 661 83 06 77

6 GENEVILLA–LAGUARDIA

After briefly entering Navarre yesterday, this stage promptly leads back into the Basque Country and ends in what is officially one of Spain's most beautiful towns, Laguardia. Like most good things in life, you must work hard to reach it and the challenge presents itself in the form of a long stage crossing the mountain pass of Bernedo. Your legs will be battle-hardened by now and you have to climb to 1,000m, but the good news is that your starting point at Genevilla is already at over half that altitude. You can look forward to incredible views over Álava, Navarre and La Rioja as well as opportunities to see many birds of prey up in the mountains. That, together with the promise of Laguardia at the end of the day, will help to ease the pain.

The mountainous scenery, which gives way to the rolling vineyards of Rioja Alavesa, is probably the star today, though those walkers with an eye for nature will be distracted by raptors and maybe a deer or two. You pass directly by the Los Llanos dolmen on the latter part of the trail.

Start Iglesia de San Esteban (church), Genevilla
Coordinates 42.64454, -2.39195
Finish Laguardia
Difficulty Hard
Distance 27.5km
Duration 8hrs 30mins
Ascent 740m
Descent 725m

THE ROUTE From Genevilla's church, continue in the same direction as yesterday: following the sign southwest for Meano. At the bottom of the slope, continue straight ahead, now following signs for Marañón and Kripan, and after less than 100m on this concrete road veer left to join a wide, shady dirt track and pick up the first sign for Laguardia. Forming part of the beautiful Izki Natural Park, the rocky crag off to your right is called **La Muela** ('the molar') due to its tooth-like appearance.

The path ends after 3km and you cross a concrete yard up into the village of **Cabredo**. Note the bright building on your right before reaching the church: this is a community bar, but it is run by volunteers so not always open. Pass straight through town, following signs first for Lapoblación and Meano, and then for Marañón. On the edge of Cabredo, take the concrete road rising to your left, now sharing your path with the

A RUSTIC LUNCH

Basques really love their food and will often travel miles to source something special, whether it is a juicy steak, fresh hake or even a modest loaf of bread. On today's stage, you pass through the quiet mountain village of **Meano**, home to the **Panadería Domaica**, a gastronomic destination in its own right for two special products: bread and chorizo sausage. If you have forgotten to bring lunch, this is your chance to gorge on these local, rustic delicacies – but you'll need to arrive early. The delightful woman in charge closes up at 11.30, though she does say that if you phone the number displayed on the front door, she will happily come down and serve you. That's if she has any bread left! If not, you can always console yourself with some chorizo – spicy or mild – also sold here and made by her sister nearby.

GR-1 route and its red-and-white markings. The next bit of this trail is a favourite haunt of many insects, so some repellent is advisable.

After 1km, follow the sign to the right for Marañón, Bernedo and Laguardia. The path becomes narrow and occasionally muddy here, but is easy to follow, with windmills appearing on the hills to your left. Reaching a junction, turn sharp right, with the windmills now directly behind and **Marañón** village in your sights. However, Marañón is not on the Ignatian route, so after only 100m you turn sharp left, leaving the village behind you and with the windmills now temporarily ahead. After a few hundred metres, the path splits and you fork to the right towards the mountains – the serious climbing begins now. At a T-junction, turn left, with Marañón still visible down the path to your right. Shortly beyond the junction, ignore a road leaving up to your right and continue straight ahead. At a clearing, you will see away to your left the peak of Ioar (Joar), which, at 1,418m, is the highpoint of the Sierra de Codés range. Well before you reach the windmills, follow the sign to your right for the village of Lapoblación, 2km away.

Now the rocky path – thankfully short – climbs more steeply, at times without shade. At the top you reach the NA-7211, with views down over La Rioja and Navarre; turn right and immediately right again to leave the tarmac on to a concrete road. Note the small *boj* (boxwood) trees here, which in times gone by were popular for making utensils and tool handles. After less than 200m, double-back on yourself, taking the left turn on a wide dirt road that rises, passing through trees with rich birdlife: a cuckoo calling is not unusual. Just before you enter

STAGE 6

Lapoblación, note the **cemetery** on your left; pause a moment to ponder that there are more bodies here than in the inappropriately named town itself ('Lapoblación' means 'The Population'), its residents numbering around 12 at time of writing. Nonetheless, there are great views from the cemetery down and across to the distant mountain ranges, collectively known as the Sistema Ibérico. The distinctive cone off to your right is that of San Lorenzo, La Rioja's mightiest at 2,271m, located in the Sierra de la Demanda range. Logroño is in front of you and you can *just* spot your destination, Laguardia, off to your right, but still a long way distant. At this point you would be entitled to consider why Ignatius went from this high point to Laguardia, then Navarrete, then Logroño, rather than walk directly ahead to La Rioja's capital. The answer lies in his previous life as a soldier, as he had close connections with the Duke of Najera, whose base was in Navarrete.

Continuing straight ahead from the cemetery, you arrive at Lapoblación's church (the Iglesia de Nuestra Señora de la Asunción) and the *fronton,* with a bar behind you by the roadside (but again opening times are sporadic, so don't rely on it). The church is worth a peek for its impressive Gothic altarpiece, but sadly it is often closed. Veering left of the church, take the tarmac road as it quickly reaches a junction with the NA-7210 and continue downwards on this until the tarmac curves left, at which point you follow the sign to the right for **Meano**. Approaching

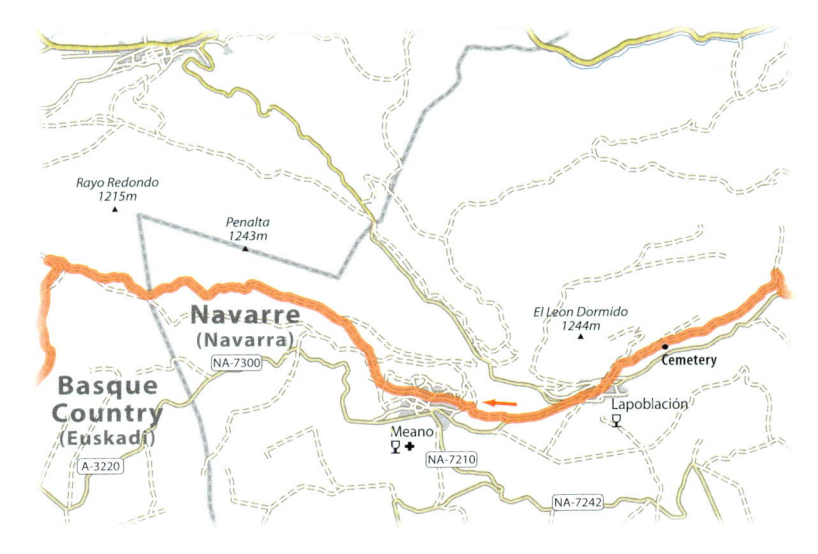

GENEVILLA–LAGUARDIA

this next village, descend past an agricultural building on the right to be greeted by the solar-panelled roof of a chorizo factory, surprisingly large for such a small place. The path continues with the village to your left, but if you need some lunch, take a left on to Calle Nueva and descend on a steep concrete path before turning right to find the bakery (see box, page 91). There is also a bar here.

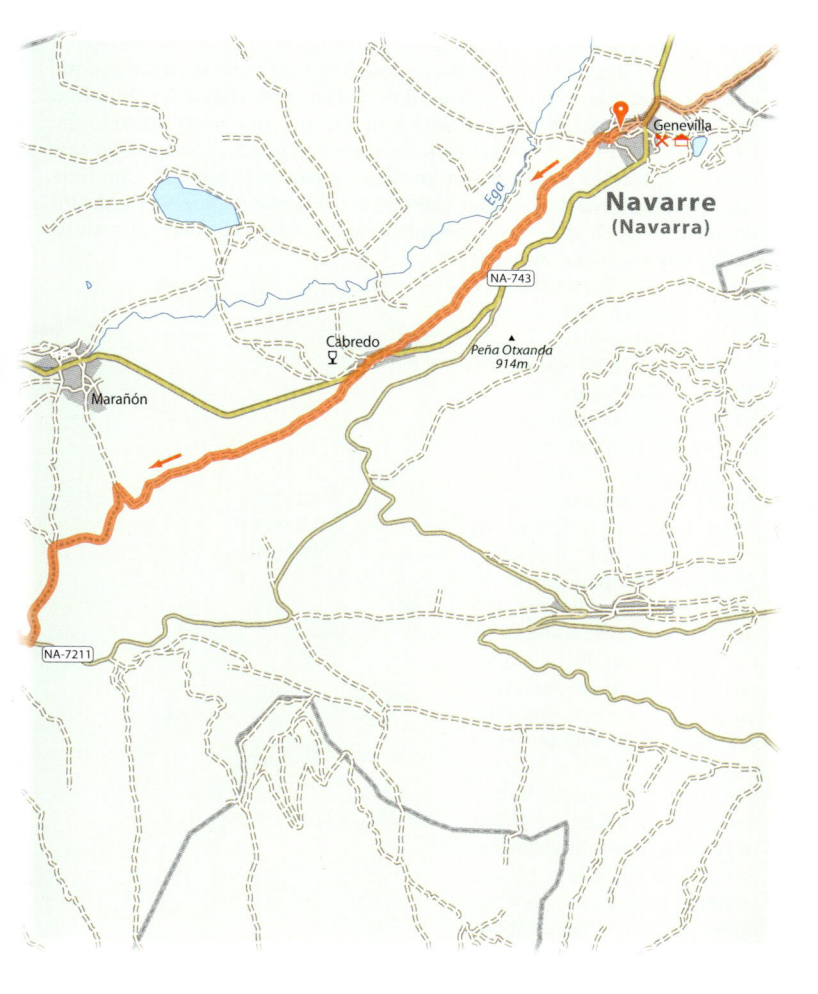

STAGE 6

If choosing not to visit Meano, simply continue straight and in less than 100m fork left for Kripan and Laguardia, soon passing the village cemetery and exiting town on this concrete road. Your path veers slightly right, with agricultural buildings on the left, and at the next fork continue right on to a path. As you walk with sheer cliff faces up to your right, do look out for the resident vultures and listen for the plaintive cry of peregrine falcons. With luck, you might also spot a Bonelli's eagle.

Soon the path angles down to the left, shortly after one of the many convenient stone benches that invite you to rest. At a crossroads, continue ahead on what is sometimes a muddy section and, after a few hundred metres, you'll reach a junction with a rough road that leads down to the left, away from the cliffs and with trees on either side. Descend on this path for a further 200m and at another crossroads turn left. Continue your descent towards the vineyards and at the next junction go right, still downwards, with your target – Kripan village – now just over 1km away.

In the distance, the elevated buildings of Laguardia are now clearer – but there is still a long way to go!

The road now joins the A-3220 (the prefix 'A-' for 'Álava' confirms that you are no longer in Navarre) and you proceed to the right. After the tarmac curves right, leave it in favour of the A-3228 for the final 500m into **Kripan**. To enter the village, veer left off the road, as it begins to bend to the right. Look for a triple-arched building on your right on the Plaza de la Barbacana: here, turn right, following the waymarking. (If you need a rest stop at this point, follow the road for a further 150m instead as it continues down to the left. The bar is by the fronton, though its opening hours are not reliable. There is also a casa rural, the

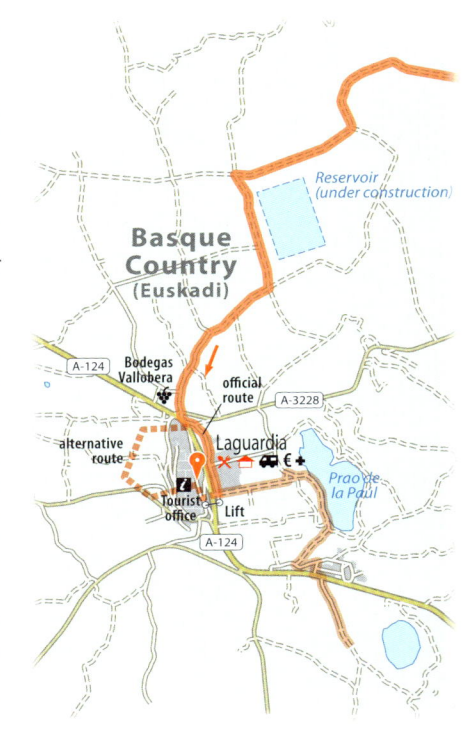

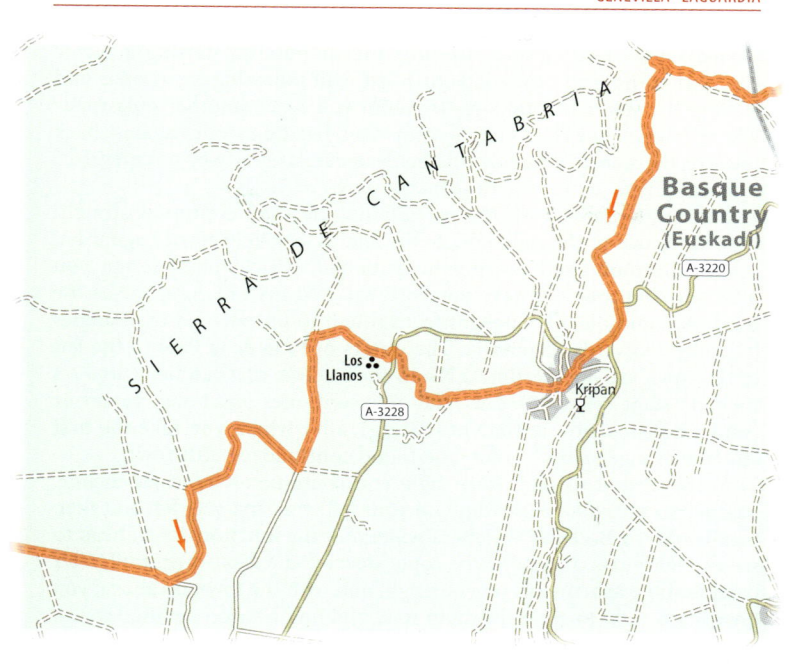

Mercedes Etxea (**m** 629 81 57 93) here, but it may demand a two-night minimum in high season.) Pass the church and pick up the signs for the Ignaciano and GR-120 with Laguardia, still a healthy 11km away. Beyond the church, note the information panel which, unusually for these rural areas, is translated into English. Your dirt track soon reaches tarmac and you now leave the road to follow signs up to the right with blue and yellow waymarking, then the more familiar red and white. The path here can be a bit overgrown, but vigilance will ensure these last markings guide you through.

In just under 1km, you reach the tarmac of the A-3228 road; turn left to then cross it and after 50m leave to the right, signposted for the **Los Llanos** dolmen. This rectangular burial chamber was only excavated in 1982 and is accompanied by a multi-lingual board with background information. The area to the north of Laguardia has many sites of megalithic interest. Beyond the dolmen, continue on the wide grassy track towards the mountains of the sierra until you reach a junction, where you turn left and descend towards the church spire of **Elvillar**. After 1km, turn right on to tarmac (continuing straight on leads to the

STAGE 6

village), now heading back towards the mountains, passing a picnic site, and at the next crossroads turn left, still following the tarmac and leaving the sierra behind you. In 500m you reach another crossroads where you take the right on to a stony road, heading – once again – back towards the sierra. Note how the fields of cereals give way to vineyards, indicating what drives the Riojan economy.

Running parallel with the mountains, the road continues straight with vineyards to the right and, to the left, a clear sighting of Laguardia. Ignore the unmarked turnings to your left, which might tempt you into thinking they will take you to town, and instead continue as the road rises and quickly changes from rough to tarmac and then angles in slightly towards Laguardia. The waters of **Prao de la Paúl** to the left of the town are now visible: a haven for birdlife, this can be visited on the next stage (page 98). The road now continues past a new **reservoir** (under construction at time of writing), after which you take the first left (the orange arrow is a bit faded) and continue towards town.

At the next crossroads, turn right and continue up a tarmac incline. Passing an agricultural building on your left, you first veer left and then turn left at the Bodegas Vallobera winery. At the junction, look ahead to see the markings on a pole: the route steers you left of town until, after passing some apartments on your right and with the town up above, you turn sharp right to cross the main road and find a welcome lift/elevator, which will whisk your tired legs up to **Laguardia**. It certainly did not exist in the Ignatian times! An alternative option to following the official route to the left of the town is to reach the main road after Bodegas Vallobera, cross it carefully, continue down the left side for 150m or so and then take the right-hand turning leading upwards into town.

WHERE TO STAY AND EAT Drawn in by its narrow streets and proximity to many world-class wineries, visitors to Laguardia will find it well equipped with characterful hotels and restaurants. It has no trouble filling them in high season, particularly August. Prices are inevitably a bit higher, too. Advance booking weeks, if not months, ahead is advisable.

Agroturismo Larretxori (4 rooms) Portal de Paganos; 945 60 07 63; w nekatur.net/larretxori. Pleasant, with great views out to the vineyards & mountains. Owners make their own wine. €50 sgl/dbl

Erletxe Casa Rural (6 rooms) Mayor de Peralta 24, Laguardia; 945 62 10 15; m 657 79 93 11; e erletxe@gmail.com; w erletxe.com. At the bottom end of town, a good choice with spacious rooms & pleasant courtyard. €45–75 sgl or dbl

Hospederia de los Parajes (18 rooms) Mayor 46, Laguardia; 945 62 11 30; e info@hospederiadelosparajes.com; w hospederiadelosparajes.com. Classy, upmarket choice, with jacuzzi, excellent restaurant, spa & atmospheric cellar bar. But not cheap! €110 sgl/dbl

🏠 **Hostal Biazteri** (9 rooms) Mayor 72, Laguardia; 945 60 00 26; e reservas@biazteri.com. Bar & decent restaurant. Another of the lower-cost choices, b/fast inc. Very central. €65 sgl/dbl

🏠 **Hotel Marixa** (10 rooms) Sancho Abarca 8, Laguardia; 945 60 01 65; w hotelmarixa.com. One of the less expensive options in town. AC rooms, some with terrace & vineyard views. Good restaurant with local specialities. Good-value b/fast. €55 sgl/dbl

🏠 **Sercotel Villa de Laguardia** (84 rooms) Paseo San Raimundo 15, Laguardia; 945 60 05 60; e reservas@hotelvillalaguardia.com; w hotelvillalaguardia.com. A short walk out of the town centre, this large chain hotel has outdoor pool, gym & spa treatments. Restaurant. €110–300 sgl or dbl

TOURIST INFORMATION

Tourist office Mayor Kalea 52, Laguardia; 945 60 08 45; ⏰ 10.00–14.00 & 16.00–19.00 Mon–Sat, 10.45–14.00 Sun. Very helpful & with occasional exhibitions inside.

WHAT TO SEE If you are planning on spending time in Laguardia before continuing, there are plenty of **wineries** to visit and the tourist office can advise which ones offer English-language guided tours. If you don't want to stray far, the **Bodegas Carlos Pedro Pérez de Vinaspre** (Páganos 44; 945 60 01 46; w bodegascarlossanpedro.com) is right in the town centre and offers tours and tastings, although they are more rough-and-ready than its grandiose name suggests.

If that's not enough, there are occasional guided tours of the **Santa Maria church**, showcasing the stunning portico and giving a potted history of the building, which exhibits various styles (Romanesque, Gothic, Renaissance) employed across the centuries, a **performing clock** in the charismatic town square, which celebrates the time with folk-dancing figurines, and some quaint shops into which to poke your nose.

Bird lovers should visit the **Prao de la Paúl** lake, to the west of town, although you will in any event pass close to it at the start of tomorrow's stage (page 98).

TRANSPORT Regular buses from Laguardia serve Logroño in Navarre and Vitoria-Gasteiz, both with connections to Bilbao. A couple per day serve Bilbao directly.

Taxis

🚕 **Bastida Taxi** (Labastida) m 629 26 16 38

🚕 **Taxi** (Laguardia) m 627 70 04 09

7 LAGUARDIA–NAVARRETE

After overnighting in beautiful, atmospheric Laguardia, the route today continues further south, leaving the mountains behind, departing the southern Basque Country and crossing Spain's longest river. Underfoot you will be mostly on tarmac roads or wide, dirt tracks; very little traffic is encountered and the handful of small towns en route provides welcome refreshment points. Much of the route is through the gentle vineyards of Rioja Alavesa and then those of La Rioja itself. By population, La Rioja is the smallest of Spain's 17 Autonomous Communities, but the wine that has given it its worldwide fame means that – economically – it punches well above its weight.

Today you will also meet up with what might justifiably be called the 'Pilgrim Superhighway', as the Camino Francès ('French Way') intersects with your own lesser-trodden path as you reach the stage end in Navarrete. This hugely popular camino is the busiest of the many Camino de Santiago pilgrim routes, carrying as many as 170,000 pilgrims annually as it wends its way westwards from the Pyrenees to the city of Santiago de Compostela in distant Galicia.

Start Iglesia de San Juan, Laguardia
Coordinates 42.55262, -2.58466
Finish Navarrete
Difficulty Easy
Distance 19.5km
Duration 5hrs

THE ROUTE From the rear of Iglesia de San Juan, exit through the heavy ornate town gate and cross the road to find the sign for the Lagunas de Laguardia. Note the inscription by the outside of the gate (see photo, opposite), which translates as: 'Peace to those who arrive, good health to those who reside, good luck to those who depart.' A fond, uplifting farewell to travellers from a beautiful town. Take the handy and totally unexpected lift down, cross the main A-124 road and pick up the Ignaciano signposting. In typically efficient Basque fashion, the waymarking today (a plentiful combination of orange arrows and Ignaciano signposts) is excellent all the way, until you reach the River Ebro and La Rioja at the halfway point. The route takes you left then right past **Prao de la Paúl**, which you will already have spotted on the previous stage and again while awaiting the lift's arrival. This lagoon holds water year-round and is favoured by common coots, mallards and great crested grebes, among other bird species.

◀ The inscription on the gate *MS*

A few hundred metres beyond the lagoon, at a signpost continue straight ahead, ignoring the deviation offered to Elvillar: that route simply leads back up the mountains you left behind yesterday. Depending on the time of year, the smell of grapes may be all around you. After a few hundred metres more you cross the A-124 again, still guided by those reliable orange arrows as you pass the **Bodegas Ubide** winery on your right, and then, after 1.5km, the **Laguna de Carravalseca** off to your left. The waters here are fed only by rainfall and 'drained' only by evaporation – there is no outflow – so, depending on the season, this lagoon can be full of water or wearing just a white salty crust, and apparently dry.

Staying on the tarmac, eventually a sharp right turn reveals the town of **Lapuebla de Labarca** ahead of you, nestling in a shallow valley. Do not rejoice just yet, as it's still a deceptively long way, but finally the route leads into its centre, onwards past the church and beyond to a modest array of bars and restaurants. (There are also a couple of lodgings here and a small, municipal hostel due to open in 2022.) Despite having a population of fewer than 900, Lapuebla hosts a dozen wineries within its perimeter. The name – literally 'the town of the boat' – derives from the old method of crossing the Ebro. While the name endures, the boat has long ago been replaced by a bridge, and to reach it continue through Lapuebla to a roundabout and follow the A-3216 road for Fuenmayor down to the river. Caution is required while crossing, as there is no pavement on the bridge.

You are now entering the Autonomous Community of La Rioja. Continue up the roadside and, immediately before the railway underpass (orange arrow on reverse of 'zona de reserva' sign), leave the road to the left on a rough path and continue between vines and the rails for around 500m until it crosses the train tracks and continues straight ahead on a

STAGE 7

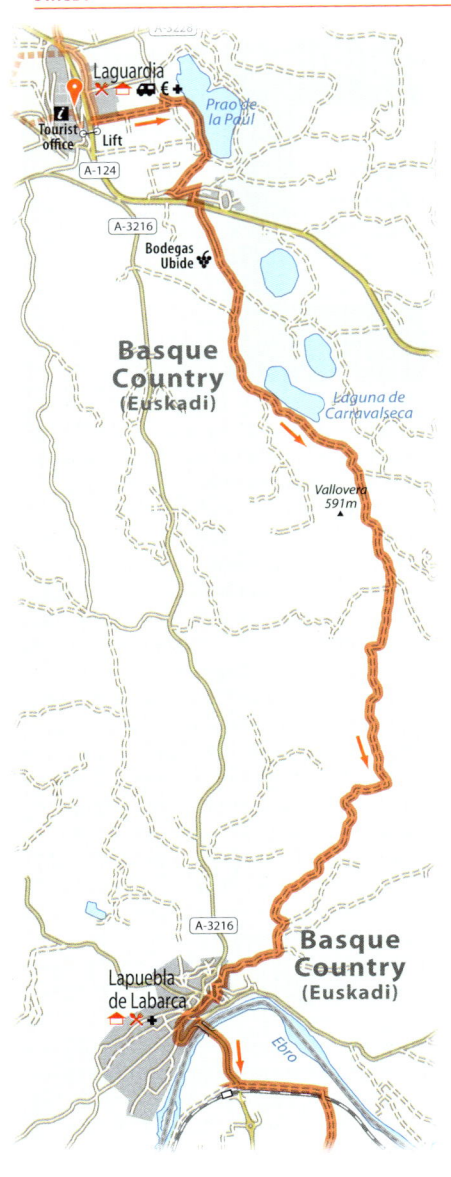

wide path through yet more vineyards. Reaching an unmetalled road, turn right, with a small tree-studded hill off to your left. Here you pick up waymarking for the GR-99, the Camino Natural del Ebro, which you follow, as orange arrows are now in short supply. This long riverside camino runs all the way from Zaragoza, and you share its route much, though not all, of the way. A river can be heard, but not seen, down to your left.

Your target is now the prominent church spire of **Fuenmayor**, ahead and slightly to your right. Waymarking is poor on reaching the town, so find the church (Iglesia de Santa Maria) and the main road junction immediately beyond. From this far side of the church, follow the sign for the N-232 (signposted Cenicero and Haro) for just 200m and then turn left on to the LR-137 for Navarrete. At the next crossroads, at a junction with the N-232, carefully cross this busy road and then turn left along it for just 120m to find a wooden signboard for the 'Camino Viejo a Navarrete' ('Old Path to Navarrete'), which runs south with a water channel parallel on its left and yet more vineyards

LAGUARDIA–NAVARRETE

on its right. Follow this wide, rough track for almost 2km until it almost reaches the AP-68 motorway and then turn right for 100m to reach the LR-137 again.

Pass through the underpass that takes this road beneath the motorway. Carefully cross the mouth of the motorway access road and immediately turn left on to a dirt track that leads past the toll booths on your left. Cross a water channel and shortly after follow the dirt track to the right towards a large stone building. This path becomes tarmac and leads you to, then through, an underpass beneath the A-12. Continue straight ahead with the outskirts of **Navarrete** already visible. Soon, you cross the main N-120 to enter town, with the first of several pilgrims' hostels visible off to your left and many other accommodations clearly signposted.

WHERE TO STAY AND EAT For its compact size, Navarrete has a good choice of places to stay and eat, particularly hostels with dorms, due

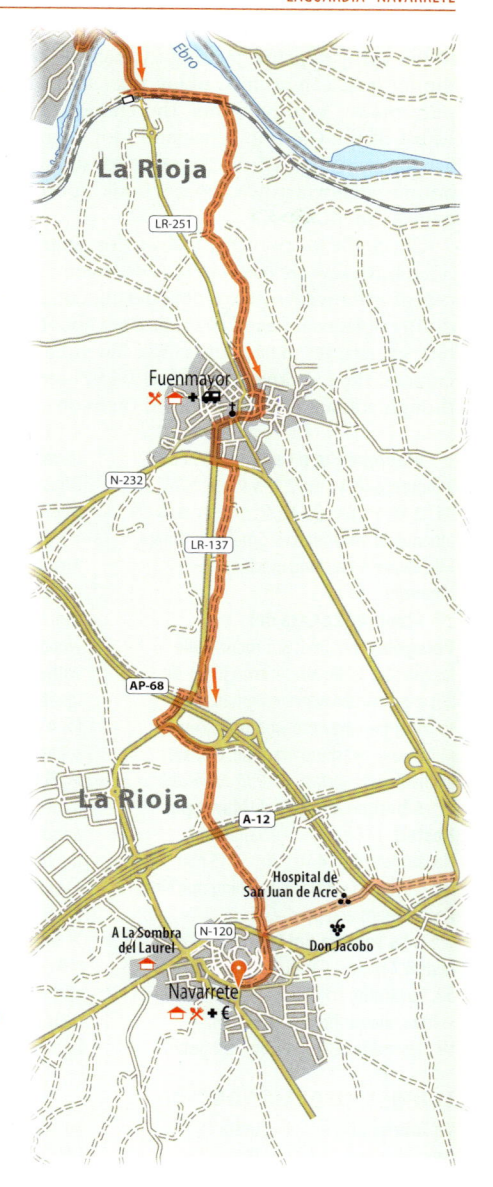

STAGE 7

to the many pilgrims passing through on the Camino de Santiago. Over dinner, you can swap walking tales and introduce the Santiago-bound pilgrims to '*your*' camino. The chances are that most will never have heard of the Camino Ignaciano, nor even noticed the orange-coloured arrows pointing eastwards – the opposite way from their own westwards-bound, yellow-arrowed route. Look upon tonight as an opportunity to educate them.

Check the tourist office website for details of all the accommodation on offer, but a few are listed here. When you are hungry, wandering the town centre will reveal restaurants offering cut-price pilgrims' menus. The two dining options here are perhaps a cut above most of the other good-value, but sometimes basic, offerings. Fuenmayor has two accommodation choices, the **Labranza** (**m** 636 41 04 97) and the **Ubeda** (**m** 663 77 96 29), though you are unlikely to need them on such a short stage.

Albergue Buen Camino (6 beds & 1 room) Calle la Cruz 2, Navarrete; 941 44 03 18; **m** 681 25 22 22; **e** reservas@alberguebuencamino.es. Small & intimate. Microwave & washing machine. *€9/35 dorm/dbl*

Albergue La Casa del Peregrino (26 beds & 1 room) Calle las Huertas 3, Navarrete; **m** 630 98 29 28; **e** alberguenavarrete@gmail.com; **w** alberguenavarrete.wordpress.com. Microwave, washing machine, blankets available, as is b/fast. *€10/30 dorm/dbl*

Albergue Municipal (Municipal Hostel) (34 beds) Calle San Juan 2, Navarrete; 941 44 07 76; 15 Mar–end Oct. Cooking facilities & washing machine. Reservations accepted. *€10*

A La Sombra del Laurel (16 beds & 7 rooms) Carretera de Burgos 52, Navarrete; **m** 639 86 11 10; **e** info@alasombradellaurel.com; **w** alasombradellaurel.com. Just out of town, clean, bright & friendly with garden. B/fast available. *€15/30/45 dorm/sgl/dbl, trpls/quads also available*

Posada Ignatius (5 rooms) Plaza del Arco 4, Navarrete; 941 12 40 94; **e** info@posadaignatius.com; **w** posadaignatius.com. A beautifully restored building, all wooden beams & exposed stone, dripping with class & character. It has a genuine Ignatian connection, as Ignatius stayed here for 4 years during his previous career as a soldier. B/fast available. *€45/55 sgl/dbl*

El Figon del Duque Contact details as per Posada Ignatius. Fine dining in an atmospheric setting, deep in the bowels of the Duke of Najera's 15th-century cellars. Mediterranean flavours; the best cuisine in town. *€17*

Sancho Calle Mayor Alta 5, Navarrete; 941 44 13 78; **w** hotelreysancho.es. Part of the Rey Sancho hotel, with a well-priced daily menu featuring Riojan specialities & local ingredients. *€15*

TOURIST INFORMATION

Tourist office Calle Cuesta el Cano, Navarrete; 941 44 00 62; **w** ayuntamientonavarrete.org. Staff can help with accommodation.

▲ The 12th-century remains of Hospital de San Juan de Acre, where pilgrims came to sleep during their journey *MC/S*

WHAT TO SEE The narrow streets in Navarrete's old town are indisputably quaint, and the 16th/17th-century church, **Nuestra Señora de la Asunción**, declared an 'asset of cultural interest' in 2020, is worth a visit. Its fine Riojan Baroque altarpiece is its standout; even if you've seen a lot of altarpieces, this one will take your breath away for sheer opulence. A short walk northeast of town are the (scant) remains of the 12th-century **Hospital de San Juan de Acre**, also passed at the beginning of the next stage. In former times a hospital was akin to a modern-day hostel or *albergue*, mainly designed for pilgrim accommodation rather than recuperation from illness.

Otherwise, the main attraction in Navarrete is engaging with Santiago-bound walkers and swapping experiences.

TRANSPORT The regular M1 bus runs frequently from Navarrete to Logroño and Fuenmayor/Cenicero in the other direction.

Taxi
🚗 **Taxi Navarrete** m 656 68 49 50

DISCOVER
LA RIOJA
Logrono
Alcanadre
Navarrete
Calahorra
Alfaro
www.lariojaturismo.com
LA
RIOJA

8 NAVARRETE–LOGROÑO

This is a very short, easy stage with negligible climb and descent, finishing in La Rioja's lively capital, Logroño. Your direction of travel changes for the first time today from predominantly south to predominantly east, and after a week of rural, often mountainous walking and small towns and villages, you reach the route's first city – though with a population of around 150,000, it is far from overwhelming. Setting out early will allow for an early finish and a chance to visit some of Logroño's attractions, which include a good museum, a few churches and plenty of bars and restaurants. Don't be put off by the modern, ever-expanding outskirts: the old town area has some real character, which is well worth absorbing.

Start Tourist office, Navarrete
Coordinates 42.42935, -2.56144
Finish Logroño
Difficulty Easy
Distance 13km
Duration 3hrs 30mins

THE ROUTE The route out of Navarrete begins from the tourist office and proceeds either along the Calle de la Cruz or the Calle Mayor Alta/Baja. These two roads merge into one before you leave town. For the first few hundred metres, simply retrace your steps from yesterday to exit Navarrete, reaching the N-120 road which you cross to descend the set of steps immediately opposite. At the foot of these, turn sharp right to join a tarmac road running parallel to the N-120. For extra reassurance, a large, black, bull-shaped advertising hoarding awaits you in the near-distance (see box, page 109). Although there are occasional orange arrows painted on telegraph poles, waymarking today comes in the form of the yellow arrows of the Camino de Santiago, which point in the opposite direction, of course. As you pass the **Don Jacobo** winery 1km from your starting point, a sign reminds Santiago-bound pilgrims that they have 576km still to travel; comfort yourself that you, as an Ignatian pilgrim, have a mere 520km left to walk before you arrive in Manresa! Before crossing the AP-68 motorway bridge, note on your right the ruins of the old pilgrim hospital of **San Juan de Acre** (page 103).

Once across the AP-68, and still using the hilltop black bull as a guide, continue straight ahead towards the hilltop figure on a wide, rough track, and cross the N-120 once more. (A new motorway is under construction here, due for a 2022 completion, but the development is scheduled to

STAGE 8

preserve the existing routes of the two caminos.) Proceeding slightly uphill, you approach the main Logroño motorway, but before reaching it cross the smaller road you're already on to find a path continuing along its right-hand side. Note here the hundreds of wooden crosses inserted for good luck by pilgrims into the wire fencing on your left. Continuing straight ahead, you will shortly see the **Embalse de la Grajera** reservoir, with the conurbation of Logroño beyond. Ignore a path to the left, and the road turns to tarmac, veering right and descending with the reservoir now away to your left. It then curves sharply left to continue its descent.

At a junction, follow the road's curve, again to the left, with the water now hidden behind trees on your right. As the road levels out, take the right turn signposted Logroño. A few hundred metres further on, turn sharp left off the path at a shelter to find a fountain and seating area. This new track takes you past a radio mast (on your right) and leads to a park closer to the waterside, a popular recreational area for the city dwellers, though swimming is prohibited. Showing pilgrim-esque restraint, you should avoid the temptation to take a dip. Ducks, geese and swans are all prevalent on the water, while orange-brown bearded reedling can also be spotted. A pavilion-style restaurant, **La Cabaña del Tío Juarvi** (CabanaTioJuarvi), is a welcome sight halfway along the waterside. Take advantage, as surprisingly you are little more than midway through today's short stage, and there are pleasant outdoor tables here at which to re-energise.

With your back to the main restaurant entrance, leave the main path and take the dirt track to your right through trees towards the water.

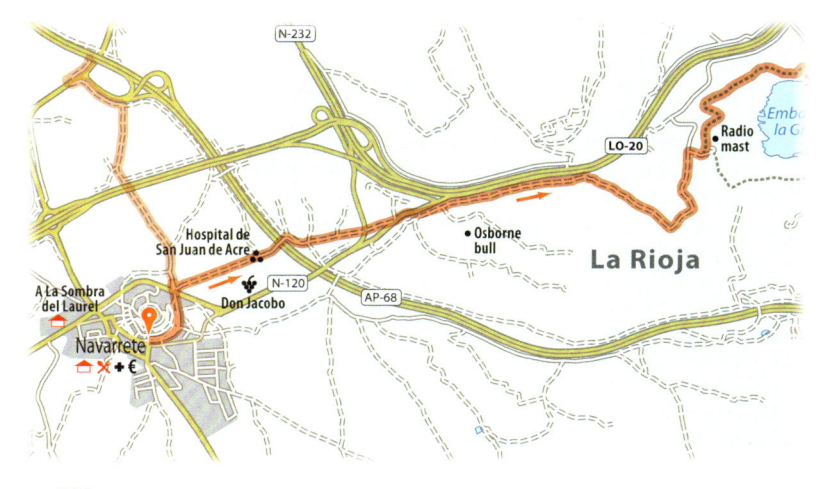

NAVARRETE–LOGROÑO

Cross a bridge over the water's edge, looking out for the resident coots, moorhens, ducks and swans, as well as for the population of lively black squirrels by the shore. Walk the length of the dam at the reservoir end, turning sharp left to descend on tarmac and then right at a children's playground to join a newly surfaced wide path for 1.5km as it crosses a bridge and leads to the city outskirts.

The path eventually reaches and runs parallel to the busy LO-20 motorway, which is crossed via an underpass bedecked with pilgrim-themed murals. Emerging at a roundabout (where the pilgrim theme continues), carry on through a small park to a further roundabout, diagonally beyond which is the beginning of a larger park, the **Parque San Miguel**, which you cross on a cobbled path. At the end, you can in theory follow either of the signs to the left: either for Avenida de

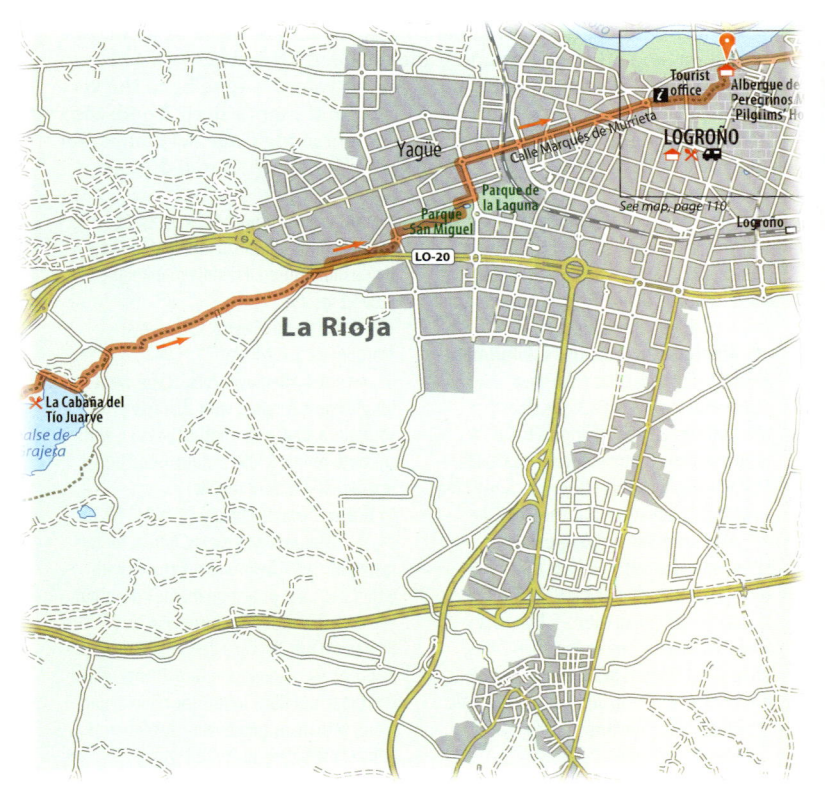

STAGE 8

Burgos or Calle Duques de Najera. Choose the former, descend on the path, turn right on to a road for 80m, first left on to the four-lane main street of Calle Portillejo, then after a few hundred metres right at a roundabout on to the Avenida de Burgos itself. Although this soon changes its name to Calle Marqués de Murrieta, maintain your direction on this road for 1.5km to eventually arrive at a roundabout and the tourist office of **Logroño**. From there, the stage continues along Calle Portales to reach the cathedral where you turn left across its square to find Calle Herrerías, then left off that street on to the Travesia del Palacio, which leads to the stage end at the municipal pilgrims' hostel on Calle Ruavieja.

WHERE TO STAY AND EAT A large-ish city like Logroño has plenty of accommodation in all categories, so if you haven't pre-booked or don't fancy any of the options listed here, make the tourist office or its website your first stop. The area around Calle del Laurel (see box, page 111) can be noisy until the small hours, so weigh up your desire to be in the very heart of the action with your need for a good night's sleep. Food-wise, you could simply gorge on the tapas all night along Calle del Laurel, but the two restaurants here offer more conventional, structured dining.

Albergue de Peregrinos Municipal (Pilgrims' Hostel) (78 beds) Calle Ruavieja 32; 941 24 86 86. The official hostel in town. No blankets, but full cooking facilities. Reservations accepted. *€10*

Albergue Privado Albas (Pilgrims' Hostel) (22 beds) Plaza Martinez Flamarique; 941 70 08 32; e albas@ alberguealbas.es; w alberguealbas.es. A little out of the centre, but easily walkable. Sleeping bag required. Microwave & washing machine. Reservations accepted. *€12.50*

Albergue Santiago Apostol (Pilgrims' Hostel) (66 beds & 7 rooms) Calle Ruavieja 42; 941 25 69 76; e ruavieja42@gmail.com; Mar–Oct. Blankets available, reception open 24hrs, no cooking. Dinners available. Reservations accepted. *€10/40–80 dorm/room, sgl or dbl*

Hostal Numantina (22 rooms) Calle Sagasta 4; 941 25 14 11; w hostalnumantina.com. A pleasant, central, modest hotel, a little dated but being modernised. Friendly management. *€35/50 sgl/dbl*

Hotel Calle Mayor (30 rooms) Marqués de San Nicolas 71; 941 23 23 68; w hotelcallemayor.com. If you want a bit of luxury, coupled with character, this is your place. In a 16th-century *palacio*, with spacious rooms & chic styling. Good b/fast (extra cost). *€65/75 sgl/dbl*

Ikaro Avda de Portugal 3; 941 57 16 14; w restauranteikaro.com. A treat for the tastebuds: a Michelin-starred choice with either à la carte or tasting menu. Pricey, but you probably deserve it by now! *€22*

Pasión por Ti Calle del Laurel 5; 941 22 00 39; w grupopasion.com. Plenty of top-end tapas, but don't ignore the main dining room, with many good-value meal choices. Genial host & decently priced wines. *€13*

THE OSBORNE BULL: A SPANISH ICON

If you have visited Spain before, the hilltop silhouette of the giant black bull will be familiar to you. Although originally conceived as an advertising tool to promote Osborne's Veterano brandy, the bull has subsequently taken on much greater significance. You will find many specimens of this bull in Spain but, like many things in this complex country, it has not been without controversy.

The bull was the idea of a Cádiz-born artist, Manolo Prieto, and was eagerly adopted by the Osborne Group to promote its drink. Nowadays, so as not to provide a distraction to traffic, the bull must by law be located at least 150m from the road and the Osborne name has been removed from the advert, leaving the simple yet imposing silhouette. An attempt to ban the bull in the 1990s was met with strong objections and Andalucía hurriedly made it part of that region's local heritage to give it some protection. Subsequently, it has been judicially acknowledged as a genuine cultural symbol and is recognised as such by both Spaniards and visitors alike. But because of its very Spanish-ness, you will find none of these bulls in either the Basque Country or Catalonia, where the strong sense of local identity trumps the national one. It also serves another, unintended purpose: as a waymark for pilgrims, as you will discover on a few of the later Camino Ignaciano stages.

▼ The iconic Osborne bull is a common sight on the route *B/S*

STAGE 8

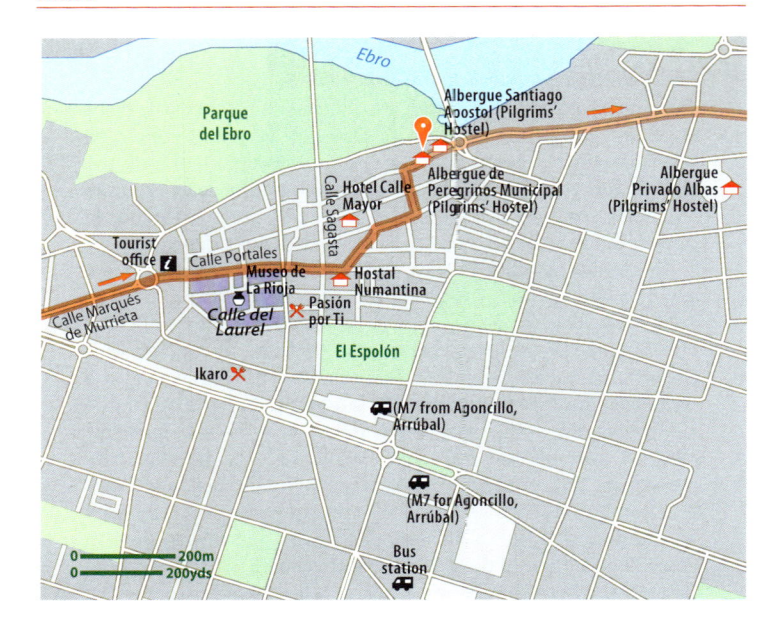

TOURIST INFORMATION

Tourist office Calle Portales 50; 941 29 12 60; w lariojaturismo.com; Jun–Sep 10.00–20.00 Mon–Sat, 10.00–14.00 Sun, Oct–May 09.30–18.30 Mon–Sat, 10.00–14.00 Sun

WHAT TO SEE The Calle del Laurel (see box, opposite) is the main event for a one-night stay, but for something more sedate the **Museum of La Rioja** (Pl de San Augustín 23; 941 29 12 59; 10.00–14.00 & 16.00–21.00 Tue–Sat, 10.00–14.00 Sun; free) is certainly worthwhile. Here, you can discover how the Romans introduced the grape and the olive to the region – two enduring products that still heavily shape the modern Riojan economy. A good way to pass an hour or two.

Logroño has its festival days on 9 and 11 June, so not a lot happens on the 10th, either. San Mateo's day on 21 September is another local holiday.

TRANSPORT There are good bus and rail connections to and from Logroño, particularly to and from Bilbao and Barcelona, if you are starting or ending your walk here. Also buses to Zaragoza and Calahorra (details at **w** lariojaturismo.com).

CALLE DEL LAUREL – THE ULTIMATE BAR CRAWL

If you try and extol the virtues of Logroño's 'party street' to any Spaniard, they will no doubt tell you that *every* Spanish city has such a raucous place. And it is true, Spaniards are never short of a venue focused on enjoyment. But Logroño's Calle del Laurel (and its intersecting Travesía del Laurel) can match up with anything other cities can offer. This little urban gem is stuffed with bars, each of which proudly trumpets its own divine culinary specialities. And boy, are they special. Although it is best to go unstructured and just dive in anywhere you fancy, a favourite for fungi lovers should be **Soriano** (Travesía del Laurel 2), where a man (or woman) studiously fries up garlic mushrooms at the end of the bar, while **Letras de Laurel** (Calle del Laurel 22) tempts with its 'black sirloin lollipop'. There: that's got you started – the rest is up to you, just browse and graze.

▼ Calle del Laurel is Logroño's 'party street' MS

RIOJAN WINE

Even if you have never set foot in La Rioja before, you will surely have tasted the delicious wines that share their names with the region. Rioja is Spain's best-known wine, available in every decent Spanish bar for little more than €1 per glass. A source of confusion and curiosity for beginners is that not all Rioja comes from the Autonomous Community of La Rioja. True, the vast majority (70%) does, but approximately 20% is produced in Álava province in the Basque Country, with the remainder of Rioja-denominated wine originating in Navarre. Ninety per cent of Rioja wines are red, although the region's whites are also well respected. Wherever it comes from exactly, Rioja is exported across the world and enjoys great economic importance.

Of course, wine is entirely a matter of taste. Any Riojan wine labelled *joven* (literally 'young') will have matured in wood for only a very short time, or perhaps not at all. Many drinkers' preference in choosing a red is to opt instead for *crianza* (wine that has been aged for at least two years), as a glass of this is better quality and only slightly more expensive. Wines labelled as *Reserva* or *Gran Reserva* will have aged for longer, but both are more expensive and will rarely be available by the glass in bars. You can treat yourself to a whole bottle from a *bodega* or supermarket, though!

One more tip, as you lick your lips in anticipation: many red wines in Spanish bars are kept in the fridge, so if you want a warmer drink specify it to be *al tiempo* (pronounced *al-tee-em-po*).

Taxis

Tramos (Logroño) 941 10 14 10

Uni Taxi (Logroño) 941 50 50 50

9 LOGROÑO–ALCANADRE

After two relatively short stages, you now face a longer, flat trek eastwards along the wide Ebro Valley, mainly on tarmac and through a mix of agricultural and industrial landscapes. If truth be told, the first half of today's stage is not the finest, with a stretch right along the side of a busy main road that can't be avoided. Things pick up considerably once you reach Agoncillo, however. If today's distance looks too challenging to walk in one stretch, there is the opportunity to shorten it by adding an extra day and splitting it in two. You could even enjoy a day's walking free from the burden of your backpack (see box, page 120). If you choose to divide this stage in two, an alternative to returning to Logroño for an extra night is to stay at the roadside hotel in Agoncillo, or the pilgrims' hostel in Arrúbal. If choosing the latter, take your own food to prepare, as there are currently no evening dining options in town.

> **Start** Albergue de Peregrinos Municipal, Logroño
> **Coordinates** 42.46844, -2.44394
> **Finish** Alcanadre (or Agoncillo/Arrúbal if you shorten the stage)
> **Difficulty** Easy, though long
> **Distance** 30.5km to Alcanadre, or 15.5km to Agoncillo, 19.4km to Arrúbal
> **Duration** 7hrs to Alcanadre, or 3hrs 30mins to Agoncillo, 4hrs 30mins to Arrúbal

THE ROUTE From the pilgrims' hostel, cross the roundabout to join Calle San Francisco and continue straight ahead as it becomes Calle Madre de Dios, passing the university. After around 1.5km you cross under the A-13 motorway, then turn immediately left into a small park, followed by a right after 50m, picking up the orange directional arrows on a tarmac path that takes you to a bridge across the River Iregua – one of more than 200 tributaries that feed the Ebro along its journey to the Mediterranean (see box, page 114). Across the water, turn left to join the signposted, tarmac Camino Natural del Ebro (GR-99) with the fast-flowing Ebro initially prominent to your left. You are unlikely to meet too many pilgrims today, as this route to Santiago is much less popular than yesterday's Camino Francès route. As a result, the yellow waymarking is not as well maintained, and your own Ignatian orange arrows are also in short supply.

Pass by some small *huertas* (allotments) and smallholdings which make good use of the Ebro's waters. At one time, *norias* (waterwheels) would have punctuated this flat landscape, ensuring a supply of the river

SPAIN'S MIGHTIEST RIVER

Flowing for 910km from Cantabria before reaching its outflow in the Mediterranean, the Ebro is the longest river located entirely within Spain. But perhaps the most significant, long-lasting contribution of the river derives from its name. Ebro has morphed from the Latin names for the river (*iber*), which of course gives its name to the Iberian Peninsula.

As it accompanies you for several days of walking along your Ignatian route, for the most part its ample width means it is a gentle, meandering companion. But further back upstream, as it rushes through the Cantabrian gorges where it rises, it can be a much busier, noisier affair. It draws waters from over 200 tributaries along its way, some joining from the Pyrenees in the north, while the smaller rivers arriving from the south originate in the vast Sistema Ibérico mountain ranges, which themselves stretch nearly as far as the Mediterranean.

Despite the impression of this being a fertile territory, the fields of crops partially mask the fact that much of the soil in the Ebro Valley is actually quite poor: stony, thin and diminished by salt from lagoons prone to evaporation. Nevertheless, the intricate network of irrigation helps to allow cultivation along the river and provides livelihoods for many.

One resident of the Ebro – although you are unlikely to meet him – is the huge but ugly carnivorous Wels catfish (*Silurus glanis*), not a native species but one that can comfortably reach 1.5m in length and weigh 20kg. It can be found in the Segre tributary as well as the Ebro and, although fished for sport, it is not treasured for its taste!

waters to the fields. Today, these have been long superseded by canals and sluice gates, and the fine produce is exported all over Europe; bottling and canning have been important economic activities since the mid 19th century. Where you reach a Y-junction, take the right-hand fork, still on tarmac and, upon reaching another junction, turn left then immediately right and continue in the same direction as before, down the length of a long stone building. Just short of reaching the motorway, turn left to continue on tarmac running parallel with the speeding traffic up above. A modern, arc-shaped bridge is ahead, but well before reaching it turn right through an underpass to cross beneath the motorway, still in the same direction as before. The juxtaposition of fruit trees to the modern roadway reminds us how Spain has transformed its infrastructure in the past half-century, accelerating rapidly from agricultural backwater into the industrial age.

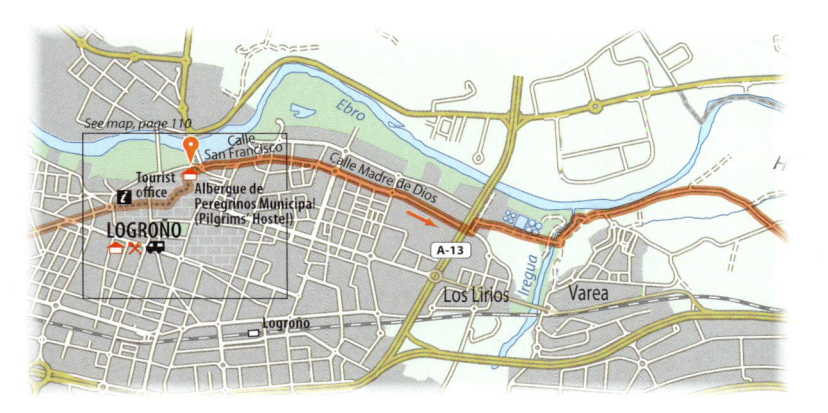

After just over 1km, you pass beneath the motorway again and continue in the same direction. The tarmac ends but the wide GR-99 track continues straight on past a large industrial building on the right and once again you hear the rushing Ebro waters on your left as you return briefly to the riverside. From here, the path rises slightly to turn left on to a wide, tarmac road, with a barrier and the buildings of a largely disused military base in the near-distance. Head towards it, but look out for a partially abandoned road on your right, 400m after joining the tarmac. Take this road (next to a 'Zona Militar' warning sign) and after a few metres, cautiously cross the railway track to arrive at the main Logroño–Zaragoza road (N-232). Turn left on to this, using the wide pedestrian lane. This is the town of **Recajo**, devoid of facilities apart from the petrol

▼ The impressive Aguas Mansas castle MS

STAGE 9

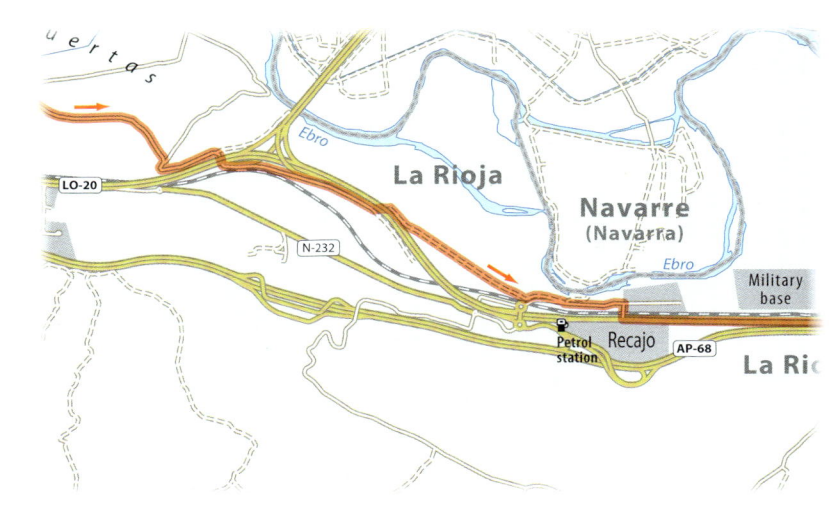

station with its shop, just behind you. Extreme caution is now required, as you must follow the N-232 for over 2.5km, sharing the route with the speeding vehicles. As you reach the sliproad signposted for the airport, you may choose to leave then rejoin the main road via the other slip road as a short respite from the vehicles. Temporarily, we have road, camino, railway and airport runway – off to your left – all running in parallel.

Continue on the main road and cross the bridge over the River Leza before immediately taking a concrete slope down to the left. (If staying at the Hostal El Molino in Agoncillo (page 120), ignore the slope and continue instead on the main road for a further 400m.) This descent soon becomes tarmac and curves to the left, passing through a narrow tunnel and then bending back right to enter the town of **Agoncillo** after 1.5km or so. Continue down Calle la Ermita, ignoring any sideroads to reach the square, church, bars and shops. Far more impressive than any of these is the chunky medieval Aguas Mansas castle, built in the 13th/14th century, but in great condition thanks to a thorough renovation as recently as 1990. It now houses a number of administrative departments but occasionally hosts an exhibition or two. It is thought that a fortified building of some sort has been on this site as far back as Roman times. Although the town is on the railway line, trains are so infrequent as to be of little use to any pilgrim; should you need a motorised escape, buses are a much better bet, and the timetable is displayed in most of the town's shops and bars.

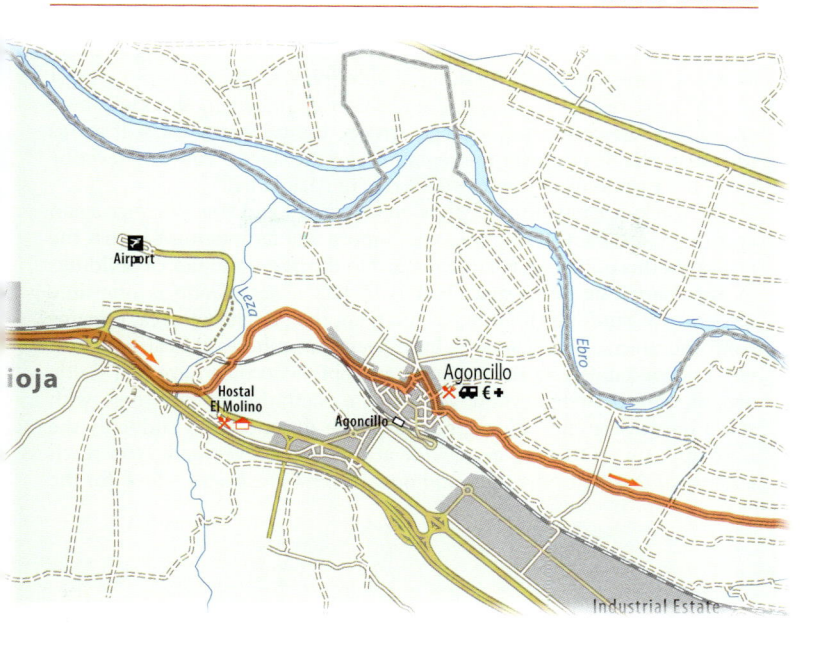

When you are ready to continue beyond Agoncillo, go behind the church and take the road to the right, shortly reaching a roundabout at which you turn left; continue with the railway away to your right. Without any deviation, this road will take you ever closer to the church spire of **Arrúbal**, already visible although still 3.5km away. Along the way, note again the intricate web of water channels and sluice gates. Beans, potatoes and tomatoes are some of the vegetable crops favoured here, while pears and almonds are also cultivated. When the road ends at a T-junction, cross the footbridge ahead to climb up to the church, with its pilgrims' hostel (page 120) cleverly concealed beneath. The town square, bus stop and Bar los Amigos (which may have a few tapas) are only a few metres away. The shop in Arrúbal is open until 19.00 Monday–Friday if you are splitting the stage here, or want to pick up supplies en route. From the church's elevated location, enjoy the view back along the valley and over to the rugged Basque hills you crossed only a few days before.

To continue the stage from Arrúbal, take Calle Calvario as it leaves eastwards from the Bar los Amigos/bus stop area. The second half of this stage is devoid of main roads and motorways – a pleasant walk, even if you're tired. Pass the cemetery on your right and continue on the

STAGE 9

tarmac as it turns right towards the railway. Just before reaching a GR-99 signpost, leave the tarmac, taking a wide track to your right to almost immediately reach the railway line. From this point on, although there are only a few comforting orange arrows, the railway track will act as the most reliable guide for the remainder of the stage – you will never be more than 100m from it until you arrive in Alcanadre.

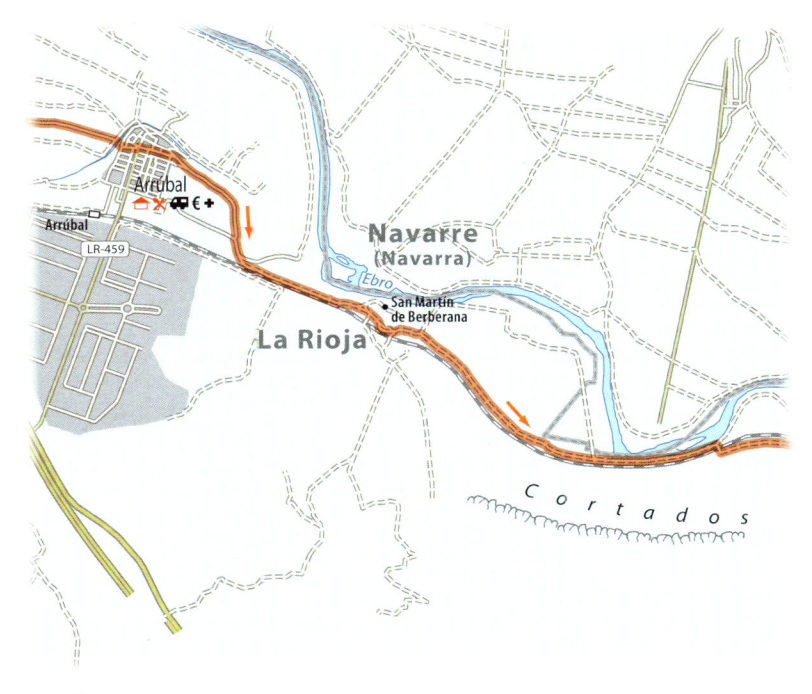

The tracks are now immediately on your right and you will once again encounter some GR-99 signposting. Ignore any temptation to cross the railway at this point, continuing instead to the large complex of buildings of **San Martín de Berberana**. This is in fact a *despoblado*, a one-time settlement abandoned for one reason or another. Archaeological remains from the Bronze and Iron ages have been found here, indicating that it was once inhabited by the Berones, a people who may have had Celtic origins. Immediately beyond, you reach a plantation of fruit trees, with some impressive cliffs now apparent in the distance, and suddenly the Ebro appears on the left, quite wide at this point. Eventually, you reach a railway crossing to the right and now traverse the tracks – look for the orange arrow. With the tracks and river to your left now, a new range of jagged cliffs appear around a corner. These Cortados de Aradón, as they are known, are steep, chalky strata and popular with the local avian wildlife. Ignoring a railway crossing on your left, continue to reach a gap in the cliffs where you will see the bright, white-painted **Ermita de Aradón** chapel up to the right, once the site of an abbey. Pilgrimages are made here in May and September, but otherwise it is closed.

At the junction for the chapel, you turn left here, following the signpost to Alcanadre, to cross the railway again via an underpass, encouraged by another orange arrow. Continue with the railway now once more on your right, and soon the sound and then sight of the Ebro re-emerges on your left. A **bird hide** offers the opportunity to spot some griffon vultures (*Gyps fulvus*) which nest on the cliff faces above. Ignore a further railway crossing, instead continuing slightly left on the same wide path with the train tracks never far distant to your right. In less than a couple of kilometres, the buildings of **Alcanadre** make their first appearance; continue straight, staying left of the railway and right of the river, and upon reaching a junction, with the buildings of the town off to the right, cross a bridge and find the station and the town beyond. This is a true 'stopover' town for walkers, with little of interest for the casual visitor. The 'Al-' prefix of the town's name is of course Arabic, corrupted from 'Al Qanatir', meaning 'the bridges'.

WHERE TO STAY AND EAT Book ahead, as accommodation is a bit thin on the ground both in Alcanadre and along the way. At the time of writing, the pilgrims' hostel in Alcanadre was closed, with no date set for reopening. The dining choices are, at best, passable: those listed here are done purely on availability, not merit – but sadly, there is little else.

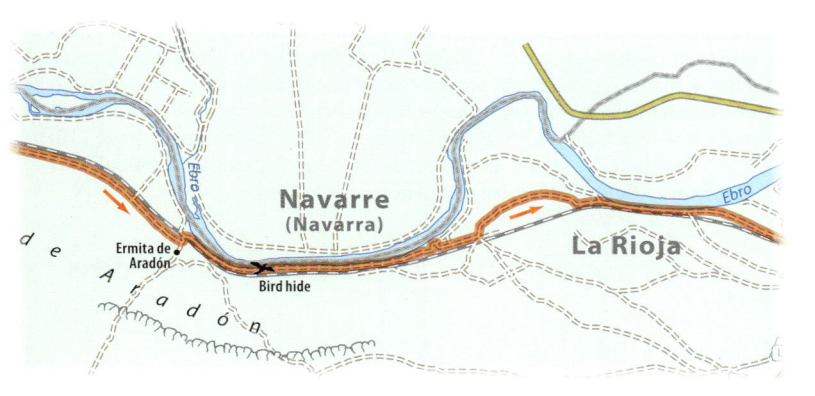

STAGE 9

🏠 **Albergue Municipal de Arrúbal (Pilgrims' Hostel)** (26 beds) Plaza de la Iglesia, Arrúbal; ☎ 941 43 12 23. A halfway option if you are splitting today's stage. Call ahead to make reservations; no permanent staff presence, no English spoken. Kitchen & laundry facilities. *€5 pp (suggested)*

🏠 **Antigua Bodega** (13 rooms) Calle de San Isidro 32, Alcanadre; ☎ 941 16 54 73; m 667 71 06 91. Pleasant & good-value *casa rural*, spread over 2 buildings. B/fast available. The **Brasa de Baco** restaurant next door has outdoor tables, but food quality is variable. *€25/50 sgl/dbl*

🏠 **Casa Azul** (8 rooms) Trasera de Pilares 29, Alcanadre; m 686 73 01 87 or 669 46 15 01; e info@lacasaazulalcanadre.com. Delightful owners, beautiful *pension*. Kitchen facilities, or dine at the very basic **Bar la Unión**, under the same ownership, nearby. No English spoken. *€47/57 sgl/dbl*

🏠 **Hostal El Molino** (14 rooms) KM11, Carretera de Zaragoza (N-232), Agoncillo; ☎ 941 43 13 16; e siembe@hotmail.com. On main road, just off the camino route, this basic roadside place is useful if you are splitting the stage. AC, private bathrooms. Food gets mixed reviews & is unsophisticated but belly-filling. Restaurant closed Sat & Sun evenings. *€25/50 sgl/dbl*

TRANSPORT If you decide to split this long stage in two, you can overnight in either Agoncillo or Arrúbal (see above) and continue from either of those to Alcanadre the following day. Alternatively, book yourself into accommodation for *two* nights in Logroño, walk to Agoncillo or Arrúbal on day one (without your backpack, if you have a daypack), take the Metropolitano M7 bus back to Logroño in the afternoon, then take the same bus back to where you left off and continue on to Alcanadre. It takes a bit of planning, but a day without your pack can be very rejuvenating. Bus timetables can be found at **w** larioja.org/transportes/es, and you'll find the relevant bus stops in Logroño marked on the city map, page 110.

Although trains from Logroño do stop at Agoncillo, Arrúbal and Alcanadre, they are not very frequent (**w** renfe.com).

Taxis
🚕 **Pradejón** (Alcanadre) m 619 96 41 41

🚕 **Taxi Pachicho** (Alcanadre) ☎ 948 69 30 55

10 ALCANADRE–CALAHORRA

This stage is flat and of medium length, taking you from sleepy Alcanadre to less sleepy Calahorra, La Rioja's second-most-populous town. En route you cross imperceptibly in and out of Navarre before returning to La Rioja, but note that there are no opportunities for food or even water after you set out, so be well prepared. Although waymarking is fairly sparse, you will again be helped by the Camino de Santiago yellow arrows pointing in the opposite direction. The presence of the AP-68 motorway and the railway also ensure that finding your way is trouble-free. Anyone seeking a rest day at this point could choose Calahorra, which offers just about enough in the way of museums and restaurants to fill a relaxing 24 hours.

Start Bar la Unión, Alcanadre
Coordinates 42.40348, -2.12053
Finish Calahorra
Difficulty Easy
Distance 21.7km
Duration 5hrs

THE ROUTE Head south on Calle Los Pilares to cross a junction with the LR-260. Continue straight ahead and, when the tarmac ends, continue straight on a rougher track with a large warehouse immediately to your right. Shortly after you will pass some solar-energy panels, again on your right, and the track now rises gently. Be sure to turn around to get a panoramic view of the surrounding cliffs. When the road divides at a Y junction, take the concrete route to the right and, on reaching the top of the gentle climb, take the right-hand fork as the road again divides at another Y. After a few hundred metres, at a further Y junction, the route turns right on to a concrete surface leading down towards the now-visible AP-68 motorway. Cross the traffic on an overpass, then double-back slightly to your left to join a dirt track, which runs parallel to the motorway. A motorway sign soon indicates your temporary transition from La Rioja to Navarre.

After a couple of kilometres on this path you reach the NA-123 road, which you cross and turn right on to briefly, passing the slip-road entrance after 100m and turning back sharp left to find the dirt path resuming its direction beside the motorway. Don't be tempted by the four large pipes crossing under the road – there's a risk of getting stuck! – instead, only 100m further on, turn left through an underpass to reach the other side. Emerging from this tunnel, turn immediately right to continue in the

STAGE 10

same direction as before and, after 1.5km and with a motorway bridge only a few hundred metres ahead, turn sharp left on to a fenced bridge to cross the railway track, then immediately take a right along a dirt track through scrubland. A modern aqueduct is soon visible on your left, then later the wider water-channel of the **Lodosa Canal**, after you descend on to a smoother path and go under a narrow bridge. This canal runs for nearly 130km, its direction paralleling the river as it spans La Rioja, Navarre and Aragón. It helps to distribute water to grow the region's many vegetables: peppers, tomatoes, artichokes, asparagus, beans, peas, spinach… the list is almost endless.

The Cathedral of St Mary stands tall over Calahorra
MR/S

STAGE 10

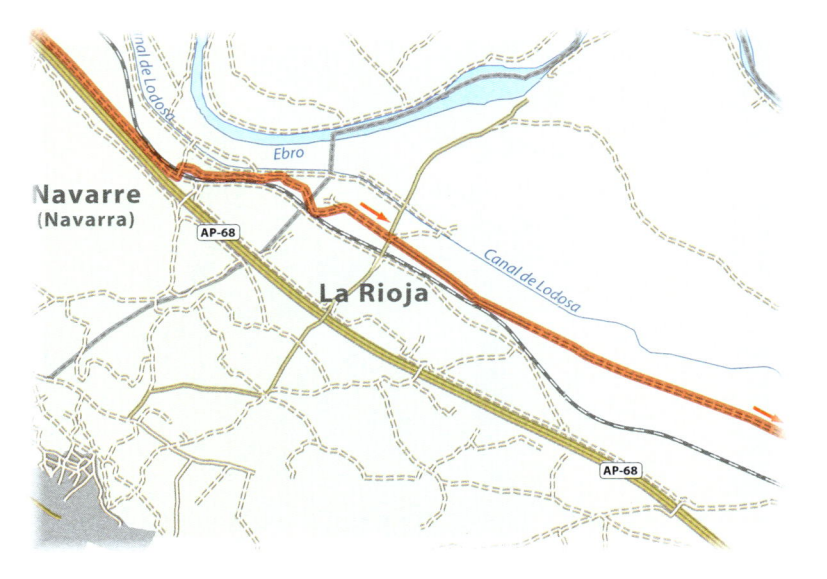

Continue your eastwards journey, picking up the occasional GR-99 signage once again. Cross an intersection with a main road, continuing on wide tarmac – the train tracks to your right are now a useful guide until just before you reach Calahorra. When the tarmac runs out, simply continue on the rougher track through olive groves. Pass a **quarry pit** on the right and then dog-leg slightly right to continue in the same direction. The turreted but modern **Castillo Maitierra** is your next marker, unmissable on the left. This brand-new 'faux-castle' does not offer visits, but, despite its lack of history, it does hold some interest as it is focused on the development and production of Riojan white wines in an area more renowned for its reds. Soon the track comes to an end, curving slightly left and meeting the paved LR-482 main road. Here, turn right to cross the railway tracks over a bridge and continue on the road until the first apartment blocks of **Calahorra** become visible. Cross straight over a roundabout with the LR-134 and continue upwards into town on Carretera de Murillo, then turn left on to Calle San Millán as it becomes Calle Ruiz y Menta. Turn right when it reaches Paseo del Mercadal, at the end of which take the left on to Calle de los Martires, first becoming Calle Grande then Calle Mayor. This takes you to the Plaza del Raso, where you'll find the tourist office. Dive into the maze of old town streets to find, 300m beyond, the San Francisco convent, church and pilgrims' hostel.

🏠 **WHERE TO STAY AND EAT** All the establishments listed here are in Calahorra itself.

🏠 **Albergue de Peregrinos 'San Francisco'** (9 rooms) Calle Rasillo San Francisco s/n; ☎ 941 59 05 11; **m** 637 73 61 08 or 637 73 61 09. In the old town, an absolute treat for pilgrims, no need to slum it in a dorm. Bright, clean accommodation arranged in twin rooms, all with private bath. Wi-Fi, heating. Laundry facilities. Discount at El Albergue restaurant next door. *€12 pp*

🏠 **Ciudad de Calahorra** (25 rooms) Maestro Falla 1; ☎ 941 14 74 34; **e** info@ciudaddecalahorra.com; **w** ciudaddecalahorra.com. A medium-priced, medium-quality option with restaurant. *€68 sgl or dbl*

🏠 **Parador Marco Fabio Quintiliano** (60 rooms) Paseo del Mercadal s/n; ☎ 941 13 03 58; **w** parador. es. At the northern end of the vast, wide pedestrian square, this modern building has pleasant rooms though no history other than to be named after a Roman

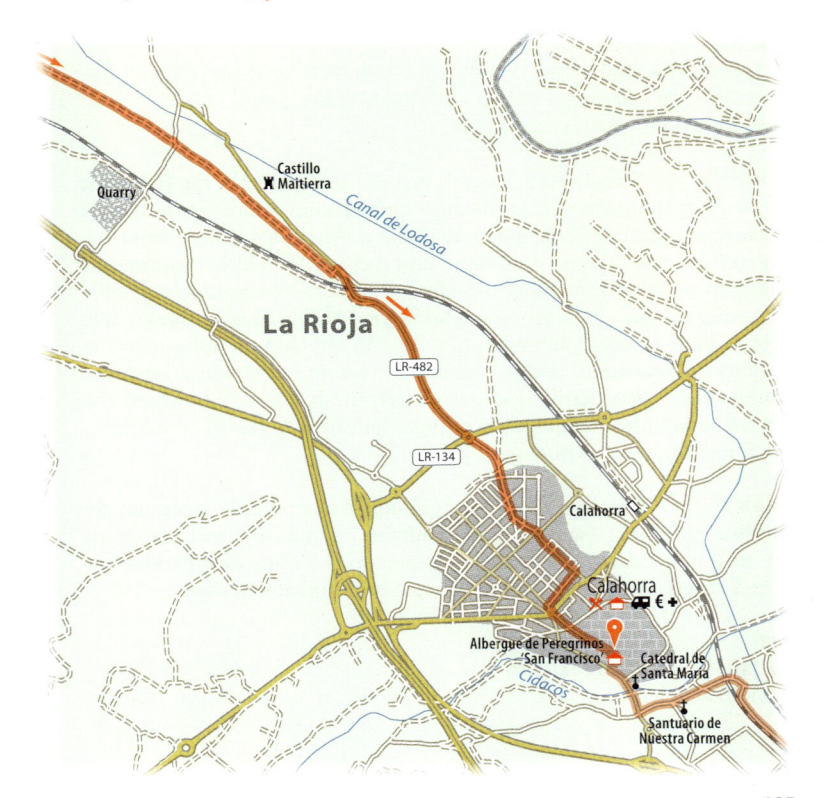

STAGE 10

emperor. The restaurant has good service & reasonable food, but is a bit pricey (€18). *€95 sgl or dbl*

🏠 **Pension Teresa** (9 rooms) 1st Fl, Calle Santo Domingo 2; ☎941 59 11 29. A lovely, affordable, fairly central option with simple, clean, well-looked-after rooms; shared bathrooms. Café downstairs. Owner has good nearby restaurant recommendations. *€30/42 sgl/dbl*

✖ **Cafeteria Avenida** Avda Valvanera 9; ☎941 14 68 74; ⊕ 07.00–midnight daily. Handy if you are staying at the Teresa or Ciudad Calahorra, this place offers no-frills fare but with a huge choice at good prices. *€8*

✖ **El Albergue** Calle Rasillo San Francisco s/n; ☎941 59 05 11; **m** 637 73 61 08; ⊕ lunchtimes Mon–Fri, evenings Fri–Sat. Superb cuisine at bargain lunchtime prices, set in modern surroundings with a large terrace enjoying panoramic views. Highly recommended. *€13 (menú del día)*

✖ **Taverna La Cuarta Esquina** Calle Quatro Esquinas s/n; ☎941 13 43 55; ⊕ closed Wed. Often cited as the town's best restaurant, with top-notch cooking in an atmospheric setting. *€18*

TOURIST INFORMATION

ℹ Tourist office Plaza del Raso 16; ☎941 10 50 61; **w** ayto-calahorra.es. ⊕ 10.30–13.30 & 16.30–18.30 Mon–Fri, 10.00–14.00 & 16.00–18.30 Sat, 10.00–14.00 Sun. Helpful English speakers.

WHAT TO SEE Should you choose a rest day in Calahorra, the **Old Town** (Casco Antiguo) is worth exploring – though somewhat run down and its labyrinthine nature demands that you collect a town map from the tourist office as soon as possible! – and there are a couple of museums that also come recommended. The first of these is 'Spain's only vegetable museum', the self-explanatory and self-styled **Museo de la Verdura** (Calle Cuesta de la Catedral 5; ☎941 14 74 23; €3), which pays homage to the region's 'Magnificent Seven' vegetables: onion, asparagus, cardoon, cauliflower, pepper, lettuce and particularly the artichoke. Elsewhere, the **Museo de la Romanización** (Calle Angel Oliván 8; ☎941 10 50 63; free) documents the town's Roman origins.

TRANSPORT Buses to and from Calahorra are mainly operated by Autobuses Jiménez (**w** jimenezmovilidad.es) connecting to Logroño to the west and Zaragoza to the east. Trains to the same destinations are comparatively infrequent, but details can be found at **w** renfe.es.

Taxi

🚕 **Taxi** (Calahorra) ☎941 13 00 16; **m** 618 01 91 56

11 CALAHORRA–ALFARO

This is another relatively easy stage, fairly long but without any elevation and with the railway to guide you. The town of Rincón de Soto provides a handy refreshment stop at just over the halfway stage and, depending on the time of year, you may have the opportunity to see Alfaro's famous storks (see box, page 128). This stage could also be split in two, and can be done without a backpack, as there are both train and bus links between the start and end points.

> **Start** Tourist office, Plaza del Raso, Calahorra
> **Coordinates** 42.30135, -1.96142
> **Finish** Alfaro
> **Difficulty** Easy
> **Distance** 25.6km
> **Duration** 6hrs

THE ROUTE The route begins from the tourist office, heading through the old town with a descent from the pilgrims' hostel along Cuesta de la Catedral to reach the cathedral itself, surprisingly sited *below* the town's elevated position. The River Cidacos is a languid affair, but despite it often lacking water, you still have to cross it on the road bridge and turn left after around 150m, signposted for the *cementerio* (cemetery) and the 17th-century Baroque **Santuario de Nuestra Carmen**. Pass this sanctuary on your right and cross beneath the railway, following the road to the right and then taking the first right (signed Sendero de Campo Bajo) to meet the railway and continue parallel to it. Cross the Lodosa Canal, staying on tarmac and veering left away from the rails. The route at this point is shared with the Senderos de la Verdura ('vegetable paths') and, sure enough, you will see all sorts of fruit and vegetables on the left as you progress.

After less than 1km, you reach a junction and choose the left-hand fork to continue on a tarmac road for 5km. To leave the road, turn right at a ruined building on to a dirt track, roughly in the direction of a distant church spire ahead of you – this is in the village of Aldeanueva del Ebro, which is not on the route. A few hundred metres beyond this turn-off, ignore a track leaving to the right and continue with a vineyard now on your left. On reaching the railway after 1.5km, turn left to walk parallel with it. Pass under a new bridge after around 750m, and with another spire, that of Rincón de Soto, now in front of you. Upon reaching a second new bridge just 1.2km later, use it to cross the railway and turn left to orientate again towards the town centre.

127

A STORK'S PARADISE

Perched on every conceivable part of Iglesia Colegiata de San Miguel church – on ledges, roof spaces, cornices, and every nook and cranny – the giant nests of Alfaro's part-time avian residents conspire to create what is claimed to be the 'world's largest urban colony of white storks'. These elegant birds can of course be found in many places in Spain, but Alfaro is perhaps most closely associated with them. And the town certainly gets great value out of the 100+ pairs who return every year to nest and then rear their new chicks. Those who designed and built the 16th/17th-century church can surely never have imagined that their opus would acquire its fame as a residence for white storks.

First, some statistics: these birds can weigh up to 4.5kg, measure up to 100cm in length and stretch to an impressive 1.5m in height. With the average number of chicks between one and five, the maximum population of birds in town can peak at around 500. The storks start to arrive in town at the beginning of December, with the stragglers flying in from sub-Saharan Africa as late as the end of February. Catching the thermals on their way, the birds can cover up to 350km per day. They return to Africa between the end of July and mid-August. Work begins on arrival: a week or two of reconstructing the nest, a task undertaken by both parents and using all types of natural and manmade materials. The incubation period is up to 32 days and the eggs are twice the size of a chicken egg. In nesting season, the birds' distinctive sound resonates throughout town, a sort of cross between a woodpecker and a two-stroke motorcycle engine. Look overhead, as they majestically glide in to land, mouths full of vegetation.

But why is Alfaro the 'go-to' destination for these distinctive, elegant birds? The Ebro Valley is rich in irrigated farmlands, a perfect habitat for the white storks who feed on the prodigious quantities of insects residing in the wetlands and marshes of the valley. The biggest attraction as a food source is the invasive freshwater crayfish (*Procambarus clarkii*), which favours streams and the irrigation channels, many of which you pass on your camino route. The popularity of the storks among humans is in part due to the fact that the crayfish's burrowing can cause enormous damage to both crops and waterways, in a region where agriculture is so important, so the storks' appetite for them keeps things under control.

Perhaps, therefore, it should be no surprise that Alfaro honours the storks with a festival, held each year in February. A local rhyme asserts

▲ Storks cover almost ever inch of Alfaro's Iglesia Colegiata de San Miguel MS

'*por San Blas, las cigüeñas verás*', meaning 'You will see the storks by the day of Saint Blas' (which is 3 February, celebrating the patron saint of woolcombers and… throat disease). With climate change, though, this is perhaps not so certain anymore, as they may arrive later!

STAGE 11

Arriving in **Rincón de Soto** with the railway now on your left, turn left on to Avenida de Aldeanueva to reach the centre. Your immediate target is the signposted *ayuntamiento* (town hall), then Avenida del Principe Felipe, the main thoroughfare on which you will find the town's smattering of restaurants and cafés, a pharmacy and a bewilderingly large assortment of banks. Continue to the end of this street and, before the railway crossing, turn left and follow the tarmac road as it curves right, then take the right-hand fork at a Y-junction to pass some hefty fruit and veg producers; cauliflowers and pears are mainstays around here.

Cross beneath an arched bridge and after 6km the dirt road turns to tarmac. On reaching a junction with the next Camino de Santiago sign on your left, turn sharp right towards the railway and the N-232 beyond. Cross an irrigation channel and then turn right to cross the railway, turning left immediately afterwards to walk alongside the N-232 to reach **Alfaro**. At the town entrance, arrive at a roundabout and take the first exit to cross the River Alhama, soon passing the bus station on your right. Upon reaching the bullring (Plaza de Toros), turn left and follow the road as it then bends to the right. At the next junction, the narrow Calle Mayor is soon ahead (turn left off it, on Calle Losada, to find the main square, tourist office), while the pilgrims' hostel is signposted left.

WHERE TO STAY AND EAT

Albergue de Peregrinos Municipal (Pilgrims' Hostel) (10 beds) Paseo de Florida 23; **m** 666 04 19 58 or 601 27 85 21. Basic hostel with kitchen & laundry. If no reply, contact the tourist office, the *ayuntamiento* (941 18 01 00) or the next-door police station! *Payment by donation, €5–10 pp suggested*

Hotel HM Alfaro (20 rooms) Calle San Antón 32; 941 18 00 56; **e** reservas@hmalfaro.es. Very centrally located, a few metres from the main square. Possible discounts for pilgrims. *€40/50 sgl/dbl*

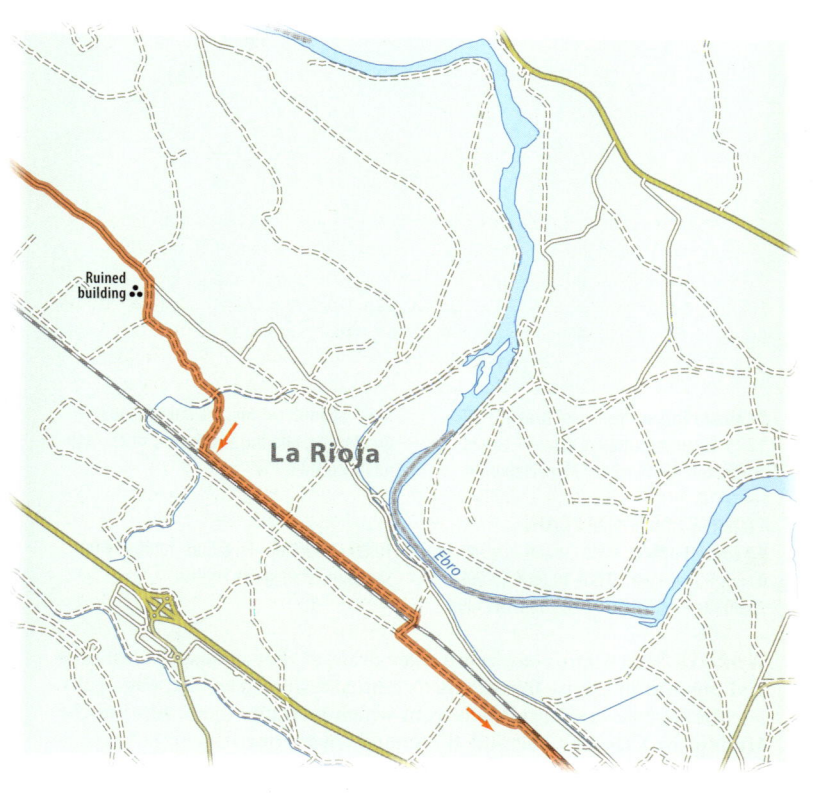

Hotel Palacios (67 rooms) Avda Zaragoza 6; 941 18 01 00; **e** info@palacioshotel.com; **w** palacioshotel.com. Large, well-run establishment, prominent as you enter town on the camino. Mexican restaurant & bar on site. B/fast inc; possible discounts for pilgrims. *€45/70 sgl/dbl*

✗ Graccurris Avda de Zaragoza 29; 941 18 04 75; lunchtimes daily, evenings Fri & Sat. Artistically presented, tasty Spanish cuisine. Not too hard on the wallet, given the quality on offer. Close to the Hotel Palacios. *€18*

STAGE 11

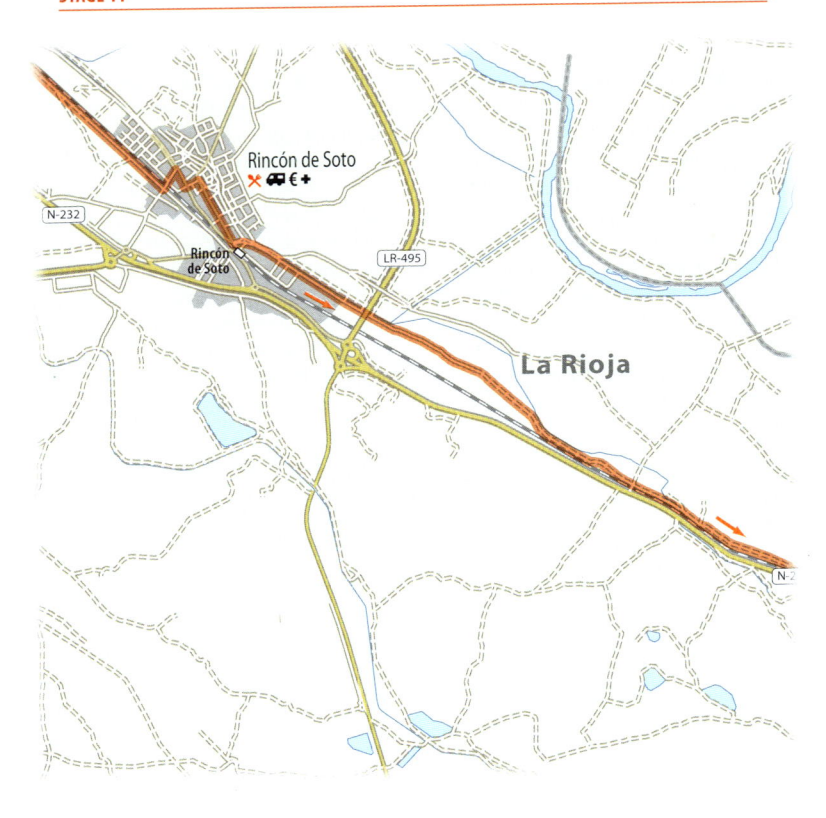

✕ **Morro Tango** Calle las Pozas 18; ☎ 941 18 15 33; w morrotango.com; ⊕ closed afternoons Sun & all day Mon. Elaborate north Spanish cuisine; the daily menu is great value, offering a variety of small, high-quality dishes. €17

TOURIST INFORMATION
ⓘ Tourist office Pl de España 1; ☎ 941 18 01 33; ⊕ Jul–Sep 10.00–14.00 & 17.00–20.00 Tue–Sat, 10.00–14.00 Sun, Oct–Jun 10.00–14.00 Tue–Fri & Sun, 10.00–14.00 Sat. Some staff speak English.

WHAT TO SEE Alfaro's storks are a key draw, as they choose to nest here and provide an excuse for the town's annual festival (see box, page 128). For the best viewpoint in town from which to watch them, head to the **Mirador de Cigüeñas** (behind the church, with open access). There is

132

also the **Centro de Interpretación de la Naturaleza** (Pl de España; ✆941 18 29 99; ⏱ Jul–Sep 10.00–14.30 & 17.00–20.00 Wed–Sat, 10.00–14.30 Sun, Oct–Jun 10.00–14.30 Wed–Sun), next to the tourist office, where you'll find information on the Ebro and its vegetation, as well as more background on the storks. Best of all, you can access the webcam, which gives you a close-up of the giant birds in their nests.

TRANSPORT Alfaro is on the main railway line between Logroño and Zaragoza, though trains stop here fairly infrequently. Autobuses Jiménez buses (page 126) run to and from Calahorra, Logroño and Zaragoza and the bus station is on the right as you enter town from the west.

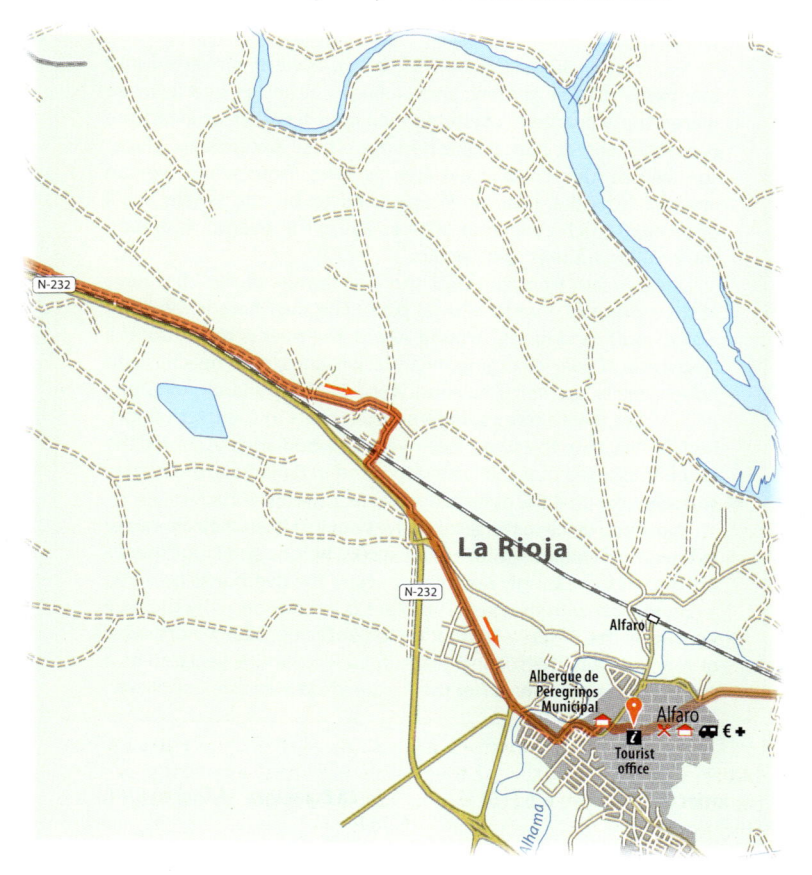

SOTOS DEL EBRO

Over time, agricultural needs have shaped the Ebro Valley to the detriment of the original vegetation. But the riverbanks around Alfaro and in a few other places (page 137) have managed to preserve their natural, wooded state to some degree, despite the many transformations they have been subjected to at the hands of mankind. In days gone by, forests covered the Ebro Valley, then one of the most fertile in the whole of Europe. But the trees were ruthlessly cut down and cleared and the underlying, rich alluvial soils were transformed into precious agricultural lands. Gravel was removed, rivers were canalised and water defences were built.

As a result, the wild banks of the Ebro were converted into manmade market gardens and orchards, although in a few rare places the valuable ecosystems managed to resist or avoid the consequences of human interference. These exceptional places survived as lush enclaves, known as *sotos*, from which we can imagine how the river landscape used to be and where you'll encounter a rich collection of trees along the riverbank, among them willows, alders and poplars.

Downstream from Logroño, the river waters of the Ebro have at their disposal a wide, alluvial plain. The river here is rambling and its outline sinuous. Around Alfaro, the river is made up of a landscape of ever-changing meanders, islands, river beaches and flood canals. The *sotos* have survived in this dynamic medium, rich copses where trees submerge their roots in the river's floodbed. Although in the past those riverside woodlands occupied the entire flood-bed that the Ebro deposited in Rioja Baja, today they scarcely take up 4.5% of its surface area, a mere 840ha.

The importance of the *sotos* derives not just from their character as havens of wildlife – look out for storks, herons and kingfishers – but also as increasingly rare places where the riverbanks preserve a connection with the past. These are good reasons why the area known as the Reserva Natural de los Sotos de Alfaro, northwest of town, is only the second place in La Rioja to be declared as a natural protected area, after the Parque de la Sierra de Cebollera.

Taxis

Javier Gil (Alfaro) **m** 626 31 06 12

La Esperanza (Alfaro) **m** 678 61 70 29

12 ALFARO–TUDELA

Today the route leaves La Rioja and its vineyards, Alfaro and its 'stork paradise', and – after the Camino Ignaciano's previous fleeting visits to Navarre on earlier stages – properly enters into the third of our five Autonomous Communities. Once a great kingdom that encompassed parts of both modern-day Spain and France, today Navarra (as it is called in Spanish) is reduced in status to being a large region with lingering regal pretensions, but in reality it is a very spacious Autonomous Community with a small population. The camino cuts a swathe across the southern tip of Navarre, and your destination is the city of Tudela de Navarra, usually just called Tudela. Modest in size yet still Navarre's second-biggest conurbation after Pamplona, the town was created by the Muslims in the 9th century as a 'new city' that flourished for some 300 years. It's a place rich in multi-cultural history, with sights of interest if time permits.

Today's route is quite long, though you stay relatively free of contact with highways, using the underused railway track as your navigational guide. The path keeps you in occasional contact with the Ebro, with opportunities to see some of the rich birdlife it supports.

Start Tourist office, Alfaro
Coordinates 42.17848, -1.74974
Finish Tudela de Navarra
Difficulty Easy
Distance 25.5km
Duration 5hrs 30mins

THE ROUTE From Alfaro's tourist office on the Plaza de España main square, find the aptly named Plaza Chica ('little square') and proceed down Calle Araciel, which in turn becomes Calle Castejón and leads out of town to a roundabout with a pilgrim sculpture in the middle. From here, take the LR-288 road to the right as it leads all the way to Castejón. As a pilgrim, you will feel well looked after because, in addition to the sculpture, to the right of the road is a specially made path that stays separate from the traffic. The railway is also off to the left and remains with you for much of the day. After 5km on this welcome path, you reach a roundabout and, taking care, as you cross the N-113, you enter Navarre, continuing straight ahead once across the road to reach the first buildings of **Castejón**. A large *bodega*, the Marqués de Montecierzo (see box, page 136), is on your left – worth visiting if you have the time. Continue along Calle de Pablo Sarasate and then – in the same direction – Calle Navas de

STAGE 12

A BODEGA WITH STORIES TO TELL

You can hardly fail to be impressed by the building occupied by the **Marqués de Montecierzo** (☎ 948 81 44 14; w marquesdemontecierzo.com), directly on your left as you arrive in Castejón. But inside, the *bodega*'s history is even more intriguing. If you are passing after 10.00 on your morning walk towards Tudela, a visit is well worthwhile. This is a family-run business, the building restored to its current stunning condition by the Lozano-Melero family, who used the original stone from its ruined state only 20 years ago.

Its multiple-award-winning wines are 100% organic. Reds, whites, rosés and even vermouth are crafted from the 28ha of vineyards surrounding the *bodega*. And the building? A century ago it was built to serve as a flourmill, but in the Civil War was commandeered as a prison by Franco's Nationalists and used to hold Republican captives. They were put to work on the railroad, as the town has always been an important railway junction. It is said that over 3,500 prisoners passed through this building in the 1930s. After the war, it was returned to its original purpose, but eventually closed and fell into disuse. By the time current owner Joaquín Lozano bought it in 2002, it was crumbling to dust. Marvel at the photos on the wall, touch the old machinery and, if the family are available – they are very open to visitors – you can take a guided tour. It's also popular with storks, nesting on the roof.

Tolosa (see box, opposite). Remember there are no refreshment stops or shops between here and Tudela.

Pass a park and, when the road ends at a junction, turn left to ascend on to a road bridge that crosses the railway. Before actually crossing the *main* railtrack, however, turn right *off* the bridge on to a dirt road that runs parallel with it. Continue on this path for over 5km, until the route turns to tarmac and crosses a bridge over the railway. Once across you have a choice: if already tired, simply continue along the road with the tracks now immediately on your right, or alternatively add an extra 2km to the stage by taking a more scenic route down by the Ebro.

The former option needs no instructions. If choosing the river walk, which gives a break from road-walking and offers wildlife-spotting opportunities, then as you come off the bridge double-back to your left on a dirt track which disconcertingly – but only briefly – takes you back in the direction in which you have just come. Fear not! The path soon curves right and you follow it, taking the right-hand branch at the first fork. The thickening vegetation ahead alerts you to the proximity of the Ebro and, on reaching it, you follow its gentle flow as your path runs parallel. This is an area where you will encounter more *sotos* (see box, page 134). Passing a solitary house on your right, continue straight on

> ### A BATTLE FAR AWAY, IN TIME AND PLACE
>
> 'Navas de Tolosa' is a very common street name across Spain, and with very good reason. Even here in Castejón, Navarre, a street will proudly bear the name of this famous battle that took place not only centuries before – in the year 1212, to be exact – but also many hundreds of kilometres away, north of Jaén in distant Andalucía. So why is this skirmish fêted in so many street names, so far away? Because the Battle of Las Navas de Tolosa is regarded as a key turning point in the Christian Reconquest of Spain, marking a significant defeat of the Muslims of the Almohad Caliphate who were then occupying a huge part of the Iberian Peninsula. Any differences between the rival kingdoms of Castile, Aragón and Navarre were temporarily set aside for the fight, as the Caliph Muhammad al-Nasir's forces were routed. Christian losses were, by comparison, very small. Such a crucial military engagement in the making of modern-day Spain certainly deserves to be remembered by the many streets that now bear its name.

STAGE 12

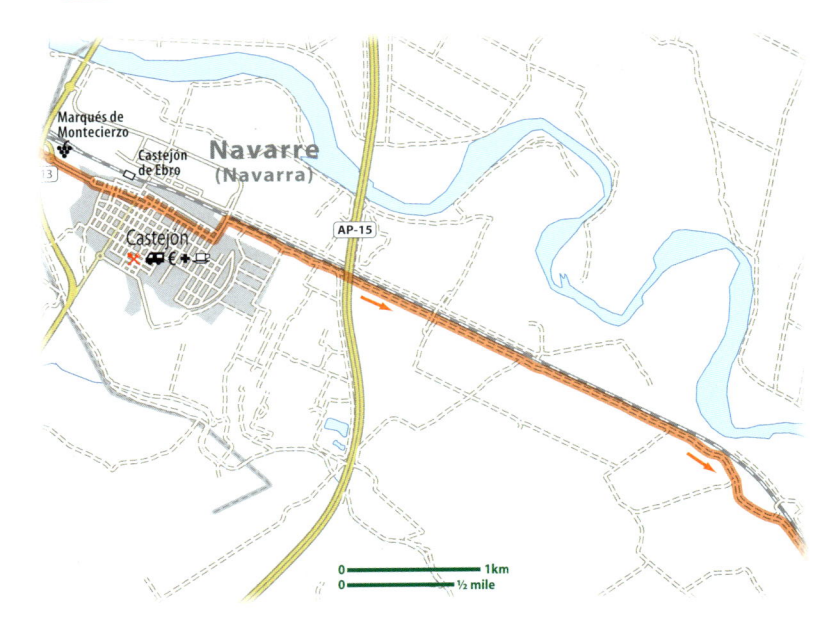

as the path briefly distances you from the water. On reaching a group of run-down buildings, you first fork left (the right fork follows up the side of fruit trees) then follow your chosen path as it curves to the right in front of the houses. Pass with them on your left and then immediately beyond them you turn to the left, keep to the right fork a few metres later as the path divides again to take you between a thick wooded area and vegetable fields.

You are soon returned to the riverside, where you continue straight until the path again veers right to take you once more away from the water. Passing through more dilapidated farm buildings, the path curves left beyond them, giving you – on a clear day – your first sight of the outline of Tudela. Fifty metres beyond the buildings, fork left and continue until the path takes a 90-degree turn to the right, which will take you back to rejoin the tarmac road you left earlier. Before reaching the road, note to your left the new **Soto de los Tetones** bird observatory, which is worth the very short detour as it is well situated, looking down on a reedy section of the Ebro. Species to look out for here are grey heron, Western marsh-harrier, hoopoe, crested lark and common kingfisher. If you earlier chose the tarmac option (page 136), do look out for this site, signposted left off the road, as your detour to enjoy it will be only a few hundred metres.

Your route into Tudela now follows the tarmac road, with the railway on your right. You come close to the Ebro for one final time today, as you soon approach a **dam**. A couple of hundred metres beyond it, look out for the low stone bridge on the left, which you can cross to then turn immediately right and walk on a dirt road that runs parallel to the tarmac road you've just left. To your left are some impressive *huertos*, or allotments, highlighting that this is a region that really venerates its vegetables. Artichokes and asparagus top the list of celebrities in this region.

The entry to **Tudela** is a pleasant one, with no need to traverse industrial estates nor walk in the shadow of apartment blocks, as is sometimes the case. When the dirt road ends after approximately 2km, briefly rejoin the tarmac road on your right before turning right underneath the railway and following the signs for the *ayuntamiento* (town hall), *oficina de turismo* (tourist office) and cathedral down the quaint Calle Fosal, which soon

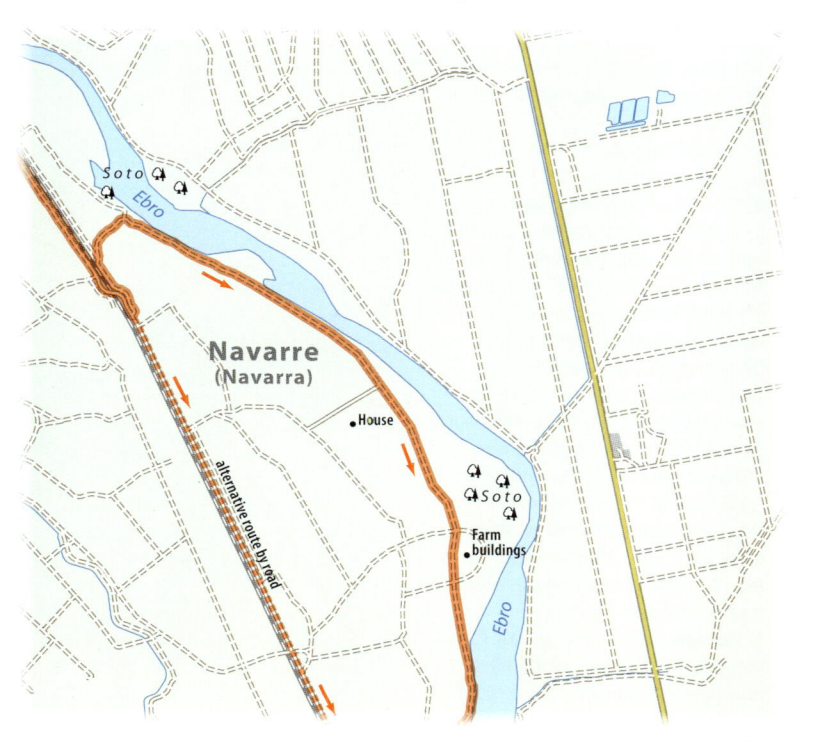

STAGE 12

becomes the cobbled Calle Portal. If you want to follow the official route to the cathedral, continue straight on; if the tourist office on Plaza de los Fueros is your destination, turn left on to Calle Magallón and follow the signs for it.

WHERE TO STAY AND EAT

As a medium-sized town, Tudela has a number of accommodation options, though no actual bespoke pilgrims' hostel.

Albergue Juvenil de Tudela (Youth Hostel) (8 rooms & 16 dorm beds) Calle Camino Caritat 17; **m** 670 82 44 90 or 664 63 61 75; **e** alberguetudela@gmail.com. Situated on the outskirts of town on Stage 13. Advance reservations required. *€12 (pilgrim rate), sheet hire €3.50*

Hostal Remigio (35 rooms) Gaztambide Carrera 4; 948 82 08 50; **e** info@hostalremigio.com; **w** hostalremigio.com. A reliable stalwart & super-central, with a good-value restaurant (see below). AC, heating & TV. *€48/70 sgl/dbl*

Hotel Santamaria (50 rooms) Camino San Marcial 14; 948 82 12 00; **e** info@hotelsantamaria.net; **w** hotelsantamaria.net. One of the better central choices, modern with good facilities. AC, satellite TV, restaurant. *€70/80 sgl/dbl*

✕ Mesón Julián Calle de la Merced 9; 948 82 20 28; **w** mesonjulian.com. Pricier than some, but has delivered quality for many, many years. Often showcases the region's famed vegetables, alongside hearty meat & fish dishes. *€20*

✕ Remigio Gaztambide Carrera 4. Part of the *hostal* of the same name, this offers an extensive menu enjoyed by middle-aged

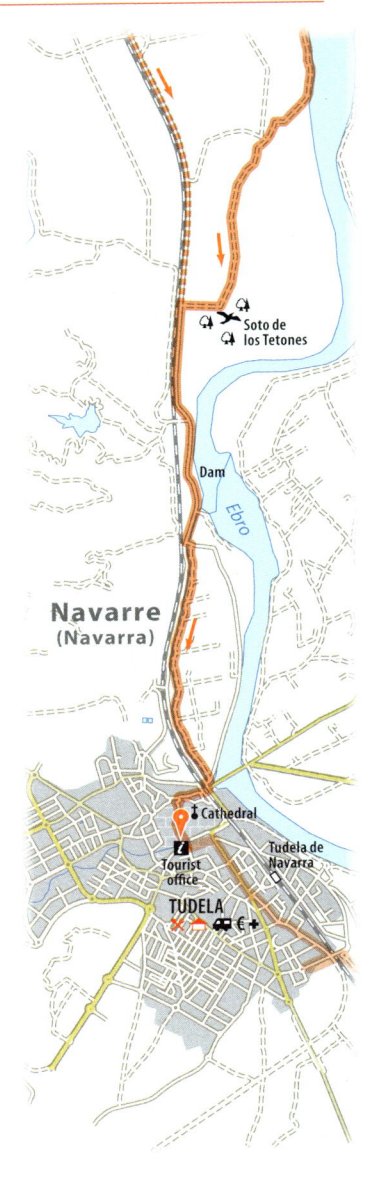

FRANCIS XAVIER, CO-FOUNDER OF THE JESUITS

Although the Camino Ignaciano takes its name from Ignatius, a native of the Basque Country, neighbouring Navarre is inextricably linked with the *other* co-founder of the Society of Jesus: **Francis Xavier** (Spanish: Francisco Javier), who was born in 1506 in the town of Javier some 50km east of Pamplona, and is recognised as one of the greatest missionaries of all time, canonised in 1622.

At the age of 19, Francis's studies took him to Paris where his paths crossed with Ignatius. In 1534, having taken the necessary vows of poverty, chastity and obedience, Francis then went on to study theology and was ordained as a priest three years later. Soon after the founding of the Society of Jesus, Francis – some say somewhat reluctantly – answered the call from the King of Portugal to spread the faith in that country's overseas territories and his missionary work began in 1541 in southern India, before progressing in later years to Ceylon (modern-day Sri Lanka), southeast Asia and Japan.

His death is remembered each year on 3 December, during the Day of Navarre. At other times, the imposing 10th-century Castillo de Javier castle and museum – his birthplace – is a major visitor attraction, and the site of a massive pilgrimage each March. Along with San Fermín, Francis Xavier is the co-patron of Navarre and much revered in the Autonomous Community and across the world.

---

locals in a wood-panelled dining room. Quaint & atmospheric. *€15*

✕ Sua Carnicerias 11 bis; 948 00 30 86; **f** restaurantesua. 'Death to the tablecloth' is the restaurant's motto, appropriate for a place where food takes centre stage & table linen is indeed scarce. Basque-influenced, but with local vegetables also prominent. Great wines. Recommended. *€16*

TOURIST INFORMATION

Tourist office Pl de los Fueros 12; 948 84 80 58; **w** www.tudela.es/turismo; 10.00–14.00 & 16.00–19.00 Mon–Sat, 10.00–14.00 Sun. English-speaking staff.

WHAT TO SEE If you arrive early, leave late or take a day off here, a coffee in the **Plaza de los Fueros** – originally constructed for bullfighting, and adorned with coats of arms – is a good place to begin to plan your day. The top visitor draw in town would be a combined visit to the **Museo de Tudela** (948 40 21 61; €4) and the adjacent 12th-century **Cathedral de**

STAGE 12

Santa Maria, with Romanesque features. As well as archaeological finds and religious iconography, the museum houses a reproduction of *La Manta*, the canvas which recorded the names of those Jews who agreed to convert to Christianity. Sobering. However, in medieval times, Moors, Christians and Jews lived contentedly side-by-side in Tudela and this harmony is celebrated annually in September with the town's Mercado Medieval Tres Culturas (Three Cultures Medieval Market) festival.

TRANSPORT Tudela's train and bus stations sit snugly side-by-side, a 10-minute walk southeast from the centre. Services run east to Zaragoza, west back to Logroño, and between and beyond.

Taxis
Asociación de Taxis de Tudela (Tudela) 948 82 20 27; m 638 12 14 78
Jesus Maria Diaz Mendoza (Tudela) m 615 01 14 74

Taxi Castejón (Castejón) m 636 47 16 72

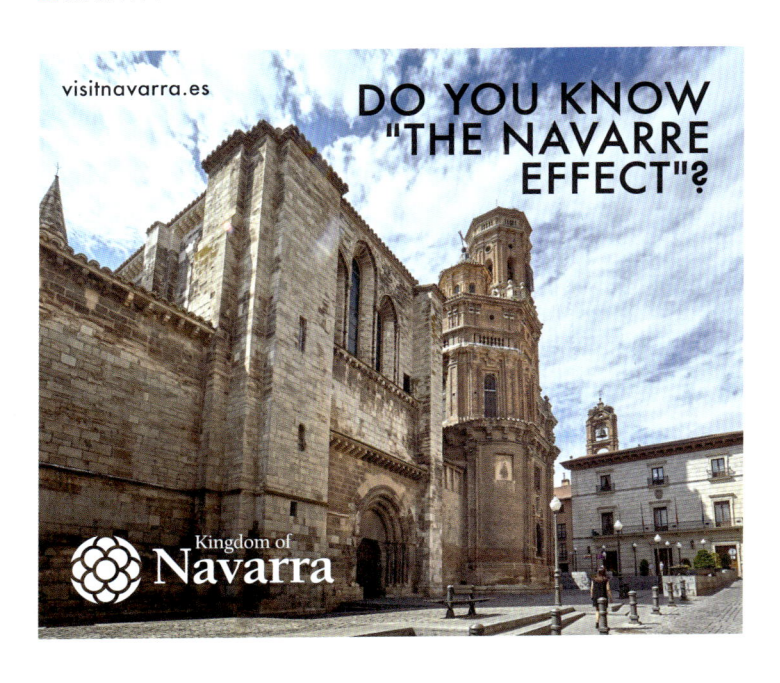

13 TUDELA–GALLUR

If you stick to the official guidance, today's hefty route will be the longest of all the Ignatian stages. There's an attractive alternative of dividing it over two days by overnighting in Mallén (see box, below), but this does require some advance logistical planning. At the three-quarter mark of the stage, the camino says goodbye to Navarre and enters into the route's fourth Autonomous Community, that of Aragón. Note that much of the walk today is spent by the side of a canal, which attracts biting insects; long trousers and insect repellent are advisable. And the good news? The terrain is very, very flat and Cortes has an interesting castle.

> **Start** Tourist office, Tudela
> **Coordinates** 42.06145, -1.60561
> **Finish** Gallur (but options for splitting the stage)
> **Difficulty** Easy
> **Distance** 39.2km (29.1km if stopping at Mallén)
> **Duration** 10hrs (7hrs 45mins if stopping at Mallén)

THE ROUTE From the tourist office, head along Calle Gaztambide-Carrera and turn right on to Avenida de Zaragoza, initially in the direction of the train station. Reaching a roundabout, with the train station visible off to your left, take a left on to Camino Calle Caritat. On the pavement here are unusual painted route markings, which you can safely follow until you have crossed the railtrack – but no further. These look like waymarkings, and indeed they are, but they were in fact painted to help children find their way to school! Turn left on Calle Fustiñana and, at the end, cross the railtrack on a pedestrian bridge and turn right to walk parallel with it. Soon you pass an electricity transforming station

SPLITTING THE STAGE IN TWO

Unless you use a taxi, the options for splitting this stage over two days are a bit limited, due to the scarcity of accommodation choices along the way. One option would be to end a truncated stage at Mallén, which has one hostel. The following day, you could then make the short (10km) walk into Gallur, or take the longer (31km) route through to Alagón. A second option would be to take a bus or train to Ribaforada or Cortes de Navarra and walk the remainder of the stage. Slight cheating, but needs must.

STAGE 13

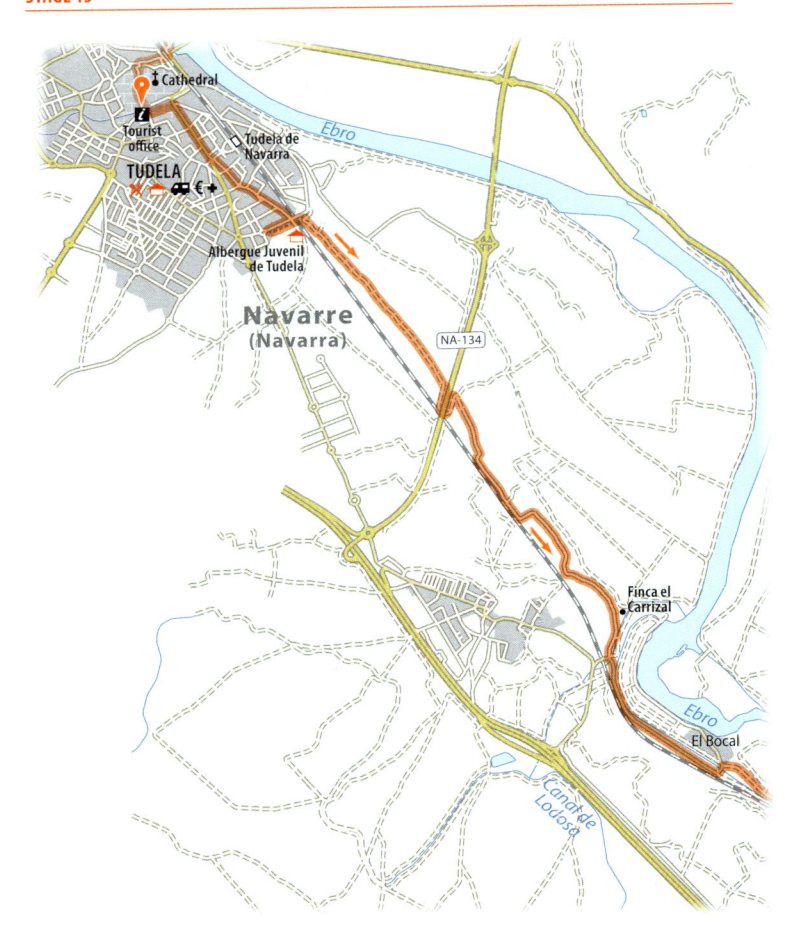

and upon reaching a road that rises to cross back over the rails, ignore it and proceed straight ahead, looking instead for the wide concrete path to its left, which continues your route parallel to the rails. Your concrete gives way to rough track and you leave Tudela behind.

The scenery here is flat and without great interest, but early mornings here bring rewards in the shape of a lively birdlife and boisterous rabbits. After around 2km you meet the NA-134 main road up above, and turn right to cross it via an underpass. Continue briefly parallel with the NA-

134, now on your left, and at a junction turn sharp right, with a windfarm in the distance to your left. The route edges close to the rails once more, before turning to paved road. Follow as it briefly veers to the left, soon passing the front gate of the **Finca el Carrizal ranch**. Shortly after, and just before reaching the railway, turn left over a bridge on to a road squeezed between the serene Canal Imperial and the tracks. After less than 1km, turn left across Formigales bridge to find **El Bocal**, the birthplace of the Canal Imperial, on your left. Ramón Pignatelli was the man responsible for the canal project in

▲ The Canal Imperial, near El Bocal *MS*

the 18th century, developed to provide irrigation and a communication route. Running between Fontellas in Navarre and Fuentes de Ebro in Aragón, it was ridiculed at the time, but Pignatelli took his revenge on his doubters by erecting a Fuente de los Incrédulos (Fountain of the Unbelievers) in Zaragoza on the canal's arrival in the city. Part of Pignatelli's education was by Jesuits and his canal is recognised as a major work of its time. At the bridge end, turn right on to a dirt road, signposted for the GR-99, and continue with the canal now on your right. Much of the birdlife here stays up in the trees, but herons can usually be spotted on the canal banks.

Your canal-side stroll continues for nearly 5km, until you cross the Puente de Ribaforada bridge into the town of the same name. The route continues straight through **Ribaforada**, past its handful of cafés, without any deviation until you meet the railway once more. Turn left without crossing the tracks, instead walking parallel to them. Note the yellow scallop-shell signs fixed to some of the houses here, indicating that you are on the Camino de Santiago del Ebro. The tarmac turns to dirt as the buildings of Ribaforada are left behind. Stay on this track for 2km, and as the road turns left towards a huge **Sofidel** factory, continue straight ahead on a grass/dirt path parallel to the railway. A bridge across the railway is our target, some 400m distant. The path here is indistinct, without markings, but just stay close to the railway and pass beneath the bridge. Beyond this, you are rewarded with a wide dirt road to continue your journey.

After a further 2.5km, the road turns slightly away from the railway. Pay attention here: leave the road as it curves left, instead staying close to

ENTERING INTO THE SPIRIT? THE CASTILLO DE CORTES

Dominating the centre of this quiet town, the much-restored 12th-century **Castillo de Cortes** (Pl de la Iglesia 2; m 676 38 15 63; e amigoscastillodecortes@gmail.com; w castillodecortes.com; ⏲ visits by appointment only; €3) has many surprises to share. Amazingly, dozens of volunteers have spent over a decade restoring this squat edifice, bought in 1997 by the town council and with a new room being renovated each year since. The work done is truly admirable. Inside the thick walls is a quaint museum, with period furniture and old agricultural and other machinery, as well as an exhibition dedicated to Bronze- and Iron-Age artefacts found at a site nearby. Restored rooms include the children's dining room, the chapel, two bedrooms and various sitting areas. There is even a tea salon, as the noble family who once resided here often travelled to London and counted both Orwell and Hemingway among their friends. To round things off are the gruesome dungeon, a suspiciously shiny suit of armour and, of course, a *fantasma* or ghost. No doubt to the delight (and fright) of visiting youngsters, she is revealed by a volunteer opening a wooden door with a cunningly concealed remote control. No English is spoken, but there may be a translated information sheet available.

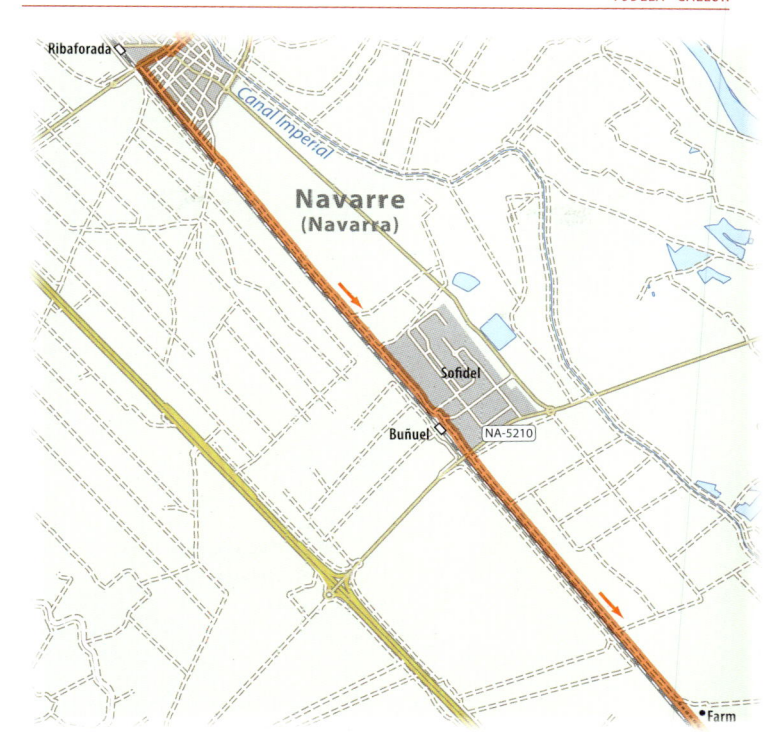

the tracks and passing a multiple-siloed **farm** on your left. After 400m or so, just beyond the farm, rejoin the dirt road which has now reappeared on your left. After a further 500m, the dirt track again veers away from the tracks, and this time you follow it. You now have a long, straight, 5km haul into Cortes, passing a number of in-use and disused buildings focused on livestock farming. Eventually reaching a roundabout, follow the sign into **Cortes**. The road turns slightly right and, although the waymarking here is not great, there are signs for the San Juan Bautista church and castle to your left. If you've phoned ahead, your castle visit will provide an interesting diversion (see box, opposite). Next to the castle is a beautiful park with swans and ducks – a good place for a rest before continuing your journey.

With the castle entrance on your right, follow Calle San Miguel to its end. At the crossroads, continue straight ahead, signposted for the train station and Mallén. You will shortly leave Navarre and enter Aragón. Pass

STAGE 13

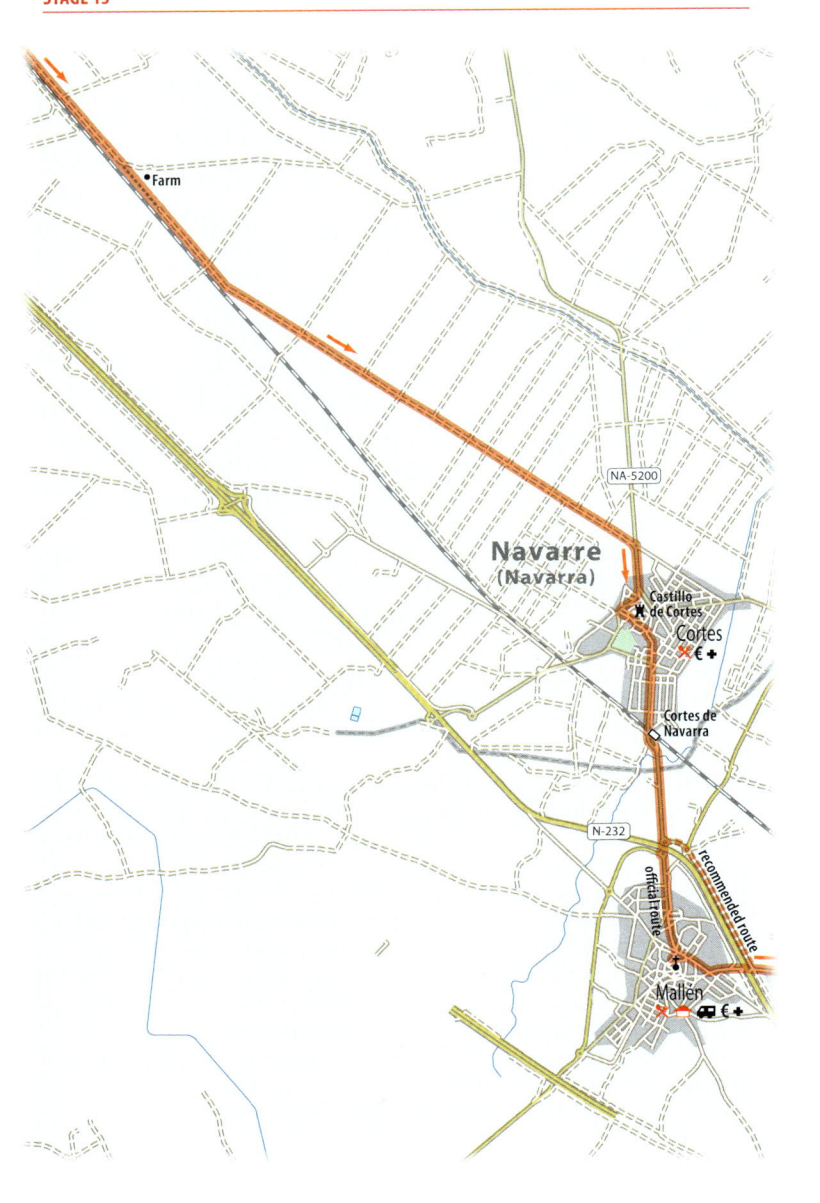

beneath the track via an underpass and continue straight ahead, with the buildings of **Mallén** appearing up ahead. Cross a roundabout, and on reaching a triangle-shaped children's playground, veer left as the road curves to the right. The church is now directly ahead, and on reaching it you can continue straight and slightly right to find the town's bars and services; if you're not stopping here, turn left at the church and soon take another left on to the Camino de Santiago street, heading back towards the busy A-68/N-232 road – extreme caution is required. (An alternative, safer route is to turn left at the roundabout just before entering Mallén, on to the CP-2 road towards the industrial estate, with the motorway to your right, and turn left again at the Dia building. But this does mean you miss Mallén town centre.) Once across, continue straight through the industrial estate – with the Dia building to your right – and at the end of this road take the right fork, with olive and fig trees to your left, and then fork left to pass some agricultural buildings on your right. Cross the train tracks by way of an underpass and continue to the right, shortly turning

FERDINAND AND CATHERINE: PUTTING ARAGÓN ON THE MAP

Aragón, stuck inland without a coastline, lacks any showstopping tourist sites, apart from El Pilar in Zaragoza (page 169) and the semi-desert of Los Monegros (see box, page 179), which will surely leave an indelible impression. But anyone walking on the Camino Ignaciano will spend more time in this region than most visitors, so a bit of understanding is useful background.

Perhaps the best starting point is to look at two influential figures whose associations with Aragón have certainly put the region on the map of history with their significant contributions to the world. Born in 1452, **Ferdinand II** married Isabella, who was heir to Henry IV of Castile. He was just 17, and this youthful marriage paved the way for the 1479 union of these two Iberian superpowers and the shaping of modern-day Spain. Considering that Aragón at that time also held sway over Catalonia, Valencia, Majorca and indeed some overseas territories, its joining with Castile meant that this was the most unified that Spain had ever been. In later years, the conquest of Navarre would add another significant piece to the emerging Spanish jigsaw puzzle.

The major challenge for Ferdinand and Isabella during their early joint rule of Aragón and Castile was the completion of the Reconquista: the taking back of the peninsula from the Moors after nearly 800 years of Islamic occupation. This monumental task was duly completed in 1492. But it was not just Spain that was being created under Ferdinand and Isabella's rule. That same year, Christopher Columbus was dispatched to the Americas and two years later a treaty between Spain and Portugal divided out the world beyond the Iberian Peninsula for the purposes of

right towards some windmills. On your left is the Canal Imperial, which you cross on a stone bridge.

At this point, your navigational worries for today are over: you have 7km to **Gallur**, with the canal always on your right and never out of sight. You have the benefit of some conifers at the start of this long stretch and, if you are fortunate, a wind from the west to cool you. En route are some *almenaras*, to all appearances just little canal-side stone buildings, but with sluices to the side which helped distribute water to the fields for irrigation. When Spain lost Cuba and its sugar production to the United States in 1898, the fields around here were used to ramp up production of sugar beet to compensate and the canal was ideal for its transport. After the 29.5km mark, you can choose to take the left fork for the *centro urbano* (town centre) to find Gallur's solitary hotel, or fork right if heading for

conquest. These were seismic times indeed, with Jews being expelled from Spain, the diminishing of the rights of the country's Muslims, and ultimately their expulsion, too. Ferdinand II died in 1516, but the foundations of Spain as an entity were by then in place.

Ferdinand and Isabella's daughter, **Catherine of Aragón**, is another historical figure who – albeit against her will – can rightly be said to have changed European history. However, it is in England, not Spain, where the impact of her life would be felt. Born in Castile and widowed at only 16 from her first marriage, she then became number one in the unfortunate chain of serial spouse Henry VIII's six wives. Only one daughter survived from the six children she bore him and, as it was a daughter, Henry sought to turn his attentions elsewhere in search of producing a legitimate male heir. The problem was that divorce was not allowed by the Catholic Church, and a few cleverly constructed arguments by Henry and his advisers failed to persuade the Pope otherwise. To find a solution to this problem, Henry decided to split the Church of England away from Rome, conveniently appointing himself head of this new institution. With this self-awarded authority, he sanctioned his own divorce from Catherine and married Anne Boleyn. The seeds of Protestantism in England were sown.

Catherine herself avoided the worst of the fates that befell Henry's other wives. She was a popular figure in England, attracting great sympathy from its citizens. She would always consider herself the rightful Queen of England until she died from cancer – not beheading or other fate – in 1536.

the pilgrim's hostel next to the train station (signed *estación ferrocarril*). For those choosing the latter, look for the blue metal bridge a little further on. Across this bridge, climb a few steps to see the hostel straight in front of you, 200m away, with the train station to the right. Gallur is a pleasant little town, though without major attractions. If you've walked this stage in one day, it's unlikely you'll be looking for nightlife.

WHERE TO STAY AND EAT

Albergue Municipal Gallur (5 rooms, 16 beds) Next to the train station, Gallur; 976 86 43 96. The pilgrims' hostel also houses a bar & restaurant. *€12/25/40 dorm/sgl/dbl*

Hostel Pinocho (10 rooms) Calle Tudela 4, Mallén; 976 85 02 25. Central, basic but with a restaurant. The only option in town & the only option if you are splitting this long stage in 2. *€18/36 sgl/dbl*

STAGE 13

🏠 **Hotel/Restaurante El Colono**
(8 rooms) Constitución 13, Gallur; ✆976 86 42 75; **e** info@elconogallur.com. Very central, on the north side of the canal, with an early opening bar & restaurant. Pilgrim discounts. *€36/70 sgl/dbl*

✕ **Meson Rincón del Gallo** Calle Union General de Trabajadores 1, Gallur; ✆976 86 40 21. Hearty & elaborate at the same time, very much the place to dine in town. *€12*

TRANSPORT It's comforting that today's long stage is never too far from the railway, with stations at Ribaforada, Cortes de Navarra/Mallén and Gallur itself. Four or five trains run daily westwards to Tudela and eastwards on to Zaragoza. Alsa buses also connect Tudela to Ribaforada and Cortes de Navarra (**w** alsa.es).

Taxis
🚗 **Taxis Mallén** (Mallén) **m** 654 65 77 70

🚗 **Taxi Zueco** (Gallur) ✆976 85 73 18

14 GALLUR–ALAGÓN

This is a stage of medium length, delightful in places, with neither climb nor descent, passing through a couple of interesting small towns that offer clues as to the history of this region: first Luceni, whose Italian-sounding name stems from the Roman 'Lucius', and then Alcalá de Ebro, whose now-ruined castle lent the town its name from the Arabic al-calat, or 'the castle'. Alcalá has a bigger claim to fame as, according to famous travel writer Jan Morris, it is the inspiration for the island of Barataria over which Sancho Panza held sway in the epic, Don Quixote. *History and fiction aside, both places provide the chance for a welcome coffee or refreshment stop. One downside: the first 7km between your start-point and Luceni is along the busy VP-24 road. But this inconvenience can be avoided… read on for more!*

> **Start** Hotel El Colono, Gallur
> **Coordinates** 41.86876, -1.31789
> **Finish** Alagón
> **Difficulty** Easy
> **Distance** 22.8km
> **Duration** 5hrs

THE ROUTE To start the day's stage, find once again the tranquil Canal Imperial and the adjacent park, the Parque de Pignatelli – named after Ramón Pignatelli, who created the canal. From here, cross the main road by the canal to find the Calle Camino Real (the VP-024), almost directly opposite. (If coming from the pilgrims' hostel, head towards town, cross the canal and turn right.) It's hard to imagine the Camino Real ('Royal Way') of olden times, as it is now a busy road that leads straight to Luceni; stay aware, as traffic moves fast and there is little protection for walkers. Face the traffic (sunglasses often essential in the morning, as you will be heading eastwards) and perhaps step off on to the sloping grass verge each time a vehicle approaches: the smooth road surface encourages drivers to drive at great speed! (If this sounds too much, there is an option to take the train straight to Luceni – see box, page 154.)

After 6km, your trek along the road leads to a roundabout where you turn right to reach the first buildings of **Luceni**, then veer left on to Calle Ramón y Cajal as the main road continues off to the right. This street heads straight through this quiet town, first leading to the square – which is home to Bar Lisboa, a few shops, bakery and pharmacy. Note that there is drinkable water in the square, but not from the central fountain; look

A GOOD TIME TO CHEAT

As a good pilgrim, I am not normally one to advocate cheating, but if you wish to 'stray from the righteous path' and skip a bit of walking on the way to Manresa, then this is a good stage to choose. There are three early morning trains that will whizz you to Luceni in 5 minutes, and no-one will ever find out about your short cut. Why would you do this? Traffic is the answer. It may be that a path is eventually found that avoids the vehicles on the busy VP-024 road, but it does not as yet exist and safety has to take priority over any pious devotion to walking every step of the way. Go on: I won't tell. And indeed, this little 'cheat' seems like a fairly minor sin, when compared with something that Ignatius himself came close to perpetrating near here, 500 years ago. Here's how, according to his own account, the reformed Ignatius came perilously close to returning to his former, combative self and committing a heinous crime in defending his beliefs.

It so happened that on his route Ignatius chanced upon a Saracen (Muslim) riding a horse and, falling into conversation with him, the subject turned to that of the Blessed Virgin. Given their different faith perspectives, perhaps it is no surprise that their views diverged. The Saracen boldly ventured the opinion that, while he accepted that Mary had experienced an immaculate conception, he questioned whether she had remained a virgin thereafter. Ignatius could not persuade him otherwise, and after the stranger had gone on his way, this dishonouring of the name of the Virgin troubled and angered Ignatius, to the point where he considered whether he should follow the Saracen and kill him. Struggling to make his decision, Ignatius decided to let his own mule decide. If the mule chose to turn towards the village (Pedrola, just off the route), which was the Saracen's destination, then Ignatius would avenge the dishonour, but if the mule stuck to the main path, then Ignatius would let it pass and continue on his way. Fortunately, the mule carried straight on, or the Ignatian story could have ended differently – and perhaps right there and then.

So, give in to temptation, don't let a mule decide, just choose to avoid the traffic.

instead for the nearby *agua potable* sign. From the square, continue in the same direction as before, now on the Calle Daoíz y Velarde, picking up GR-99 signs. It is now 3.7km to Alcalá de Ebro.

Traffic on this next stretch is, thankfully, likely to be limited to a few underpowered motorbikes, driven by senior citizens and perhaps accompanied by a scrawny dog or two. The by-now-familiar thickening of the vegetation on the left announces the proximity of the Ebro, just as the twin spires of Alcalá's church appear straight ahead. The tarmac gives way to dirt road, but the direction remains the same. Your track ends after around 3km and you proceed left to approach the town centre. Look out for the **observation tower** on the left, which gives an opportunity to enjoy an elevated view both up and downstream of the Ebro. Note the storks' nests piled up on a midstream water marker. **Alcalá de Ebro** sports a few references to Miguel de Cervantes (author of *Don Quixote*), principally a mural and a couple of Sancho Panza metallic sculptures. Continue on Calle de Miguel de Cervantes and, after 500m, turn off this street to follow the sign to the left at a junction for Cabañas de Ebro and the Bar las Truchas bar/restaurant appears on your left. (At the time of writing, both bars in the town centre were closed, leaving just a bakery,

STAGE 14

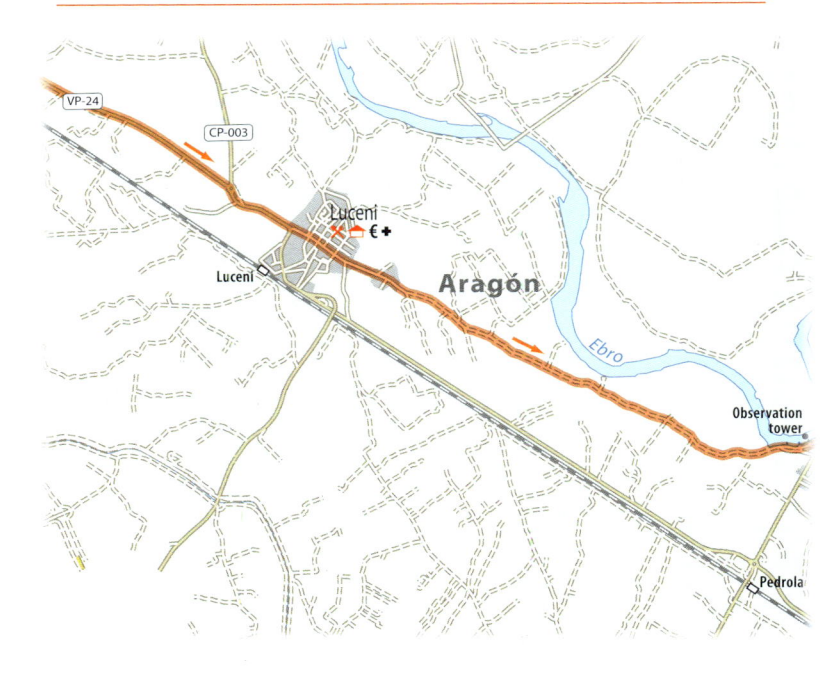

pharmacy and a hostel (should you wish to break the stage in two) to attend to pilgrims' needs.)

Soon the tarmac ends, but you continue straight ahead. Again, some tree clusters tell you that the Ebro is about to join once more from the left. Soon you approach **Cabañas de Ebro** and, before reaching a water tower, turn right and pick up the signs for the R7 path where you will find the welcome sight of the Hostal Restaurante Cubero (page 159). Continue past this on the tarmac for about 1.5km to reach a junction with the VP-24 as you meet the Ebro once again. Turn left on to the VP-24, still a busy road at this point, where the absence of a suitable pavement makes it again unpleasant. The railway and AP-68 are visible to the right, as are Alagón's buildings straight ahead.

Recent pilgrim-friendly improvements have been made to the route, and thankfully after only 500m you can turn sharp left (signposted Alagón, 4km) on to a wide dirt track which curves right behind a white wall, then left close to the river. After less than 1km, take the right turn (again, signposted Alagón) to leave the river behind you. Now following the GR-99 signs, the route curves right across an irrigation channel, then left, and eventually beneath the motorway via an underpass. You continue with no need to panic, although it initially appears that Alagón is being bypassed away to your right. Keep the faith! The wide path eventually leads past a massive factory on your right, then swings sharply right (GR-99 signs) and curves left and right to join asphalt by a white wall. Pass industrial buildings until the road rises to cross the AP-68 via a bridge, then follow left alongside the railway track. On reaching another bridge, turn left to access it and go up and over it to cross the railway, noting

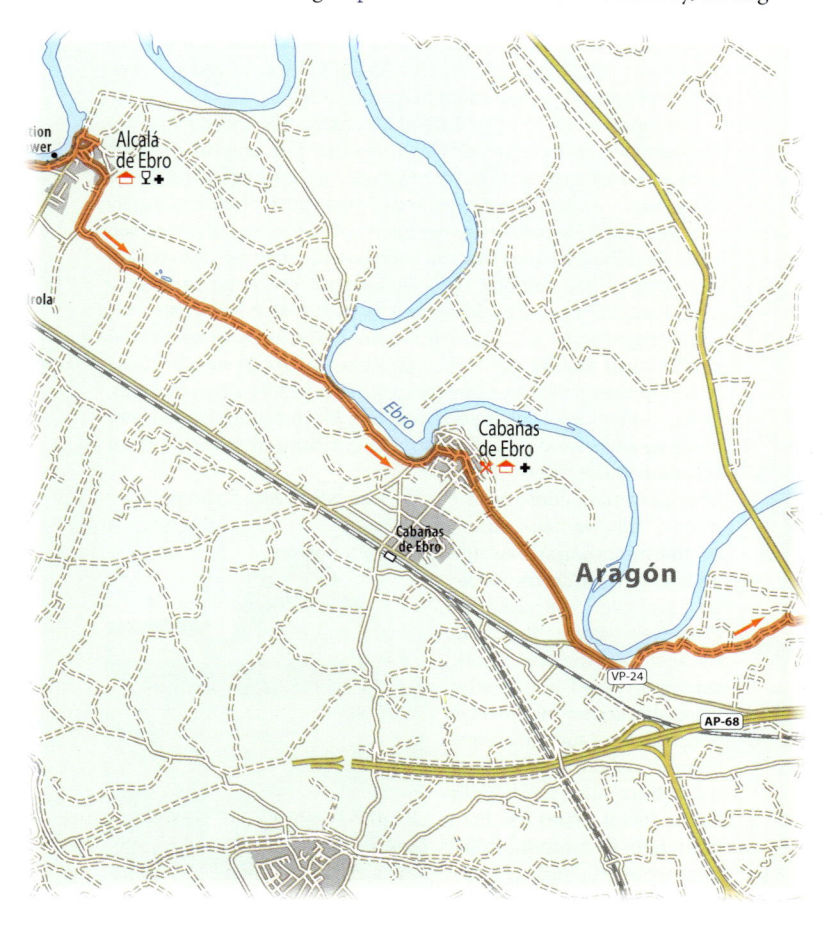

ARCHITECTURAL TRACES OF ISLAM: MOORISH AND MUDÉJAR

You would hardly expect nearly 800 years of Moorish rule in Spain to have ended without leaving some physical traces. And, some 500 years after the end of the Reconquest of Spain, plenty do remain, both direct and indirect. Anyone who has seen the Alhambra in Granada will have been blown away by that wonderful example of the tangible legacy left behind by the Moors. Much more local to the Camino Ignaciano than the mighty Alhambra is the 11th-century Aljaferiá palace in Zaragoza, beautifully preserved and now in use for regional government purposes.

In Aragón, as well as evidence of Moorish times, there are plenty of examples of mudéjar architecture, and not only in majestic Zaragoza itself, but also in lesser towns along the route. At the end of Stage 14, for example, the camino deposits you in compact, largely unexceptional Alagón, where the town's 14th-century Iglesia de San Pedro and the Ermita de Nuestra Señora del Castillo are both typical examples of the mudéjar style. Although it encompasses plenty of influences lifted and developed from the Moorish times, this architectural style also draws from elsewhere, leaning heavily on Gothic styles among its other inspirations. Buildings such as these two in Alagón stand as testament to times in history when Muslims, Christians and Jews cohabited peacefully in what would much later become what we now call Spain. Most striking in many mudéjar buildings is the extensive use of brick in their construction, a stark but perhaps easier-on-the-eye contrast to the imposing large-stone places of worship encountered elsewhere along the way. As well as the brickwork, ceramics, wood and plaster were also commonly used in construction. Mudéjar art was influential from the 12th to the 17th century, but happily in the towns along the Ebro in Aragón, its footprint is still clearly visible.

▼ Iglesia de San Pedro, Alagón *MS*

that this is where you will pick up tomorrow's stage when you head for Zaragoza. Today, however, simply follow the arrows and Camino Jacobeo signs into **Alagón**, which sports a couple of examples of the region's distinctive mudéjar architecture (see box, opposite).

WHERE TO STAY AND EAT All accommodation listed here is in Alagón, except the Cubero. As well as the restaurants attached to the Los Angeles and Baraka, there are a decent number of eating options, with most places found around the Plaza España or along the Avenida de Zaragoza, both in the town centre.

Hostal Restaurante Baraka
(8 rooms) Calle San Pedro 13; 976 61 60 11; m 649 84 27 72; e hostal@hostalbaraka.com; w hostalbaraka.com. Decent AC rooms. A surprising find is the Irish-style pub in the basement, the pride of Ramon, the owner. Restaurant closed Sun. €30/45 sgl/dbl

Hostal Restaurante Cubero
(4 rooms) Calle Joaquin Costa s/n, Cabañas de Ebro; 976 61 17 20. Ideal if you want to shorten the stage. Restaurant is open daily, lunch & dinner. B/fast inc. €20/40 sgl/dbl

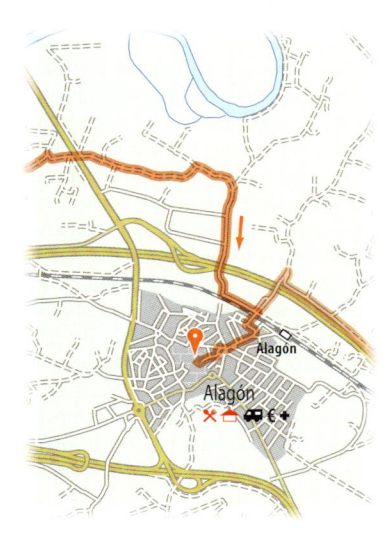

Hotel Los Angeles (30 rooms) Pl Alhóndiga 4; 976 61 13 40; e info@hotellosangeles.eu; w hotellosangeles.eu. AC & satellite TV. Popular restaurant. €35/45 sgl/dbl

Pensión Jarea (4 rooms) Calle Mendez Núnez 45; m 629 48 97 76 or 669 74 57 29. Compact rooms with private shower. €15/30 sgl/dbl

Pensión Mari Carmen (3 rooms) Calle Portillo 3; m 670 76 25 54; e puricomenge@hotmail.com. Modest rooms with shared bathroom. Kitchen & laundry facilities. €15/25 sgl/dbl

TRANSPORT Half-a-dozen trains make the 20-minute trip to and from Zaragoza, as well as in the other direction towards Gallur. Most buses from here are destined for Zaragoza, and timetables are best accessed via the Zaragoza bus station website (w estacion-zaragoza.es).

Taxis
Taxi Aguilar (Alagón) m 653 70 67 07
Taxi Angel (Alagón) m 657 52 92 69

15 ALAGÓN–ZARAGOZA

A long, totally flat route today, but with plenty of refreshment options from the plentiful feeder towns on the approach to Zaragoza. If you are craving some urban lights and delights after several days' walking through rural, small-town Spain, then starting out early will maximise your time spent in what is a much-underrated city. Firstly, the Ignatian route almost inevitably has to negotiate a number of unspectacular commuter towns, many with their own heavy industries and apartment blocks to house their workers. But the last few kilometres into Zaragoza itself are along the Ebro's right riverbank, leafy and pleasant, and with the trusty and unmissable landmark of El Pilar Basilica as your goal, orientating yourself once you enter Spain's fifth-largest city is very straightforward.

Start Plaza de España, Alagón
Coordinates 41.77062, -1.12078
Finish Zaragoza (El Pilar)
Difficulty Moderate
Distance 30.3km
Duration 5hrs 30mins–6hrs

THE ROUTE Find Calle Santiago Ramon y Cajal and pick up signs for the GR-99/Camino Jacobeo del Ebro, which shares your path but in the opposite direction. At the end of this long street, turn left on to Calle Estación and, where this road splits into two, take the left-hand fork up and over the railway before crossing a second bridge over the AP-68 motorway. Follow the GR-99 signs for Torres de Berrellén by turning immediately right at the bridge end, on a paved road, which becomes a dirt track, both parallel to the motorway. Passing (but not crossing) the next motorway bridge, the route then heads away from the traffic towards the River Jalón, a beautiful haven for birdlife. The path now turns right, temporarily leaving the water, picking up signs for the local R17 and R18 paths, which here coincide with your own camino route. You once again approach the river, marked by trees, and after a few hundred metres finally cross the river on a bridge. Follow the tarmac on the other side, then proceed as the road takes you sharply right as the buildings of **Torres de Berrellén** become visible. Enter town on Calle Garfilan to reach a roundabout with a café. The brightly painted *ayuntamiento* and church are off to the left, but your route continues straight ahead across the roundabout until you turn left on to Avenida de Constitución and then right on to Calle Cervantes to leave town. Ahead, the buildings of the next settlement, Sobradiel, are already visible.

ALAGÓN–ZARAGOZA

> ## WHAT'S IN A NAME? SANTIAGO RAMÓN Y CAJAL AND SPANISH ENCLAVES
>
> For the curious traveller, street names can act as great keys to help unlock the doors of a country's history and culture. For example, any observant visitor to France will notice the number of *avenues* carrying the name of Jean Jaurès. Knowing nothing about him, it was only the preponderance of street names – there seemed to be one named after him in every sizeable town – that eventually made me curious enough to find out something about this famous 19th-century socialist.
>
> And as the Camino Ignaciano leads you through the small Aragonese towns of Gallur, Alagón, Utebo, Sobradiel and many others, none of them misses a trick in celebrating one of their most famous sons, Santiago Ramón y Cajal (1852–1934). When I enquired about him, a local told me: 'We don't have too many Nobel Prize winners, so we like to name our streets in their honour.' In fact, Spain has had only eight Nobel Laureates, six of whom were lauded for their work in literature. Ramón y Cajal, however, worked in the field of medicine, and was famous for his research on the structure of the nervous system. He was born in Petilla de Aragón, a name that serves as a key to unlock yet another door that reveals a further Spanish curiosity. Despite its name and its location on a map, careful scrutiny shows that while Petilla is administratively part of Navarre, it forms a little enclave completely surrounded by – but not actually part of – the Autonomous Community of Aragón. Spain has many of these geographical peculiarities, usually created due to historic quarrels between different regions, which have never been resolved.
>
> Like I said, curiosity about a simple street name can lead us anywhere in our wanderings. And if lots of Aragonese towns want to fête a man whose birthplace is actually in a neighbouring region, surely that's fine?

Staying on the tarmac, cross an irrigation channel before continuing on a dirt road that veers left and continues. Eventually, the road divides either side of another irrigation channel and you stay left with the channel to the right, leading into **Sobradiel**. You dog-leg slightly, reaching the park and the church and first continuing straight ahead, then turning right and left to exit town on Calle del Pino past some modern apartment buildings. When the main road turns right after 1.5km, continue over the

STAGE 15

bridge with the AP-68, and at the roundabout on the other side take the second exit, straight ahead through industrial buildings. Turn left on a paved road as you meet the railtrack and continue on tarmac to exit this industrial zone, with the motorway away to your left and the town of Casetas on your right.

Leave the abandoned ICASA building to your left and continue to the next town, **Utebo**, 3km away. On reaching a main road, cross it and continue down a narrow, paved road with the sports stadium off to your right. At the next junction turn left on to a cobbled street, which quickly becomes Calle Miguel Hernandes and leads to the Iglesia Nuestra Señora de la Asunción, with its noteworthy 16th-century tower

WINDS OF CHANGE

You will no doubt be struck by the number of wind turbines decorating the landscape as you progress across Spain. In fact, despite having few operational *offshore* wind farms, Spain is the fifth largest in terms of installed wind power after China, the USA, Germany and India. And after nuclear, wind power is the second-biggest source of energy in the country, contributing to a whopping 20% of Spain's electricity.

Navarre, for example, lacks any coal or oil resources, has no nuclear capacity and not much in the way of significant hydro-electric installations. As a result, it has embraced wind power with great gusto (pardon the semi-pun), as before doing so nearly every energy source had to be imported. While those wind turbines might spoil your photos, their presence contributes to the Spanish economy and raises few objections from the locals.

in mudéjar style (see box, page 158) and the Nobelty bar/restaurant that makes a great lunch spot before continuing (page 168). From behind the church take a right on Calle Antonio Machado and, after 1km, cross the motorway once more to continue with the traffic now on your right. Cross an irrigation channel, previously on your right, and a wider channel appears on your right as you prepare to enter **Monzalbarba**, its church spire now your target. Where the track ends at the entrance to town, take a right and then a left on to Calle la Sagrada. Pass a restaurant and café, with a bank off to the right, and continue straight as the Paseo la Sagrada leads out of town. As the main road turns sharply right,

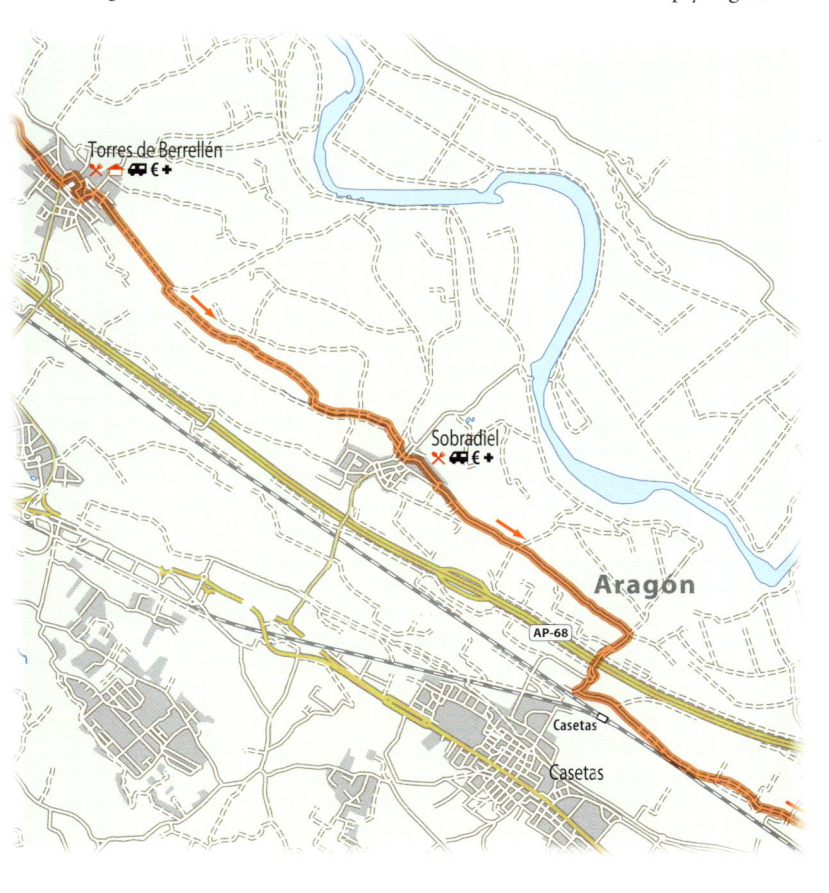

STAGE 15

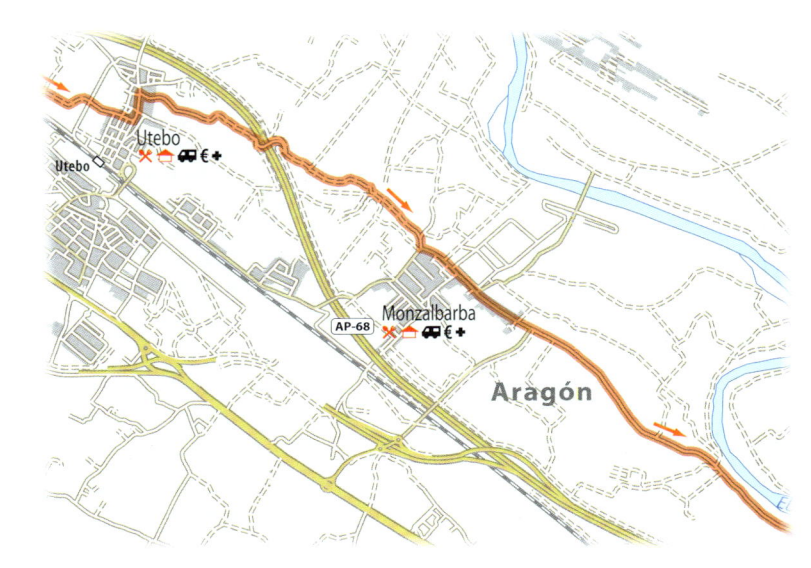

continue straight ahead instead, signposted Camino Monzalbarba, with Zaragoza's outskirts visible in the distance. Note the sign-boarded acacia tree on your left, a native of North America.

After around 2.5km, ignore a road off to the right leading to a motorway bridge and continue on the tarmac, again ignoring any deviations and another right turn leading to a further motorway bridge. As you approach the intersection of two busy motorways, the track heads over a bridge and then under a further three bridges in quick succession and finally over another, still on the same tarmac road. After several hundred metres, you reach a T-junction and turn right, delighted to see your old friend, the River Ebro, running parallel to the path and a cycle path. Follow this, with the river always on your left, all the way into **Zaragoza**. Pass under a couple of fancy bridges, with the EXPO site visible on the north bank of the river, and eventually you'll see the twin spires of the El Pilar, where the stage ends.

WHERE TO STAY AND EAT Being Spain's fifth-largest city, Zaragoza lacks nothing by way of accommodation or eating choices. The places listed here are recommended for their quality, but also for their proximity to the Ignaciano route. Nobody wants to be trailing across a large city or working out transport logistics after a long day's walking. If you

ALAGÓN–ZARAGOZA

have not pre-booked, the Avenida de Cesar Augusto has half-a-dozen accommodation options of all standards. For entertainment, the El Tubo district of the city's old town contains enough tapas bars to help any weary pilgrim relax – or worse, wear them out further. Historic **Bodegas Almau** (Calle Estébanes 10; **w** bodegasalmau.es), dating to 1870, is an atmospheric place to start your Zaragoza café crawl.

The Botanic Hostel (42 beds & 2 rooms) Calle Basilio Boggieri 78; 976 04 05 73; **e** reservas@thebotanichostel.com; **w** thebotanichostel.com. Opened in 2019, this beautiful hostel with high standards has microwaves, complimentary drinks & a communal space. *€22/40 dorm/sgl or dbl*

Hotel Catalonia El Pilar (65 rooms) Calle Manifestación 16; 976 20 58 58; **e** elpilar@cataloniahotels.com; **w** cataloniahotels.com. Housed in a 20th-century Modernist building, this 4-star chain hotel still has an old centenarian wooden lift & staircase. This a 4-star choice. Spacious rooms, each with balcony; good buffet b/fast & gym. *€65 sgl/dbl*

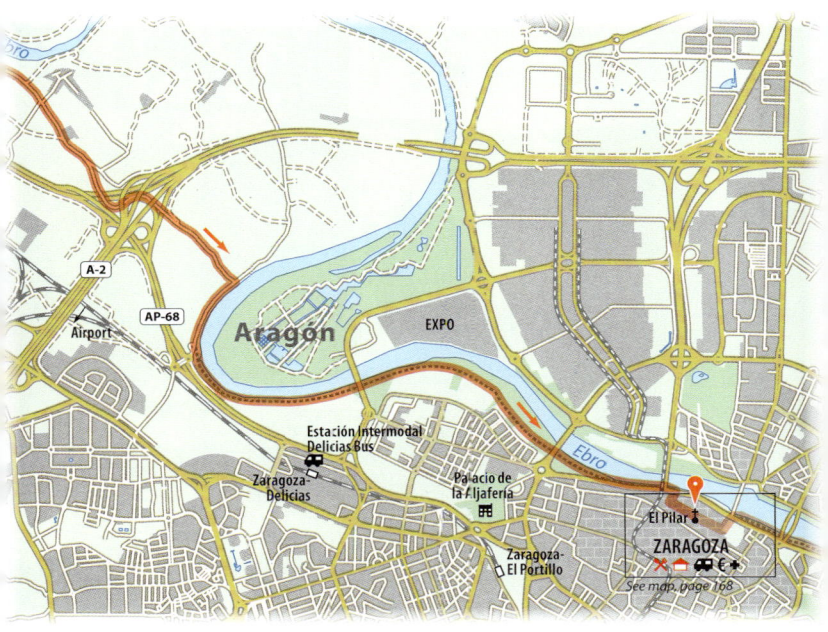

Hotel Rio Arga (38 rooms) Calle Contamina 20; 976 39 90 65; **w** hotelrioarga.es. A reliable, central option with soundproofed rooms. *€40/55 sgl/dbl*

Hotel Sauce (15 rooms) Calle Espoz y Mina 33; 976 20 50 50; **e** hotelsauce@hotelsauce.com; **w** hotelsauce.com. A truly excellent choice, this small, family-owned

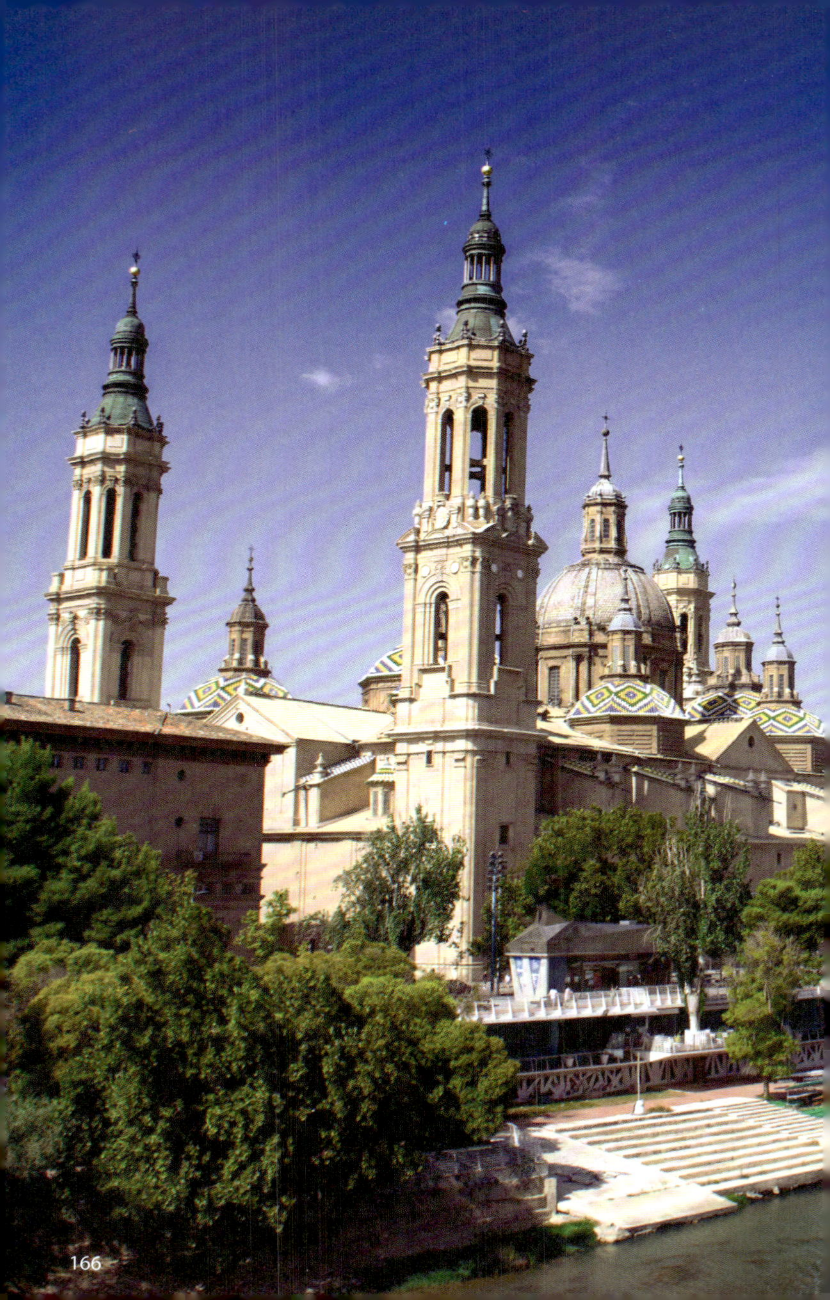

On the banks of the River Ebro, Zaragoza's El Pilar is an undisputed icon of the city *DMF/S*

STAGE 15

& centrally located gem is looked after with true love & attention to detail. Pleasant rooms, modern & spacious. Some have interior windows, guaranteeing peace & quiet. At b/fast, homemade coffee & cakes, as well as jams, add to the experience. *€40/55 sgl/dbl*

✕ **Casa Lac** Calle Martires 12; 976 39 61 96; w restaurantecasalac.es; closed Sun evening & all day Mon. A good place for a gastronomic treat, but not cheap. With 200 years of history, it's the oldest restaurant in town. Vegetables at the fore. *€20*

✕ **La Republicana** Méndez Núñez 38; 976 39 65 09. An atmospheric, museum-like tapas bar. A less-expensive option with heaps of interesting artefacts to ponder while you await your choice from an extensive menu. *€14*

✕ **Nobelty** Plaza España, Utebo; 976 54 53 39; lunch & dinner Tue–Sat. Smart place with great-value & quality *menu del diá*. Wine & bread inc. *€13*

✕ **Taberna el Papagayo** Calle Jordan de Urries 4; m 686 12 58 48; w restaurantepapagayo.com. Recommended for consistent quality, the haute-cuisine menu is short but with excellent meat & even decent seafood options, given the distance to the coast. *€20*

TOURIST INFORMATION

ℹ **Tourist office** Pl César Augusto 1; 976 20 12 00; w zaragozaturismo.es; 10.00–20.00 daily. English-speaking staff. Also another office opposite El Pilar Basilica.

WHAT TO SEE Zaragoza has some 2,000 years of history – Roman, Visigoth, Muslim and beyond – and a wealth of sights to boot. If you have the luxury of a rest day, visit the tourist office to investigate the full realm of sightseeing possibilities; everything is walkable and the terrain is flat, with many pedestrianised streets. If time is limited, however, start in the **Plaza del Pilar**, which is riverside, on your route and in the city

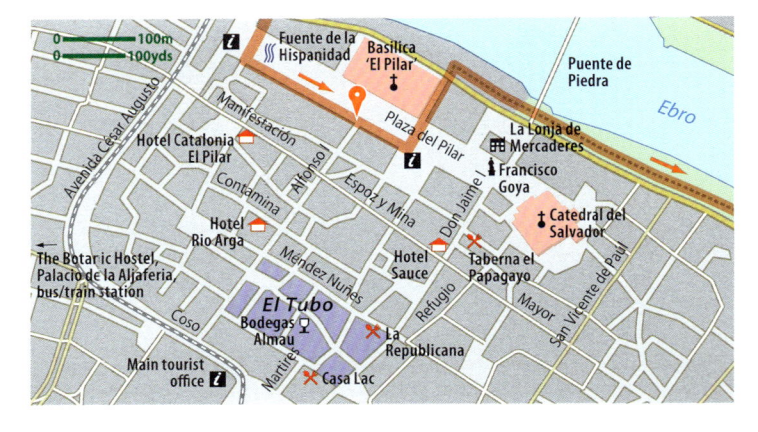

▲ The magnificent Palacio de la Aljafería is well worth a visit MR/S

centre. One of Europe's largest pedestrian squares, this is sprinkled with a few cafés and, without argument, the symbol of the city: the dominant **Catedral Basilica de Nuestra Señora la Virgen del Pilar** (happily abbreviated to 'El Pilar'). Taking the lift up one of its towers affords panoramic views over the city. Taken as a whole, it is more impressive from the outside, though you should definitely go inside to see the Chapel of the Virgin, perched on her *pilar* (column), the single ceiling fresco painted by Goya and wonder at the two wall-mounted bombs dropped on the cathedral in 1936 during the Civil War. For the best photo of the cathedral, walk halfway across the Ebro on the Puente de Piedra bridge.

Sharing the square at the western end is the eye-catching **Fuente de la Hispanidad** fountain, whose three huge blocks of marble represent the ships of Christopher Columbus; the **Catedral del Salvador ('La Seo')** at the far eastern end; and a statue of the 18th-century Aragonese Romantic painter, **Francisco Goya**, who looks suitably relaxed as he gazes down at the square's eastern end. To complete the square's main attractions, the 16th-century **La Lonja de Mercaderes** was designed in fine Aragonese Renaissance style as a venue for markets, but now serves as an exhibition hall. The tourist office can advise as to the best combined tickets, should you wish to visit several of these attractions.

Away from the square, a 10-minute walk will take you to the gorgeous **Palacio de la Aljafería** (Calle de los Diputados; ↘976 28 96 83; **w** cortesaragon.es; ⏱ 10.00–14.00 & 16.30–20.00 daily; €5). This site is actually composed of three palaces from different periods and captures much of the city's history. The first of the palaces traces its construction in part as far back as the 11th century, to the period of Islamic supremacy, though the tower pre-dates even that by 200 years. It later served as a royal residence to the kings of Aragón after the Christian Reconquest of Zaragoza. It has been restructured many times, notably after the Reconquest, and ranks only third in importance after the Alhambra and Cordobá's cathedral/mosque as an example of Iberian Islamic architecture. In much more recent times, part of the building served as a military prison; the inmates' scratchings can be seen on the walls, and there is even a chess board carved by them on the stone floor! Bringing it all up to the present day, it now houses the Aragonese Regional Assembly. English-language audio guides are available, with some guided tours in high summer. Well worth the visit.

TRANSPORT Zaragoza is home to a massive behemoth of a transport interchange, the Estación Intermodal Las Delicias (**w** estacion-zaragoza.es), which houses both the main train and bus terminals in its cavernous interior. Destinations include all the small towns nearby, as well as the major Spanish cities such as Madrid and Barcelona (both reachable by the high-speed AVE) and Bilbao.

Taxis

Radio Taxi 75 Cooperativa Zaragoza 976 75 75 75 or 976 75 14 14

Radio Taxi (Zaragoza) 976 42 42 42

16 ZARAGOZA–FUENTES DE EBRO

Exiting large cities can sometimes be an unpleasant experience on long-distance walks, but not today. Following the river, leaving Zaragoza on the Camino Ignaciano is a wildlife delight, with excellent opportunities to spot cormorants, herons and, later on, a colony or two of storks. These giant elegant birds, who you may already have met on Stage 11, are truly emblematic of Spain. You also visit the town of Cartuja Baja with an impressive façade of what was once a monastic community. This is a long stage, and there is no water or food available during the last 13km, so come well stocked or get yourself fuelled up in Cartuja Baja or El Burgo de Ebro.

> **Start** El Pilar Basilica, Zaragoza
> **Coordinates** 41.65674, -0.87849
> **Finish** Fuentes de Ebro
> **Difficulty** Easy
> **Distance** 30.1km
> **Duration** 7hrs 30mins

THE ROUTE Your route to exit the city is simple, with the Ebro always close by on your left. Pick up GR-99 signs, which also explain it is 391km to Riumar, Delta de Ebro and although that is not our destination, it gives us an idea of how long this mighty river still has to travel before it empties its waters into the Mediterranean Sea. The tarmac turns into a wide dirt track, then passes under the railway bridge. As you continue straight ahead, you'll share your route with many city-dwelling cyclists, walkers and joggers who enjoy this easy escape to the countryside. Fishers, both human and avian, also take advantage. Where the path splits into two, the left-hand branch offers the better bird-spotting opportunities, keeping you closer to the river. The path then narrows and joins up again to take you through fields, now slightly away from the water. Take note of the signage for the Camino Natural La Alfranca, which you now follow for some time. This section of the Ebro is known for its *galachos* – abandoned pools of water, caused by the river changing its course over time, rich in flora and fauna. The eastern outskirts of Zaragoza now appear off to your right, showing that you have truly left the city behind. Although temporarily no longer visible, the river remains nearby to your left, hidden behind dense vegetation. It reappears as you reach a motorway bridge, which you cross beneath, again picking up the GR-99 signage encountered on previous stages.

STAGE 16

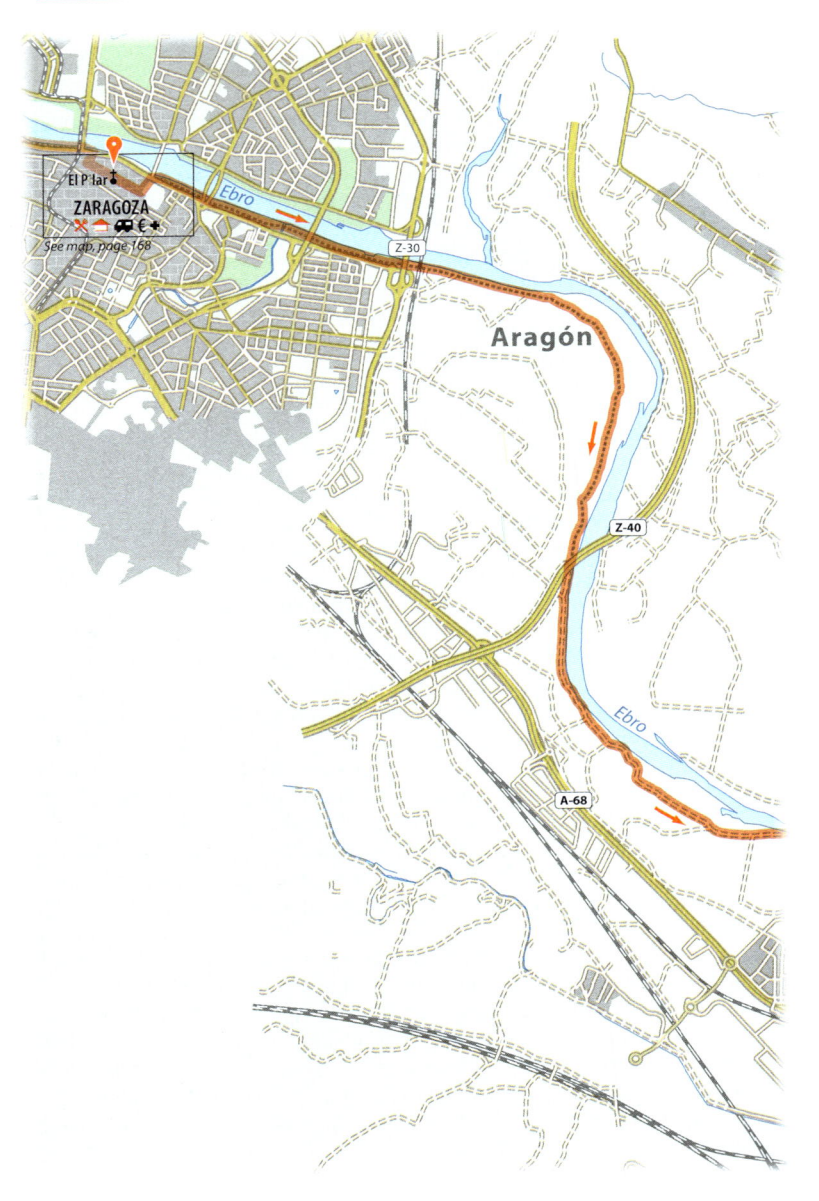

Zaragoza
El Pilar
See map, page 168

Ebro
Z-30
Aragón
Z-40
A-68

After a few kilometres, the track curves slightly right to reveal the distant spire of **Cartuja Baja's** church. As the path draws level with the spire, take a 90-degree right (signposted) to approach the town, now under 1km away. If you are not stopping here for refreshment or supplies, take the path signposted El Burgo del Ebro that veers left just 300m before you reach Cartuja's elegant town façade; otherwise proceed into town. Built in the late 17th century to isolate a monastic community from the outside world, Cartuja Baja's thick stone walls later came in handy for defence in times of trouble and also to secure prisoners during the first Carlist War (1833–40). Today the main square is an oasis of calm, and nearby you will find a café, shops and banks. After visiting, simply rejoin the path you were on.

Beyond Cartuja, the wide track gives an elevated view down over the river valley and the next few kilometres are decorated with many **storks' nests**, which in season provide another point of interest. These birds can often also be seen at ground level in the adjacent fields, grubbing around for delicacies. More GR-99 signs and the occasional orange arrow guide you and you take an underpass beneath a road, then a slightly ascending right fork at a junction. Two kilometres beyond Cartuja, continue straight ahead at a junction and soon the motorway and railway join from the right. Eventually a bridge running parallel to the motorway takes you across a stream and the track dips down to a roundabout and carries on straight ahead on a rising dirt track. Your path now runs parallel to the tarmac road as it leads into **El Burgo de Ebro** via another roundabout.

STAGE 16

Remember: this is your last opportunity for provisions until the stage's end. Carry on down the main road until, towards the edge of town, some orange arrows take you off at an angle to the left, past tennis courts and a football field. Where the road then splits at a Y-junction, continue to the left between the two rows of trees and follow the wide track as it arcs left to leave a residential development off to your right. This is the community of **Virgen de la Columna**, whose white-painted chapel you pass.

From here, the path continues in open countryside. The main ARA-A1 road appears on the horizon, and around 3km from Virgen de la Columna the path heads beneath this highway. Continue to the right of an irrigation channel towards a huge industrial estate, ignoring any temptation to cross the water and instead staying on the tarmac until the very end of the estate. When the tarmac eventually turns sharp right, continue straight ahead, crossing a water channel on a wide dirt track with the buildings and church spire of Fuentes de Ebro now in front of you in the middle distance. The path curves right a couple of times, each time nudging you closer to town. A road bridge over the railway appears, but before reaching it take the left-hand fork where the road splits, veering away from the bridge. Your path soon reaches the railway and runs parallel with the tracks, passing between two buildings and then reaching a second bridge, over which you cross the tracks.

Continue up Calle Doctor Fleming towards **Fuentes de Ebro**'s church spire. As you reach the junction with the main N-232a road (Paseo del Justicia), which acts as a ring road around the north of the town centre, all the town's accommodations are helpfully signposted.

Fuentes de Ebro has a decent enough infrastructure for an overnight stay, but is a small town of around 5,000 people with no tourist attractions.

WHERE TO STAY AND EAT All four accommodation options here have restaurants.

Hostal Elena (12 rooms) Avda Santiago La Puente 9; 976 16 02 67; m 628 47 81 99. Neat, budget place on the main road; discounts for pilgrims offered. AC rooms, bar & restaurant on site. *€35/55 sgl/dbl*

Hostal Restaurante El Patio (15 rooms) Calle los Sitios 37; 976 16 09 15 or

STAGE 16

▲ Cartuja Baja's thick walls came in handy for defence in times of trouble FR/WC

976 16 06 40; **m** 640 20 61 49. At the top of the town, with simple, clean rooms, some with balcony. Restaurant, bar downstairs. *€30/50 sgl/dbl*

🏠 **Hostal Restaurante Texas** (18 rooms) Calle Mayor 13; ☎976 16 04 19; **e** jarogascon@hotmail.com; **w** hostaltexas.

es. Basic place with spacious AC rooms. *€25/42 sgl/dbl*

🏠 **Hostal Texas II** (18 rooms) Paseo del Justicia; ☎976 16 10 70; **m** 686 96 07 53. Spacious rooms with some arty murals. Small b/fast inc. *€35/65 sgl/dbl*

TRANSPORT Four or five buses daily (Line 310) connect Zaragoza with Fuentes de Ebro, calling at Cartuja Baja and El Burgo de Ebro (**w** consorciozaragoza.es). Connections are fewer at weekends. Trains run to Zaragoza, but services are infrequent.

Taxis

🚗 **Sonia Rubio** (Fuentes de Ebro) **m** 627 57 42 90

🚗 **Taxiva** (Fuentes de Ebro) **m** 627 57 42 90

⓱ FUENTES DE EBRO–VENTA DE SANTA LUCIA

Today's stage brings a different walking experience, as you part company with the River Ebro and its accompanying Camino del Ebro path and cross the southern part of the singular, desolate landscape of the Los Monegros semi-desert. Logistically speaking, this stage also demands a bit of thought and planning, as there is no accommodation at the end of what is a hard, near-30km trek. The section on page 183 sets out the available options to ensure you don't get stranded. The weather is also a consideration, as this is not a stage to undertake in either high heat or strong winds, both of which are common. Should you be doing your journey in winter, this is a region which can ironically also be fiercely cold.

Daunted? Don't be! The dirt road across the desert is easy to follow even without much signage and the avid pilgrim will have saved their most profound thoughts for contemplation while they traverse this barren but atmospheric land.

> **Start** Junction Paseo del Justicia (N-232a)/Avenida Lorenzo Pardo, Fuentes de Ebro
> **Coordinates** 41.51247, -0.62797
> **Finish** Venta de Santa Lucia (on N-II road)
> **Difficulty** Moderate/hard, depending on weather conditions
> **Distance** 29.7km
> **Duration** 7hrs 30mins–8hrs

THE ROUTE From the Paseo del Justicia (N-232a), find the Avenida Lorenzo Pardo and follow it until you meet the Camino del Baño on the right. When this road ends at a junction, dog-leg slightly left and carry on in the same eastwards direction as before, with the tarmac soon becoming a wide dirt road. A few painted orange arrows guide you. Pass a stone **quarry** on your right and, where the road forks, take the right-hand branch, heading straight for an underpass beneath the AVE high-speed railway track. If you are lucky on timing, you might see one of these sleek trains bulleting above you at speeds of up to 310kmh. Running between Madrid and Barcelona, they make few stops in between, and certainly not at sleepy Fuentes de Ebro!

Once you're through the underpass, the path takes you left, up and over the second set of tracks reserved for the slow train between Barcelona and Zaragoza. At the bridge end, cut back to follow the dirt road that runs parallel to these slow tracks, which you follow for around 3km, ignoring both a bridge and a railway crossing and with the tracks always on your

LOS MONEGROS OR LAS VEGAS? A NEAR-DISASTER IN THE SEMI-DESERT

If you've ever been to Las Vegas, you will either have loved it or hated it, I suspect. But one thing that most people who have driven there will surely agree on is the amazing way that the gambling-mad city suddenly emerges out of the nothingness of the Nevada desert.

Back in 2008, reports emerged that the Aragón government had approved a plan for a British-based consortium to build a casino complex in Los Monegros, swallowing up some 2,000ha of the desolate landscape. Yes, this was to be Europe's very own Las Vegas. But when you look closely at the proposed numbers, perhaps it is no surprise that the project never progressed. The cost? A cool €17 billion. Number of hotels, casinos and restaurants? That would be 70, 32 and 230 respectively. And perhaps most ridiculously of all, number of foreign visitors expected annually? A projected 20 million – nearly half of Spain's total population. Throw in a proposed James Bond Theme Park, replicas of Egyptian pyramids, the Pentagon, Roman temples... you get the idea.

'Los Monegros is a place of great natural biodiversity, with a huge range of species from Africa and Asia that have been very well conserved over the last five million years,' said Julio Barea of Greenpeace, at the time. 'In the last five years alone, 200 new species have been discovered there.

'In any other country, it would be a national park, strictly protected. What the politicians in Aragón are doing is shameful – telling voters that there is nothing there worth protecting, when it is in fact a zone rich in animal and plant life.'

Since 2008, the Gran Scala project, as it was known, has disappeared without leaving a trace, apart from perhaps a smudge of embarrassment on the faces of the local government who approved the farcical, fanciful project in the face of fierce criticism over its expected environmental carnage.

So it seems that the only way a hardened gambler could ever have hit the Gran Scala jackpot would have been to have bet that the over-the-top project would never happen. And thankfully, it did not, and surely now never will.

right. Just after passing the crossing, the path turns slightly left away from the tracks, soon crossing one irrigation channel and then another. A road joins from behind from your right but ignore this and, after

STAGE 17

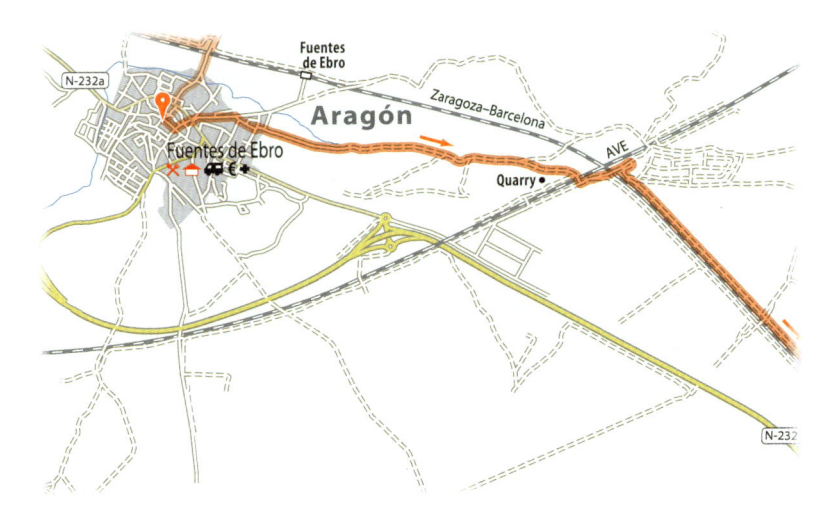

100m, turn left on a path through fields to see the thickened vegetation ahead – signalling your imminent reconnection with the River Ebro. At a T-junction a few hundred metres on, turn right to follow the river downstream. Soon the spire of Pina de Ebro's church comes into view, as your path then curves right but with the river still close – though not always visible – on your left. After a few hundred metres, you find a GR-99 sign, one of the last ones you will see as you will part company with this 'contraflow' camino.

Eventually your path turns to the right, again towards the church spires. After 1km, you reach the A-1107 road, turning left on to it to cross the Ebro on a long bridge, at the end of which you turn immediately right on to a dirt road, parallel with the river, which leads towards **Pina de Ebro**. You reach a tree-filled park and, once level with the tower on the left, divert into town to find the main plaza with its numerous bars, banks and a shop. (You need to stock up here with water and food, or phone ahead to confirm if the Venta de Santa Lucia is open; see, page 184.) Beside the church, follow the Calle de la Iglesia until you turn left on to Calle Fernando el Católico to follow this long road out of town.

Eventually you rejoin the A-1107 road with the prominent COOPINA building ahead of you; on reaching it, use the dirt road parallel to the A-1107 to keep clear of traffic. After less than 1km, look to the right to spot the 19th-century **Ermita de San Gregorio** up above you, the end point of a pilgrimage that takes place on 9 May. Cross an irrigation channel

FUENTES DE EBRO–VENTA DE SANTA LUCIA

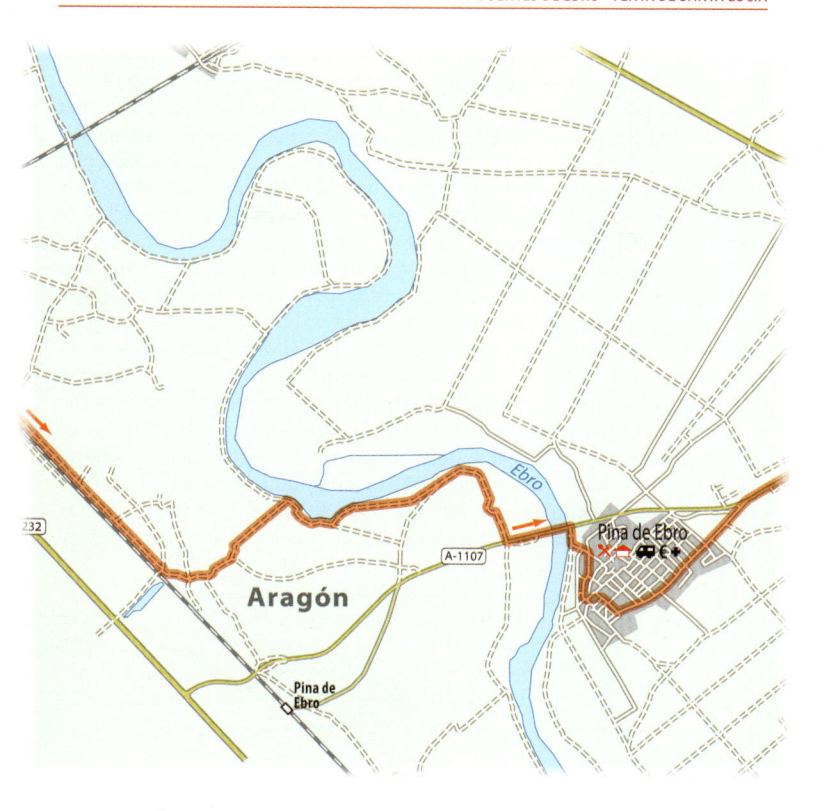

and turn right, initially following a sign for the Mirador de San Gregorio but then continuing on the left-hand, wider path when it splits only 50m later. You are now heading towards the buildings of the industrial estate straight ahead. On reaching the first building, turn right on the tarmac, then left after 100m, now accompanied by those familiar orange arrows. The road curves left and shortly you take a dirt road arrowed off to your right, following a line of electricity pylons. (Note: there is a tarmacked road immediately to your left.) Already you can see how bleak the landscape has become. A cut-out black bull advertising hoarding, familiar from our Navarrete stage (see box, page 109), awaits you in the distance, and the main road is off to your left.

At the point where your path almost converges with the road, and as you ponder how Spain seemingly has been taken over by a plague of

STAGE 17

articulated lorries, the path thankfully turns away from the thunderous traffic and heads up into the desolate **Los Monegros**. The landscape looks lifeless at first, but keep an eagle eye open for the hardy wildlife that has adapted to this semi-lunar environment: snakes and lizards on the ground, and skywards for lesser kestrel (*Falco naumanii*). After 3km you reach some dilapidated animal shelters on your left, continuing onwards and ignoring a road that departs to the right. Apart from the track and a few scattered buildings, the human imprint up here is light. But the cry of an occasional raptor, a scampering rabbit or some mysterious footprints that cross the sandy track (a fox, perhaps?) show that you are not entirely alone. After less than 1km, ignore both a track going off to your left and a dusty path exiting to the right shortly afterwards. Very soon, at another fork, keep right, heading now towards some impressive rocky pillars sculpted by the elements. You ignore another path to the left as you approach these rocky outcrops and leave them all on your left-hand side. You now reach another split in the road, this time taking the left fork towards a plateau and further outcrop to its right. You eventually pass both of these, leaving them to your right-hand side; as the road reaches level with the plateau, it curves right and rises slightly with the plateau still on your right. The road now continues for another 3km, without deviating left or right, down to the white-painted **Venta de Santa Lucia** and the N-II road.

WHERE TO STAY AND EAT There is no accommodation at Venta de Santa Lucia, or anywhere nearby, so you need to have a plan worked out in advance to reach Bujaraloz (page 188) or else be prepared to sleep rough. Some walkers may be happy to sleep out under the stars after a 30km walk, but I am not one of that hardy band. As this is really the only Camino Ignaciano stage on which such an arrangement might be necessary, it would involve carrying a lot of equipment a long way just for one night spent in the open. So here is an alternative plan. First, pre-book your accommodation in Bujaraloz for *two* nights. Start early on Stage 17, preferably at dawn, to ensure that you arrive at Venta de Santa Lucia by 16.00. At the time of writing, there was one bus which *passes* the Venta at 16.26 and arrives in Bujaraloz around 15 minutes later. Note, carefully, the word 'passes'. The bus stops only on request, so you will have to be frantically waving your hand to prevent it thundering past, as the driver will most likely not be expecting to pick anyone up in this remote location. (If you miss the bus, you can call a taxi out from Bujaraloz.) Stay overnight

STAGE 17

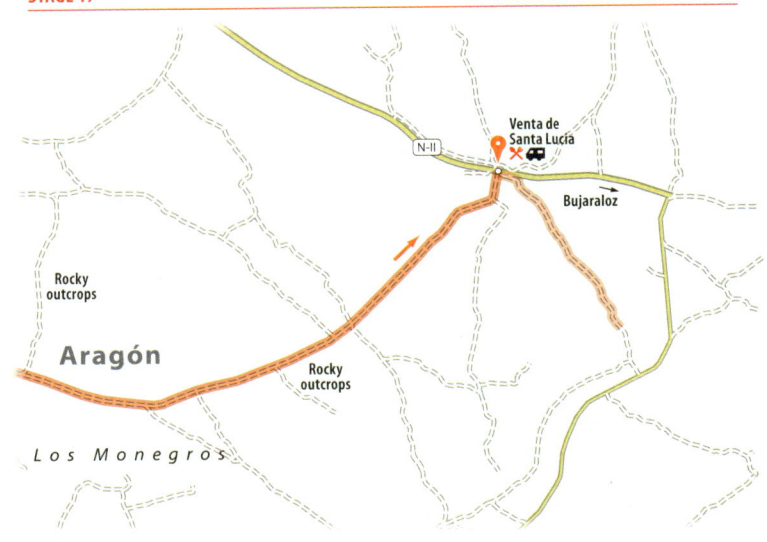

in Bujaraloz, then get the bus back again to the Venta the next day. At the time of writing, there was one bus from Bujaraloz at 09.20, which allows you to get off at the Venta and walk back to Bujaraloz on Stage 18. You can even enjoy a day without most of your luggage, by leaving it in your Bujaraloz accommodation.

For food, if taking the bus through to Bujaraloz to spend the night, see page 188 for that town's dining choices. Otherwise, you can fill up at the Venta de Santa Lucia.

✕ Venta de Santa Lucia On N-II at KM372; ✆ 976 16 20 01; ⏲ 08.00–23.00 Sun–Thu, 08.00–17.00 Fri, but phone ahead to check &, in any case, have some back-up snacks with you. A real truck stop, with friendly staff & no-nonsense, filling food. Most importantly, somewhere to shelter you while you wait for the bus. *€11*

TRANSPORT The bus between Zaragoza and Lleida, operated by Agreda (✆ 976 30 00 80; w agredabus.es), stops on request at the Venta de Santa Lucia. It also calls at Bujaraloz. (See page 183 and above for times.)

Taxis

🚖 **José Maria Franco** (Pina de Ebro) m 618 54 37 67

🚖 **Taxi Jesus** (Bujaraloz) ✆ 976 17 31 04

🚖 **Taxis Monegros** (Bujaraloz) ✆ 976 17 35 51

18 VENTA DE SANTA LUCIA–BUJARALOZ

Anyone who is suffering from yesterday's long desert trek will be grateful for today's relatively short, easy and flat walk into sleepy Bujaraloz. A petrol station provides the only opportunity for drinks or snacks, around the halfway point. In truth, there is not much to see along this stage, but not only is it less physically demanding than Stage 17, it is nearly impossible to lose your way: you can relax mentally too, except for the crossing of the N-II road towards the stage end. By the time you get there, you will need no reminder about what a busy road this can be. Just count the trucks.

Start Venta de Santa Lucia (on the N-II)
Coordinates 41.49659, -0.36733
Finish Bujaraloz
Difficulty Easy
Distance 22.4km
Duration 5hrs

THE ROUTE It is possible to begin today's stage by simply heading eastwards along the N-II all the way to Bujaraloz – but one look at the traffic should deter you against this option. It is simply not advisable. Far better is to take the arrowed dirt track to the left of the venta building (as

STAGE 18

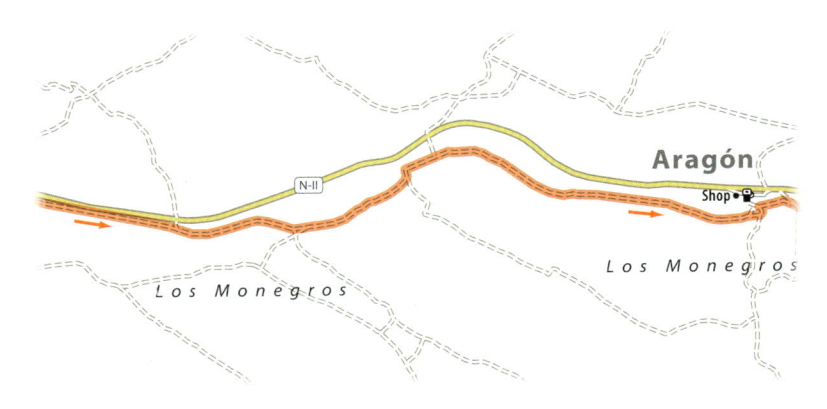

you face it) that leads away from the road at an angle. Continue along it as it passes a couple of abandoned houses and, after just over 1km, it ends at a junction with the A-1105 road. Turn left on to the tarmac, heading back towards the N-II, but thankfully just before reaching it a dirt road goes off to the right, running parallel with the main road. This is your path for most of the day.

The bleak Los Monegros landscape is off to your right today, but the route does not really penetrate its interior today. The N-II road actually carves through the middle of this barren land, with much of the desert located to the north. Despite the presence of over 5,000 species, there is no official protection in place here, and the sight of the occasional tractor will tell you that farming has made some encroachment in recent times. Where the dirt track reaches a Y-junction, 500m from the start of the dirt track, stay left, parallel with the main road. After another 5km, a **petrol station** sign appears, signalling that you are now over halfway to your destination. This is your one chance before Bujaraloz to get water or food. Don't be impatient: rather than fight your way through the undergrowth (think snakes!), wait until you reach the white tower just beyond the station and you'll find that the path turns left to give you easier access.

From the petrol station, the route continues eastwards, and after around 4km you can see the **Ermita San Jorge** on your right. Unfortunately it is usually closed, denying the casual visitor the sight of the impressive mural of St George (San Jorge) slaying the dragon. If you happen to be passing on 23 April, it might be open for those who come here to celebrate the saint. After a further 1km, the path turns left to meet the N-II and you must now cross this busy road. Once across, turn right and continue with the thundering traffic now on your right. As the track rises slowly, the buildings of **Bujaraloz** come into view. On entering town, you will notice the signs for some of the accommodations, located by the highway to the right; if staying at Las Sabinas, continue into the town centre, heading for the Santiago el Mayor church. Bujaraloz was certainly settled in Roman times, but takes its name from the Arabic, Burx-al-arús. The town was under Muslim sway for five centuries, until the Reconquest. It celebrates its annual festival at the end of August, when the streets are enlivened by strolling minstrels.

▼ The Ermita de San Jorge stands alone in the Los Monegros desert *JA/S*

STAGE 18

WHERE TO STAY AND EAT

El Español Hostal, Buffet & Bar (11 rooms) Carretera Nacional (N-II); ☎976 17 31 92 or 976 17 30 43; **e** eledspanol@grupovaquer.com; **w** www.grupovaquer.com. Large, friendly roadside place on the main road as you enter town. Open buffet meals & snacks. AC rooms fully renovated. Discount for pilgrims (on meals only). Early b/fasts available. *€30/45 sgl/dbl*

Hostal Cafeteria Los Monegros III (6 rooms) Calle la Luna 7; ☎976 17 35 47; **e** info@hostalmonegros3@hotmail.com; **w** hostallosmonegros.es. Centrally located. AC rooms; also provides lunches & snacks. *€30/45 sgl/dbl*

Hostal La Parrilla Los Monegros II (6 rooms) Carretera Nacional (N-II), KM390.5; ☎976 17 35 22 or 976 17 32 30. Closed at the time of writing, not clear whether temporarily or permanently. Perhaps contact them as a last resort. *€30/45 sgl/dbl*

Las Sabinas (6 rooms) Calle Santa Ana 6; ☎976 17 93 28. Has the advantage of being in town, rather than on the main highway. AC rooms, restaurant & bar. Good b/fast (small extra cost). Discount for pilgrims. *€30/48 sgl/dbl*

TRANSPORT The bus between Zaragoza and Lleida, operated by Agreda (☎976 30 00 80; **w** agredabus.es), stops at Bujaraloz once daily, in the afternoon. In the opposite direction, the bus leaves in the morning.

Taxis

Taxi Carlos (Bujaraloz) **m** 608 78 26 16

Taxi Jesus (Bujaraloz) ☎976 17 31 04

Taxis Monegros (Bujaraloz) ☎976 17 35 51

19 BUJARALOZ–CANDASNOS

This is a pleasant stage – the first half through gentle countryside and farmland awash with birdlife – with a convenient halfway refreshment stop in pretty Peñalba. The N-II serves as a guide for much of the way, though thankfully mainly at a polite distance. The two accommodations in Candasnos were closed at the time of writing, so unless you are sleeping under the stars, you will have to lengthen today's stage and shorten tomorrow's, by adding 2km extra and choosing to overnight at the quirky but recommended Hotel Cruzanzana.

> **Start** Santiago el Mayor church, Bujaraloz
> **Coordinates** 41.49807, -0.15260
> **Finish** Candasnos (or Hotel Cruzanzana)
> **Difficulty** Easy
> **Distance** 22km (or 24km to Hotel Cruzanzana)
> **Duration** 5hrs 30mins (or 6hrs to Hotel Cruzanzana)

THE ROUTE From the southeast corner of the Santiago el Mayor church, follow Calle Mayor as it becomes Calle Baja, passing the **Ermita Virgen de las Nieves** sanctuary on the left and proceeding straight on past agricultural buildings into open countryside. The busy N-II is parallel, off to the right. If you have been wondering why all the heavy traffic is on this route, rather than the better, faster AP-2 just to the north, the answer is that lorries pay tolls on the latter. After 2.5km the path rises to the right, but instead follow the fork immediately to the left. The bushes here conceal seemingly endless birdlife, content to entertain walkers with

STAGE 19

their aerobatic displays; crested larks in particular are common in this area. Continue on the wide dirt track as you pass a small white building on your right. After several kilometres the path nears the N-II again, with a long, low animal shed to your left, but your direction never wavers.

▼ Look out for crested lark on this stage *t/S*

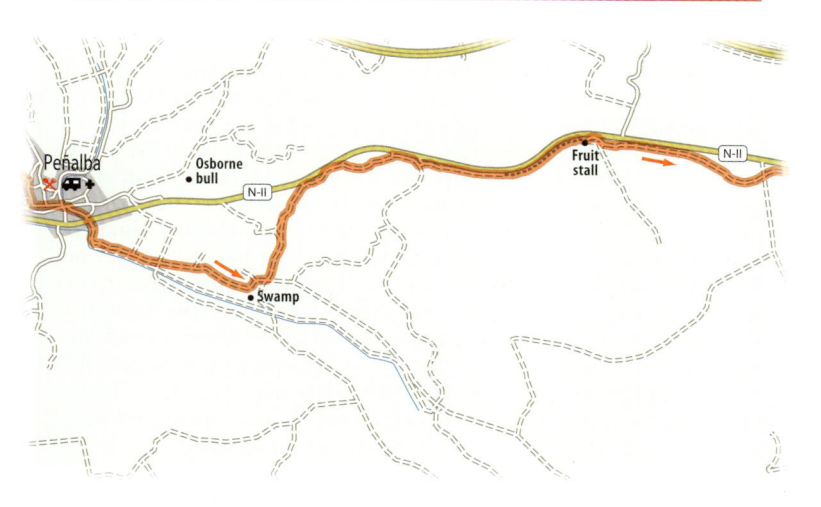

Cross a stream at a four-way junction and continue on the path which now ascends. At the top of the rise, with the animal shed now immediately to your left, turn right. After a few hundred metres, the path curves left and you ignore a narrower track to the right. Now you enter a pretty, peaceful section, with no traffic in view or noise to assault your ears. After a couple of kilometres, the path rises, passing beneath two long sheds (your nostrils may protest that there are animals inside!), after which you turn right on to the tarmac A-2213 – note your 'guardian angel' on the near horizon, the **Osborne bull** from earlier stages (see box, page 109). After 100m, leave the tarmac on a road leading downhill to the left. Turn right at the bottom, with the buildings and spire of **Peñalba** now visible ahead.

Continue down, picking up Calle Joaquin Costa, which takes you past the La Posada bar, serving simple meals and with an outdoor terrace. From the bar, follow the road round to the left towards the town centre. The road becomes the Calle Ramón y Cajal and leads to a deeply set water channel, which you cross on a bridge. Turn right towards an arched bridge carrying the N-II highway and pass beneath it. Continue on the asphalt with the water on your right and soon the black bull off to your left. After several hundred metres, the asphalt becomes dirt and you pass a reedy **swamp** on the right (sometimes with water, sometimes not). The track leads uphill to the left towards electricity poles and, on reaching the first of these, turns sharp left to continue uphill, ignoring the main path which continues to the right (the occasional orange arrow reassures you).

STAGE 19

At the top, turn right just before the path meets the N-II and, after 100m where the track forks, take the left-hand, narrower path to continue walking parallel with the highway. A few hundred metres further on, descend with a forest visible straight ahead, and at the bottom meet the highway once more to again turn right, parallel with it. Soon you cross a small bridge, heading straight on back towards the N-II but again taking a dirt track parallel with it. Now you have a difficult choice: you can either take this path for around 800m, accepting that it is in poor condition and can be very muddy in places if there has been rain in the previous few weeks, or trudge up the side of the N-II highway with endless trucks screaming at your back. In dry times, choose the path. The highway is never more than 25m to your left, and you always walk with the tree line immediately on your right, so there is no question of getting lost. It is a bit jungle-like, with puddles that can swallow you up to ankle-height; perhaps use a stick and a few stones to try and warn any waiting snakes of your approach. There is also a ditch to your left on occasions. But despite these hazards, it is probably still preferable to the road. And, if it gets too muddy, you can always turn back and do Plan B.

If you do choose path over road, you will emerge close to the N-II where the path turns away to the right to reach a picnic/resting place with a **fruit shop** (⊕ Apr–Oct). From here, follow the wide track, once again parallel with the N-II, which after 1km will reveal Candasnos's buildings in the distance. Closer to town, with the Candasnos sign visible on your left, leave the dirt track and join first asphalt then tarmac to reach the centre. **Candasnos** is ultra-sleepy, but the 12th-century Romanesque-style Iglesia de Candasnos is worth a peek; Gothic styling from the 14th century is

▲ Sleepy Candasnos is the end point of this stage *JA/S*

also evidenced in its construction. You can check to see if the El Pilar has reopened, but otherwise you must continue to the recommended Hotel Cruzanzana (see below). To reach it, head for the church and then follow the first part of the directions for Stage 20.

WHERE TO STAY AND EAT

Hotel Cruzanzana (23 rooms) Carretera Nacional (N-II), KM412; 974 46 30 44; e hotelcruzanzana@gmail.com. You may have to add a bit of extra walking & cross a busy, busy road to get here, but you won't regret it. On first sight, this is the trucker's standard roadside sleepover, but once you are inside, there are wide stone-floored corridors, rooms with full-size baths, a communal pool table & table football, & (yes, really) a small outdoor zoo with an alpaca, wallabies, pigs & more. As it's a truck stop, you can eat at any time from a cheap, basic menu. Ask for pilgrim discount. *€30/45 sgl/dbl*

El Pilar (10 rooms) Calle Zaragoza 13, Candasnos; 974 46 30 17; closed Sun. On the camino route, as you enter town. It may not reopen its rooms post-pandemic, so phone ahead, but the restaurant will remain in service, serving basic meals. *€25/40 sgl/dbl*

TRANSPORT Buses leave from the stop beside the church, running (infrequently) to Peñalba, Bujaraloz and Zaragoza in one direction and to Fraga and Lleida in the other. See w alsa.com for times and prices.

Taxi

Taxi Romera (Peñalba) 974 47 16 73

20 CANDASNOS–FRAGA

Even if you have shortened your stage by walking 2km extra yesterday, today's trek to Fraga may seem even longer than it is. There is not much to see and be aware that there is little shade available, making it difficult if it is hot. There are no intermediate towns to break up the day. At the stage end, the medium-sized town of Fraga welcomes you – they even provide you with free accommodation if you don't mind 'going basic'!

> **Start** Iglesia de Candasnos, Candasnos (or Cruzanzana)
> **Coordinates** 41.50366, 0.06402 (41.51367, 0.09102 if starting at Cruzanzana)
> **Finish** Fraga
> **Difficulty** Moderate
> **Distance** 27km (25km if starting at Cruzanzana)
> **Duration** 6hrs

THE ROUTE From the church in Candasnos, take the wide asphalt road (marked with the occasional orange arrow) as it leaves town parallel to the N-II. After 2km it reaches a bridge across the AP-2 motorway, which here intersects with our old friend the N-II, lying a few hundred metres beyond. Across the bridge, you will see the **Hotel Cruzanzana** (page 193)

THE MONEGROS DESERT FESTIVAL

Since 1994, a barren piece of the Los Monegros has been temporarily transformed into a kaleidoscope of colour and the surrounding desert peace overwhelmed by a storm of noise. Welcome to the Monegros Desert Festival, which established its true rave credentials during its first incarnation when it began as an illegal gathering, masquerading as a 'family barbecue'. With 250 attendees, that was some 'family' and some 'barbecue'. Billed as the 'Rave in the Desert', the festival is usually held in July on a piece of land that was lost, and then won back, by its owner on the turn of a card in a poker game. Quite ironic, given the attempts to convert another part of Los Monegros into a European Las Vegas (see box, page 179).

Up to 50,000 people now flock to see over 50 acts perform across seven stages in a non-stop, 24-hour period. Music featured here moves with the times, but rave, hip-hop and other styles have often been prominent. It has certainly progressed from its 'family barbecue' days. More details can be found at **w** www.monegrosdesertfestival.com.

STAGE 20

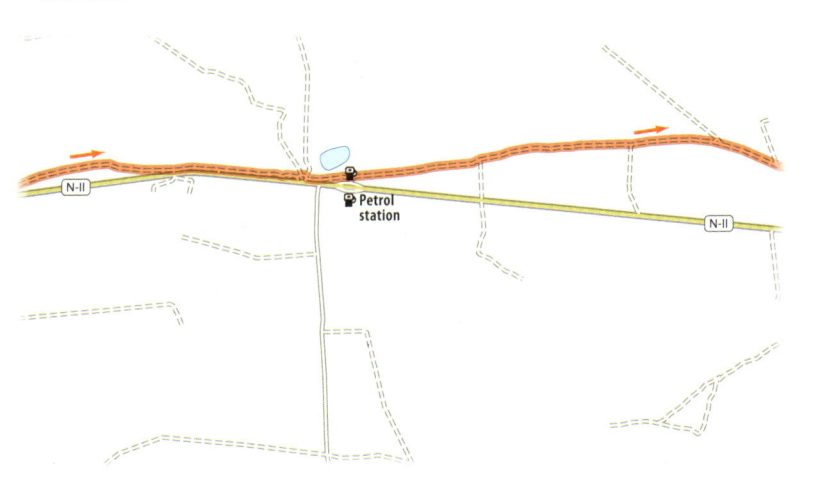

and a petrol station off to the left. (If staying the night at the hotel, turn left at the bridge end and cross the N-II: extreme care required!)

Your route continues parallel with the N-II, still on the left, and after 3km the path dips to a tunnel underneath the highway. On the other side, turn right and follow the dirt track that then rises to your left. Turn sharp right at the top to follow parallel with the N-II, which is of course now on your right. The site for the annual **Monegros Desert Festival** (see box, page 195), held in July, is close by on the left.

After around 6km you reach some abandoned buildings and then a **petrol station** on the right, which can provide refreshments or snacks. (Note also the **pond**, to your left, as it is sometimes hopping

A FREE NIGHT IN FRAGA

The Fraga municipality really loves pilgrims – so much so that they will let you stay one night here for free if you book in at the Trébol (page 198). Book directly with the *hostal*, then present yourself at the door next to the Iglesia de San Pedro (St Peter's Church) in the old town east of the river, show your passport and your *credenciál* (page 32) and you will be solemnly given a voucher to present back at the Trébol. The church office is only open 16.00–19.00 Mon–Fri, so outside these times you will have to accost someone at one of the church services!

with frogs!) Continue eastwards for a couple of kilometres as the path briefly distances itself from the highway before returning to its side again at a large layby, home of the ramshackle **Ventorillo y Estruch bar/restaurant** (**m** 677 38 14 55; ⊕ closed Mon). It is quirky, full of character and favoured by locals, but opening hours are sporadic. From here, stay parallel to the N-II for only 100m before the route takes you away again and, after a few hundred metres more, next to the tallest of half-a-dozen electricity towers, fork right. Ahead to the right, the scenery becomes greener as the N-II descends into the Cinca Valley. Your barren desert days are over!

On reaching a four-way junction immediately beneath some electricity lines, take the path that descends to your right as the town of Fraga appears in front of you. Just before reaching the valley bottom, curve sharp left, ignoring the path straight ahead, and after only 200m take the path off to your right, signposted for Fraga, now just 3.2km away. Continue to descend, finally crossing an irrigation channel and continuing on asphalt. At a T-junction with the main A-131 road, turn right for 100m to a roundabout where you turn left on to the long, tree-lined Avenida de Aragón, which crosses the River Cinca and leads directly into **Fraga** town centre. This road – along with the Avenida de Madrid, which intersects it at a roundabout – contains most of the town's accommodations and restaurants. The official stage end is actually across the river at the *ayuntamiento* (town hall), but that can wait until tomorrow.

STAGE 20

WHERE TO STAY AND EAT Fraga's accommodations are mainly situated west of the river, as are most of the town-centre restaurants, which cluster around the Avenida de Madrid/N-II as it passes through town. A few more modest places are on the east side of the river.

Hostal Trébol (13 rooms) Avda Aragón 9; 974 47 15 33; **e** info@hostaltrebolfraga.es; **w** hostaltrebolfraga.es. Very basic, but very handy as it is directly on the route &, if you can muster enough energy to cross the river to the Iglesia San Pedro, armed with your passport & *credenciál*, you can get a certificate that will let you stay here for free (see box, page 196). Who knows, the Wi-Fi may even be working… *Free (with voucher), otherwise €25/40 sgl/dbl*

Hotel Casanova (108 rooms) Avda de Madrid 54; 974 47 19 90; **e** casanova@gargallohotels.es; **w** gargallohotels.es. Good-quality hotel, fully renovated in 2020, part of a small chain. AC rooms. No discounts for the amorous, despite the name, but b/fast is free for pilgrims. *€45/55 sgl/dbl*

Pensión Restaurante Olles (8 rooms) Avda de Madrid 33; 974 45 38 34; **m** 622 34 04 38; **e** hostalollesweb@gmail.com; **w** pensionolles.com. Basic offering with shared bathrooms. Good-value bar/restaurant below (lunchtimes only; €10). Small discount for pilgrims. *€22/38 sgl/dbl*

Borau Avda de Madrid 11; **m** 637 59 40 31; closed Tue. Probably Fraga's top spot in terms of service, presentation & food quality. Modern Spanish, French & European cuisine. Great-value lunch & weekend menus. *€15*

Restaurante Braseria Jeff Calle San Quentin 12; 974 45 35 90. On the east side of the river, its 07.00 opening makes it a good spot for b/fast. Also grills, tapas & daily menus. *€12*

▲ The town of Fraga marks the end of Stage 20 n/S

TOURIST INFORMATION
Tourist office Paseo Barrón 5; **↘**974 47 18 76; **m** 683 14 57 02; ⊕ 09.00–15.30 Mon–Fri. Located on the east side of the river.

WHAT TO SEE Despite its medium size, Fraga does not really have any major tourist attractions to brag about. Visitors will notice that although this is still technically Aragón, many of the signs are apparently in Catalan and that region's flag can be seen hanging from many balconies. The natives speak in a local dialect, *fragati*, which is closer to Catalan than Spanish.

TRANSPORT The bus station is at the west end of the bridge across the River Cinca, with infrequent services back towards Zaragoza. See **w** alsa.com for times and prices.

Taxis
- **Taxi Fraga** **m** 607 43 44 45
- **Taxi Juan** **m** 600 48 50 20
- **Taxis Eugenio** **m** 690 62 74 75

21 FRAGA–LLEIDA (LERIDA)

This long stage marks the end of your time in Aragón and your introduction to a new language, a new culture and a new, fiercely proud Autonomous Community. Benvinguts a Catalunya! *(Welcome to Catalonia!) The route climbs out of Fraga amid the busy, industrial landscape you might expect from a small city, but things improve on the stage's latter half, with the final few kilometres into Lleida tracking the course of the mellow River Segre – a flat and very pleasant entrance to this major Catalan city. Given the length of the stage, it is worthwhile considering splitting it over two days; see box, below.*

> **Start** Former *ayuntamiento* (town hall), Fraga
> **Coordinates** 41.52093, 0.35041
> **Finish** Lleida
> **Difficulty** Hard
> **Distance** 33km (19.5km if to Alcarràs)
> **Duration** 8hrs 30mins (5hrs to Alcarràs)

THE ROUTE From the former *ayuntamiento* building on Plaza de España, take the long and winding Calle Obradores de Revolt (Workers' Rebellion Street) on the square's northern side as it climbs above town. As it comes to an end and joins the N-IIa at a stop sign, look up to the left and find a white, metal bridge, which you cross to reach the town **cemetery**. Follow the side of the main road, with the cemetery to your left, to reach a roundabout with the giant **Piensos Costa factory** off to the right. Here, take a road that curves gently left along the front of some

SPLITTING THE STAGE

Fraga to Lleida is one of the Camino Ignaciano's longer stages, but there is an option to cut it in half at Alcarràs, meaning you walk 19km the first day, and then only 14km the second. Alternatively, you can take the frequent and regular bus from Alcarràs to Lleida (see **w** atmlleida.cat/horaris/126 for timetable) and stay overnight there. With this second option, you get an extra night in this big city, which has more accommodation choices and attractions. On the following day, simply take the return bus to Alcarràs (leaving your backpack in your hotel) and enjoy the pleasant riverside stroll back into Lleida to complete the stage.

FRAGA–LLEIDA (LERIDA)

industrial buildings with the N-IIa still to your right. At the end of these industrial buildings, continue straight ahead, ignoring roads leaving to your left.

The tarmac ends, but your path continues along a dirt track through scrubland. Ignore a tunnel under the highway, with your path now rising sharply in front of you. A row of powerlines serves as extra guidance and the path soon merges with a tarmac road, which you follow in the same direction as before. As the tarmac reaches a summit, continue to follow it as it turns left and descends. After a few hundred metres, you reach a four-way junction by a cluster of electricity pylons and turn right, following a line of head-high yellow Endesa gas poles. The road descends and soon reaches a large **industrial estate**. Your path curves to the left (but not *sharp* left!) and at the next junction, after only a few metres, turn right to pass a tall industrial building, which you leave to the left. Walk the length of this industrial estate on the service road, with the busy A-2 road off to your right; at the end, the road turns left and leads to a junction where you turn right to finally exit the estate.

Continue straight at the roundabout and then turn left down the side of a further small industrial area. Pass behind the **Oasis** *hostal*/restaurant (\974 47 06 54; w oasis.es), whose gaudy exterior belies a fairly basic, but decent place to eat (or stay), of which there are precious few on this stretch. The road leads through fruit plantations as you proceed with the highway still on your right, and soon the track merges with a tarmac service road,

201

STAGE 21

parallel with the A-2. Continue along the side of this for around 1km to reach a roundabout, picking up signs that confirm that you are already in Catalonia, and take the route diagonally opposite, away from the traffic, signposted for Alcarràs and Lleida (Cami de la Cabanyera). This road rises through more orchards for almost 1km to reach a junction where you turn left and then shortly right, still following signs for Alcarràs and Lleida. This dirt track skirts a pine forest with welcome shade and descends through yet more fruit trees to end on tarmac, where you turn left, parallel once again with the highway, visible a few hundred metres ahead.

Approaching a roundabout, continue straight ahead to find a bridge across the A-2 highway. At the bridge end, double-back on yourself towards the AP-2 and take the dirt track that runs parallel with it, proceeding under another bridge and continuing straight ahead on the right-hand side of the service road as it divides. Continue as the service road merges, carrying on to reach a roundabout where you take the right. You stay on the right-hand side of the N-II, passing some large factories to reach a further roundabout where you continue straight ahead for 150m and then take a dirt track off to the right, still signposted Alcarràs/Lleida. Where the track ends at a tarmac road, turn right for 250m then left on to a tarmac road into **Alcarràs**. You enter town on Carrer Clamor, which leads left up to the N-II, also called Avinguda de Catalonia. (If you have chosen to divide this stage into two (see box, page 200) this is the road where you'll find the Can Peixan hotel and buses into Lleida.)

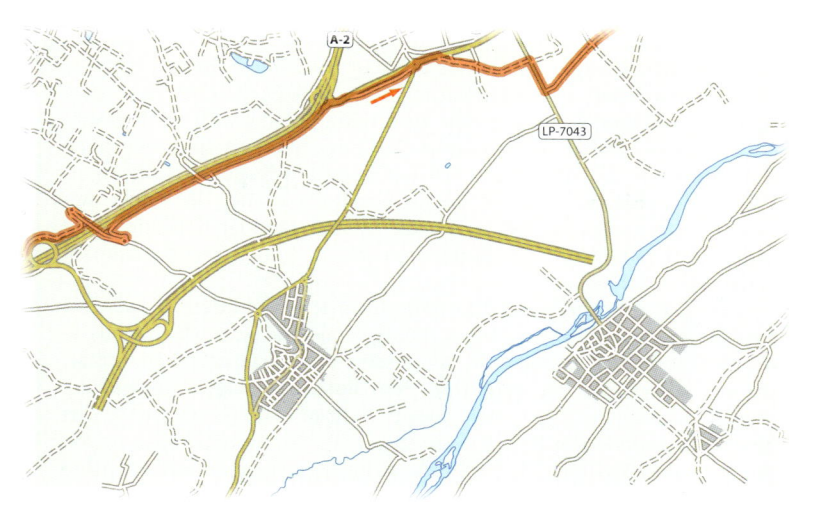

If continuing the stage on foot to Lleida today, turn right and proceed until you reach the Passeig del Riu on your right, which you take for 50m before turning left on to the Avinguda Onze de Setembre, where familiar orange arrows direct you out of town. Pass a park to reach a junction and turn right, signposted Albatàrrec/Lleida. After 50m, turn left for

TIE A YELLOW RIBBON…

Even before entering Catalonia, you will begin to notice the many yellow-ribboned symbols tied around lampposts, balconies and railings. Often these will be accompanied by the original Catalan flag, which comprises four red horizontal stripes on a yellow background. The flag of independence is similar, but also includes a white star centred on a blue triangle.

Catalan independence is a sensitive debate, very much alive and topical. A full discussion is way beyond the limits of this book. But the yellow ribbon, tied in a loop, is a symbol of protest. In the Basque Country, where your walk probably began, similar signs of a strong, regional identity are everywhere, and both in Catalonia and the Basque Country there are many reminders that Spain is still a young democracy with strong, independent constituent parts.

STAGE 21

Butsènit/Lleida and follow the signs as the route takes you on pleasant country lanes through numerous fields of fruit trees. Cross a river on a bridge and continue on asphalt to soon arrive back at the N-II road. Ignoring the tunnel ahead of you, turn right, parallel with the highway, and pass some wholesale outlet stores on your right. Very soon, you reach a roundabout and turn right, still following the Butsènit/Lleida signs. The route twists and turns, eventually becoming a sandy dirt track; after 500m on this surface, look out for the by-now-familiar Butsènit/Lleida sign, which takes you right through more fruit trees to cross a stream on a narrow, concrete bridge.

Turn left at the bridge end towards an agricultural building and then right immediately on reaching it, taking a narrow path which leads to further buildings. Beyond these you reach a wide dirt track, then tarmac, then at a junction you turn right into **Butsènit** village. On reaching the church on your right, turn sharply right to descend on a wide dirt track that leads down to the River Segre, which now accompanies you for the final 8km into Lleida. The Camino Ignaciano coincides with a leafy local path, the Camí del Riu, popular with cyclists and joggers. You might wonder why the Segre waters are flowing west, away from the Mediterranean, and be puzzled as to where the river discharges. In fact, this river originates up in the Pyrenees and then flows south and southwest to empty into the Ebro, south of Fraga. From there, the waters are taken eastwards, Mediterranean-bound.

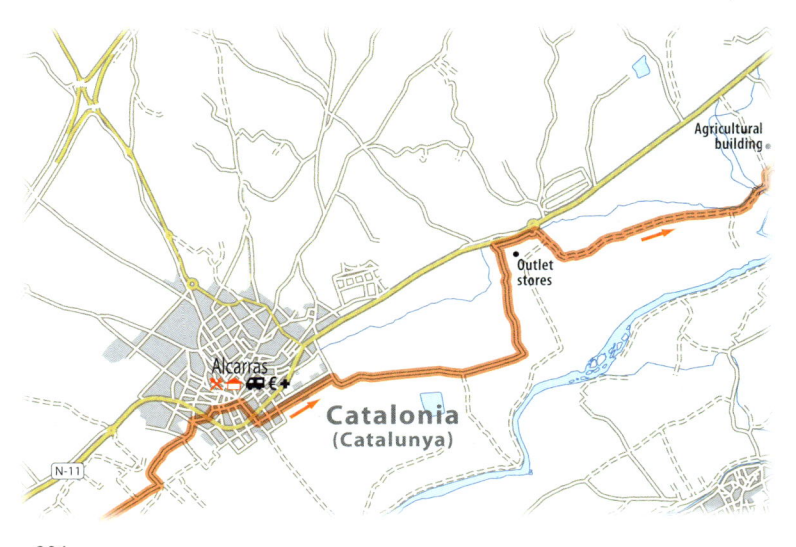

FRAGA–LLEIDA (LERIDA)

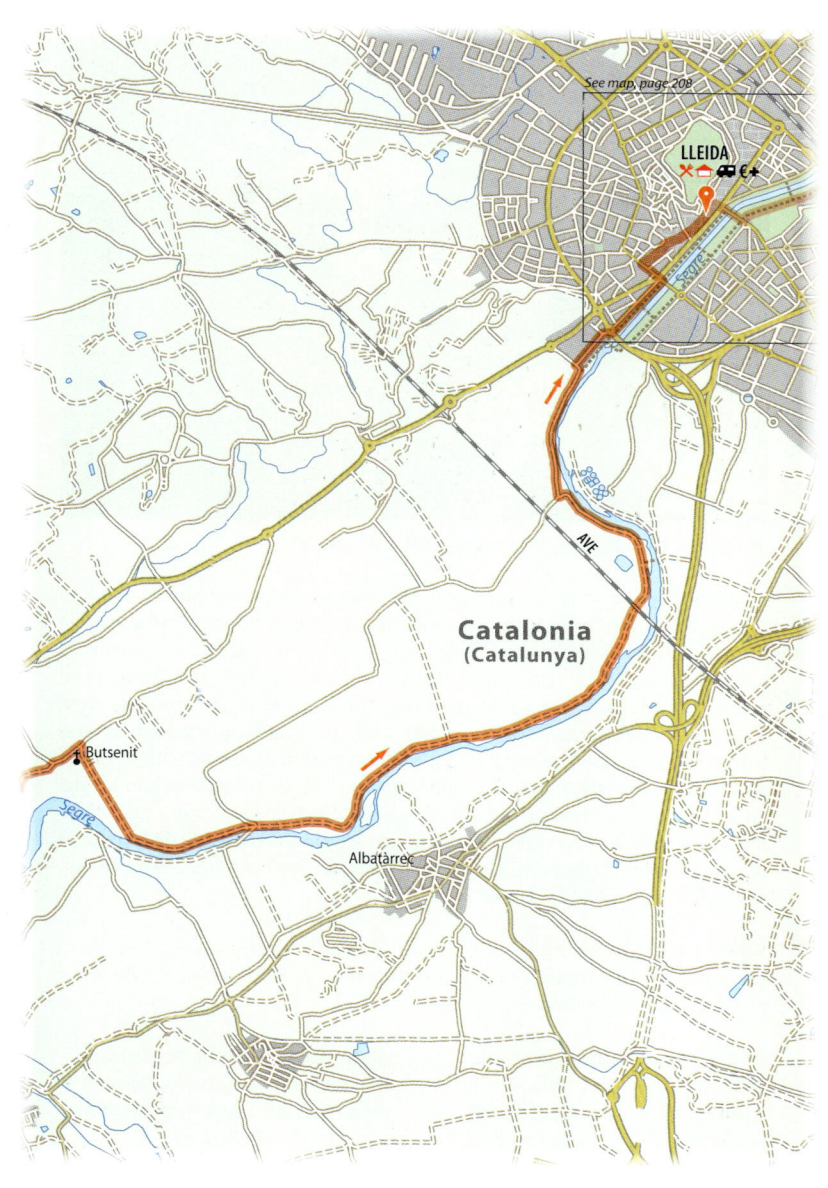

STAGE 21

▲ The River Segre accompanies you on your entry to Lleida *SR/S*

Although the river is concealed here for much of the route, you can descend after the 7km marker to see some impressive, short **waterfalls** where the river makes a downwards leap. Cormorants and egrets can usually be spotted as well. The path eventually passes beneath the AVE high-speed railway and shortly after, ignoring a bridge that tempts you to cross the river, continue straight ahead until the path ends on a tarmac road where you turn right. Take another right after a few hundred metres and, with the river always on your right, follow the path without change of direction into **Lleida**. After around 1km, take advantage of a pedestrian bridge to cross the N-II, as it itself crosses the Segre. Shortly after, turn left on to Avinguda de Catalonia and then second right on to Carrer Sant Antoni. This becomes Carrer Major, on which you will find the tourist office.

WHERE TO STAY AND EAT Although Alcarràs is a fairly small town, there are just enough restaurants and one accommodation option if you want to spend the night there (see below).

Can Peixan (20 rooms) Avinguda de Catalonia 78, Alcarràs; 973 79 10 12; e jordi@canpeixan.com. About the only accommodation choice in Alcarràs, if you are splitting this stage in 2. On the main road; AC rooms, very professional management & pilgrim discounts. Superb-value restaurant/café attached. *€28/38 sgl/dbl*

🏠 **Hotel Goya** (21 rooms) Carrer Alcalde Costa 9, Lleida; ☎ 973 26 67 88. Very handy for the city centre & bus station, this is an excellent, good-value hotel with well-appointed AC rooms. *€35/50 sgl/dbl*

🏠 **Parador de Lleida** (53 rooms) Carrer Cavallers 15, Lleida; ☎ 973 00 48 66; **e** lleida@parador.es; **w** parador.es. Though rooms are thoroughly modernised, public areas retain the stunning high ceilings, arches & stonework from the building's long-gone days as a 17th-century convent. A beautiful restaurant & the setting is matched by excellent food & slick service. Close to the centre, a worthwhile indulgence. *€90 sgl/dbl*

🏠 **Ramon Berenguer IV** (52 rooms) Plaza Ramon Berenguer IV 2, Lleida; ☎ 973 23 73 45; **e** reservas@hotelramonberenguerlleida.com; **w** hotelramonberenguerlleida.com. Slightly old-fashioned feel, but a popular, fully renovated budget choice, with good-sized AC rooms, close to the train station. *€35/40 sgl/dbl*

✘ **Aggio** Carrer dels Templers, Lleida; ☎ 973 26 61 55; **w** restaurantaggio.es; ⏰ 11.00–16.00 & 19.30–midnight, closed Mon evening & Tue. Excellent choice of tapas dishes, plus set menus. *€15*

✘ **Pinot Gastrothèque** Sant Marti 72, Lleida; **m** 673 43 27 41; **w** pinotrestaurant.com. A cosy little family place, focusing on local favourites. *€15*

✘ **Saroa** Carrer Torres de Sanui 12, Lleida; ☎ 973 09 17 01; **m** 633 49 65 62; **w** saroarestaurant.com; ⏰ closed Mon & evenings Tue–Wed. A fairly recent creation, with elaborate cuisine & fine local wines. Towards the top end of the town's price range, but a lot of love goes into the food. *€20*

TOURIST INFORMATION

ℹ️ **Tourist office** Carrer Major 31; ☎ 973 70 03 19; **w** www.turismedelleida.com; ⏰ 10.00–14.00 & 16.00–19.00 Mon–Sat, 10.00–13.30 Sun & hols. There is also an office at the Seu Vella.

SLOW FOOD IN LLEIDA

Do snails qualify as being the ultimate in 'slow food'? The highpoint of Lleida's gastronomic, or maybe gastro*podic*, year is surely the **Aplec del Caragol** (**w** aplec.org), the annual snail festival held towards the end of May. 'Frenzied' hardly seems an appropriate adjective to attach to a snail-orientated party, but an amazing 12 tonnes of these gastropods are consumed over the three-day festival and around 200,000 (human) visitors arrive in town to enjoy them, often all costumed-up and ready to get well lubricated and enjoy the many musical events and parades. But don't worry if you are not in town at the end of May as you can 'catch up' with the snails at many of the city's traditional restaurants throughout the year. Snail farms ensure a constant supply.

STAGE 21

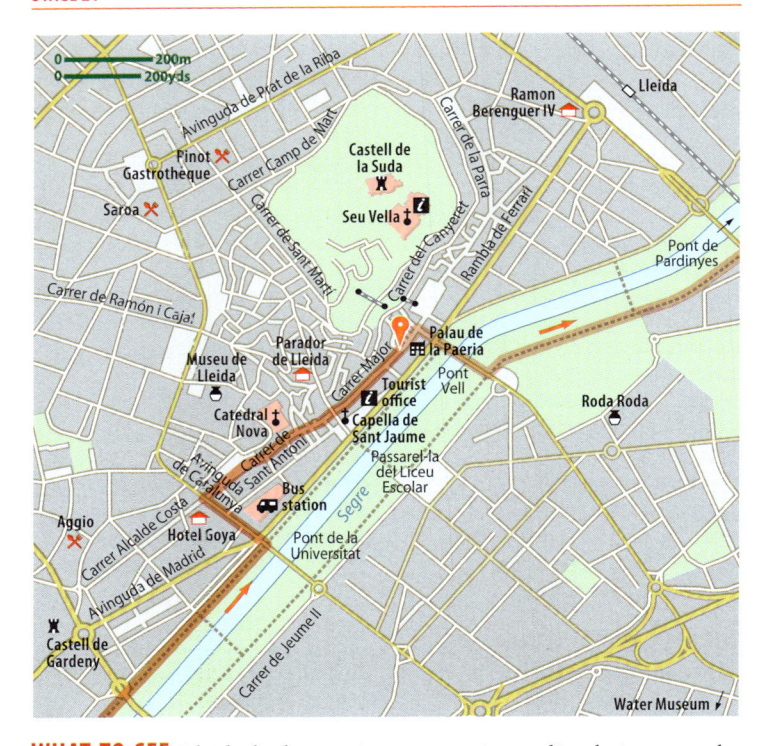

WHAT TO SEE Lleida had great importance in medieval times, as the Segre flowing down from the Pyrenees was a useful companion for pilgrims coming from the north on the way to Santiago de Compostela. Where it joins the Ebro, the devout walkers would then turn west and follow that river upstream, thus always close to water. If you have chosen to enjoy a rest day in Lleida, call in at the **tourist office** (page 207) for suggestions and opening times. The town's most impressive sight is the 13th-/15th-century **Seu Vella**, or 'Old Cathedral', which sits atop the hill that towers over Lleida. Like many churches built after Spain's liberation from the Moors, it is situated on the site of the former mosque. A visit to Seu Vella, which has English-language information panels, offers great views down over the city and its surroundings. Right next to it is the **Castell de la Suda**, the current building representing the continuation of hundreds of years of fortifications on this site. In fact, the victors in the War of Spanish Succession destroyed the dwellings around the cathedral in the 18th century, using the stones for fortifications as they took

FRAGA–LLEIDA (LERIDA)

over the cathedral for military purposes to ensure domination over the defeated Catalans. A museum and interpretation centre enhance your visit. You can take the lift up to the Seu Vella and the castle, so no need to sweat too hard on your rest day.

At a *slightly* lower level (though without any lift!), the **Castell de Gardeny** (⊕ Mar–Apr & Oct–Nov 10.00–13.30 Sat–Sun, Jun–Sep 10.00–14.00 Tue–Sun) is a castle with strong Knights Templar connections and architectural traces dating back to medieval

▲ Lleida's Seu Vella, or 'Old Cathedral' MS

times. An English-language video tells the story of the Templars. Even a stroll along the long, pedestrianised Carrer de Sant Antoni/Carrer Major will reveal historic treasures such as the 14th-century **Capella de Sant Jaume** (St James's Chapel), some **Modernist buildings** from the early 20th century, the **Catedral Nova** ('New' Cathedral), which had to be built after the Seu Vella was 'kidnapped' for military use, and the **Palau de la Paeria**. This last building, which has some intriguing features such as the remains of the Muslim docks and carvings of condemned prisoners from the 16th century, has been in constant use as the town hall for centuries.

For museums, choose from the comprehensive **Museu de Lleida** (city museum), the **Roda Roda** (dedicated to classic cars) and the **Water Museum**. All are centrally located. Lleida celebrates its big, local holiday on 11 May and its raucous snail festival (see box, page 207) at the end of that month. (It's the locals that are raucous, not the snails.)

TRANSPORT Lleida is well served by its **bus** station, with regular Alsa services to Barcelona and its El Prat airport (**w** alsa.es) and westwards back to Fraga and Zaragoza with both Alsa and Agreda (**w** agredabus.es). The latter also stops at many of the small towns along the Camino Ignaciano route. **Trains** connect the city to both Barcelona and Zaragoza and you can choose between the super-quick AVE or the slower 'regional' trains. The AVE is three-times faster! See **w** renfe.com for times and details.

Taxis

🚕 **Autotaxi Tele Radio Lleida** ✆ 973 20 30 50; **m** 680 20 30 50

🚕 **Taxi Joan** (Alcarràs) **m** 649 13 04 31

CATALUNYA.COM
WELCOME
TO YOUR
CATALONIA
EMILY
CATALUNYA
NOW AND FOREVER,
YOUR TAILOR-MADE DESTINATION.
Generalitat de Catalunya
Government of Catalonia

22 LLEIDA–EL PALAU D'ANGLESOLA

Your first stage wholly in Catalonia is a delight, traversing fields and open countryside. Be prepared, though – it is fairly long, with little shade offered and, apart from the town of Bell-lloc d'Urgell, there are no other opportunities for refreshment. For the most part, today's stage avoids any close interactions with busy highways, and the signposting is largely crystal-clear.

Start Lleida (tourist office)
Coordinates 41.61382, 0.62540
Finish El Palau d'Anglesola
Difficulty Moderate
Distance 25.6km
Duration 6hrs 15mins

THE ROUTE Today you need to choose one or another bridge to make your exit from Lleida. The **Pont Vell** carries the official route. Once over the river, cross beneath the railway bridge and then under the rather drab **Pont de Pardinyes**, after which you climb the steps to street level

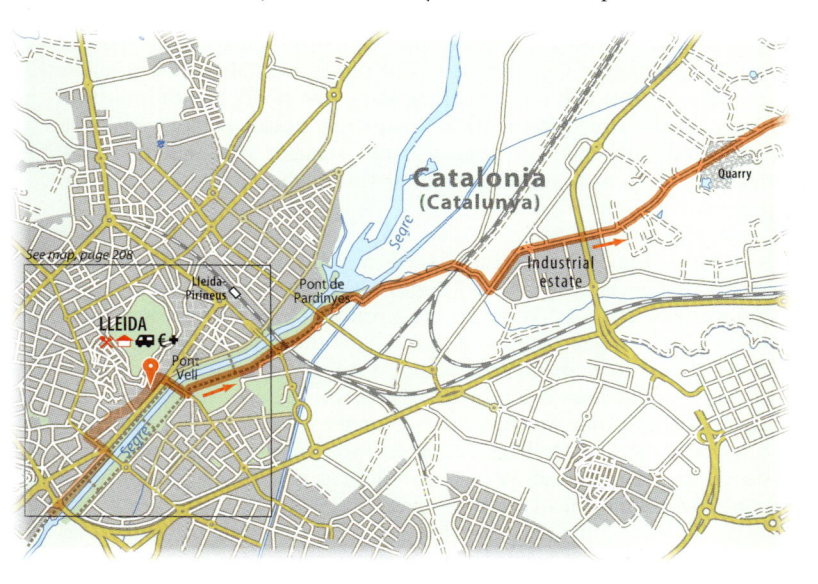

211

STAGE 22

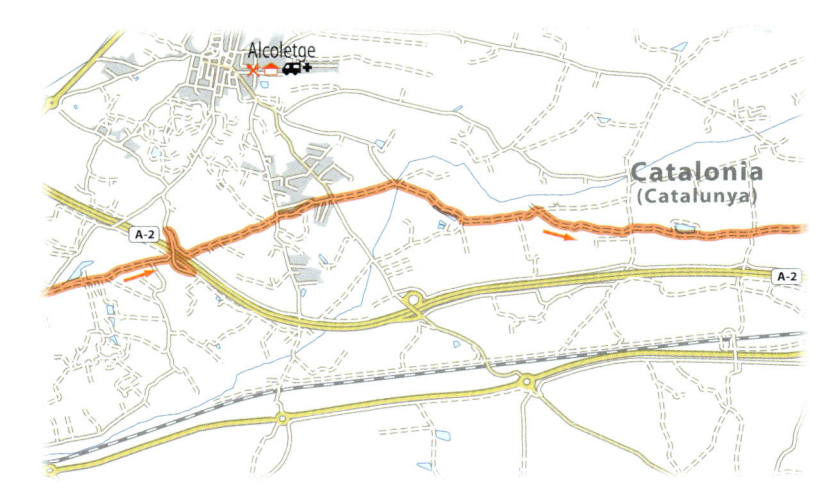

to continue in the same direction as before with the river now below you. After 300m, take a tarmac road on the right to leave the riverside, then cross a water channel and turn left towards some sluice gates. After another 500m, cross a small river and then turn right across the railway tracks. Continue along the road to reach an industrial estate and follow the orange arrows to turn left alongside a row of brick-built industrial units. At the end of these, take a road that angles off to your right, still within the industrial estate. Cross a major road junction and, reaching the end of the estate, continue along a dirt path as it passes into open countryside.

Passing through a quarry, you reach a Y-junction and pick up a sign for Bell-lloc d'Urgell/Tàrrega, which you follow to the right. After around 800m you reach the A-2 highway, where you turn right and then double-back to cross the traffic via a bridge. On the other side, again double-back to your right and then follow the path left, parallel with the highway for a few metres, before turning sharp left through fields to leave the highway behind you. After a few hundred metres, the dirt track reaches a four-way junction, where the left would lead you to the pilgrims' hostel of **Alcoletge** but, unless you are planning a stay there, continue straight ahead. Pass some buildings and, at another junction, continue straight ahead through fields.

At the next junction, veer right to follow the sign for Mollerusa/Tàrrega. You almost immediately cross a stream, and take the right-

LLEIDA–EL PALAU D'ANGLESOLA

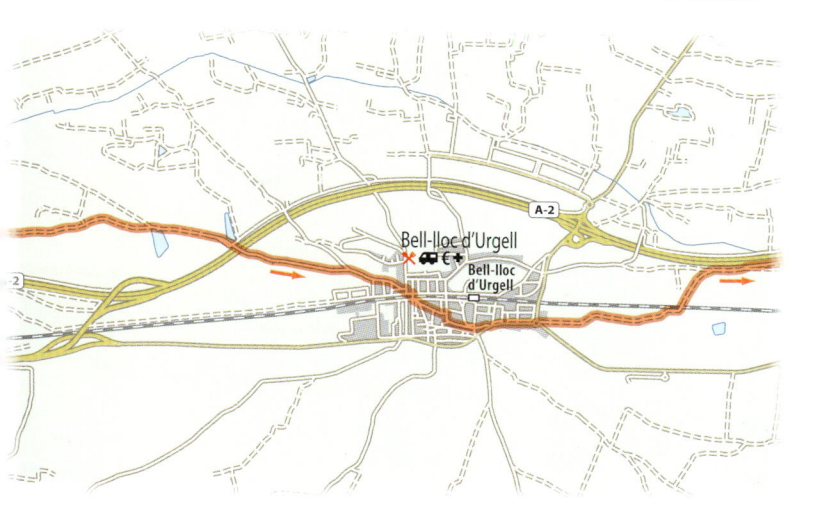

hand fork at a Y-junction with fruit trees now on your left. After a further 100m, the path curves left with a fruit plantation now on your right. Soon you see the traffic passing on the A-2 ahead. The path gradually angles closer to the road and eventually another path joins at an angle, but the

▼ A curious figure greets walkers on this stage *MS*

213

STAGE 22

direction remains as before, with a highway bridge now visible ahead. Cross the bridge, heading for the buildings of **Bell-lloc d'Urgell**. This is a service town for the surrounding area, with no great attractions, but it's worth stopping for a drink. The road ends at Camí Vila Nova de la Barca. Turn right and then left and cross the railway tracks. Diagonally beyond

> ### YOU'VE GOT A FRIEND
>
> You won't find too much of tangible historical interest in El Palau, but you will definitely encounter the pilgrim spirit. The Amics del Camí ('Friends of The Way') are a group of townsfolk dedicated to looking after weary pilgrims who stay in town. They – as opposed to the town hall – run the tiny *alberg* here and make themselves available to meet and greet. They are not a religious organisation; instead their work is inspired by a former friend who died tragically while fighting a fire. As you enter town, look out for a laminated notice directly on the route which lists the names and numbers of the members, and which notes which member is on duty to greet travellers throughout the year. Some are English speakers, but all are welcoming: this really is El Palau's precious gift to the camino.

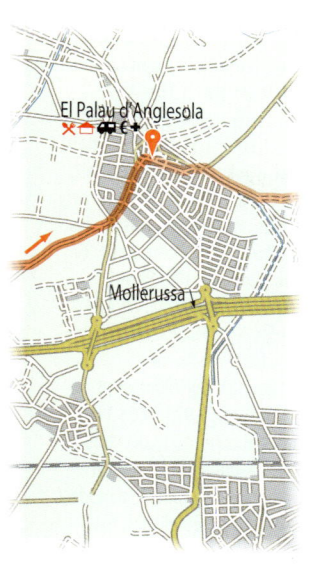

the roundabout ahead of you, follow Carrer Mina, which leads to a junction where you turn right on to Pau Casals and left on to Carrer d'Urgell to reach a junction with a rest area. Here, with the church behind you to the right, continue straight ahead (Carrer Orient) and, at a roundabout, follow a dirt track straight ahead of you.

A sign tells you that El Palau d'Anglesola is now 10km away. Even among the outskirts of a small town such as Bell-lloc, you can see signs of the industry that powers the Catalan economy. Your path forks and you choose the left, inching closer to the railway line. When it forks again, you once again choose left and soon cross the tracks to then continue straight on towards the A-2. At the highway, your path turns right to run parallel with it, now on the left. After a few hundred metres, follow the sign taking you away from the highway, through fields. After passing a farm on the left, the path leads up and over the highway and once on the other side you follow the by-now-familiar signs, taking you to the right. A strange striding figure of a giant can be seen off to the right, an odd, unmissable character who looks ready to attempt a crossing of the highway. You might consider him to be a fellow pilgrim, but in fact this structure – called the **Estatua de Sidamon** (see photo, page 213) – was erected by a construction company to mark the opening of the motorway. At a Y-junction, simply follow the signs for **El Palau d'Anglesola** to the right and the rest of the route is well signposted until you reach your destination. At one point, you pass a huge 'plantation' of solar panels and later turn right to cross a water channel and continue on tarmac. Enter town at a roundabout and follow the signs into the centre on Carrer Font, which leads to the Plaça Major (main square) where you'll find the Sant Joan Baptista church. There are a few other attractive buildings to admire, particularly the façade of the former palace (*palau*), which is located near the town centre.

WHERE TO STAY AND EAT Options today are limited, so advance booking is advised unless you want to stay at the pilgrims' hostel. If you get stuck, the town of Mollerussa is a 30-minute walk from El Palau d'Anglesola, where there are two accommodation options.

STAGE 22

🏠 **Alberg del Pelegri (Pilgrims' Hostel)** (8 beds) Carrer Major 19, Alcoletge; ☎ 973 19 67 25; **m** 625 62 01 43; **w** albergdelpelegri.cat. Some 7km out of Lleida, so perhaps of limited use. Kitchen, AC, heating, Wi-Fi, washing machine, dryer. Reservations advised. *€9 pp*

🏠 **Pension Antoni** (9 rooms) Sant Antoni 7, El Palau d'Anglesola; ☎ 973 60 21 58; **e** info@pensiosantantoni.com. Pleasant modern rooms, some on the compact side. Bar & restaurant with basic meals. Ask for a pilgrim discount. *€25/40 sgl/dbl*

🏠 **Refugi de Pelegrins (Pilgrims' Hostel)** (4 beds) Next to the municipal swimming pool, El Palau d'Anglesola; ☎ 973 60 13 14 (*ayuntamiento*); **m** 666 28 66 69; **e** amics.del.cami@gmail.com; **w** amicsdelcami.cat. A real community-run project (see box, page 214). Microwave, but no other cooking facilities. Keys, sheets & pillow covers should be collected form the Punt Bloc shop on the Plaça Major behind the church. Walk-ins only. *€5 pp*

✕ **Cal Boria** Carrer Orient 27, Bell-lloc d'Urgell; ☎ 973 56 00 14. If you time it right (& can manage a 10km walk after lunch!), this popular place in Bell-lloc provides tasty, filling meals with some sophistication, just beyond the halfway point of the stage. *€15*

✕ **El Poli Bar** Avinguda dels Paisos Catalans 1, El Palau d'Anglesola; **m** 639 52 32 34; **f** elpolibar. Modest but reliable snacks, tapas & basic meals. *€8*

✕ **Fogot** Avinguda Verge Montserrat 5, El Palau d'Anglesola; ☎ 973 04 68 31; **w** fogotrestaurant.com; ⏰ 13.00–16.00 Wed–Mon, 21.00–midnight Fri–Sat. A classy choice, surprising quality in a modest town. Choice of fish & meat dishes, plus lighter tapas options. *€15*

TRANSPORT El Palau has bus connections back into Lleida on Line 112 (**w** atmlleida.cat/horaris). Nearby Mollerussa town, 5km to the south, has connections to Barcelona city and El Prat airport with Alsa (**w** alsa.es). Mollerussa also has a train service back to Lleida, and eastwards to Cervera and Barcelona (**w** renfe.com).

Taxis

🚖 **Eurotaxi Albert** (El Palau d'Anglesola) **m** 619 60 58 05

🚖 **Miquel Bosch** (Bell-lloc d'Urgell) **m** 636 21 30 70

23 EL PALAU D'ANGLESOLA–VERDÚ

A lovely, peaceful stage that makes the most of rural back roads as it leads through the Catalan countryside. There are a couple of towns at convenient intervals to provide refreshment en route, and you finish at the lovely village of Verdú, where accommodation is limited to the pilgrims' hostel. If time and energy reserves allow, or the hostel is full, you can push on for an extra 4km beyond Verdú to reach the surprisingly large town of Tàrrega, which offers a few more overnight options.

> **Start** Sant Joan Baptista church, El Palau d'Anglesola
> **Coordinates** 41.65166, 0.88050
> **Finish** Verdú (or Tàrrega)
> **Difficulty** Easy
> **Distance** 24.7km (28.7km to Tàrrega)
> **Duration** 6hrs (7hrs to Tàrrega)

THE ROUTE Follow Carrer Sant Josep for 300m and turn left on to Carrer Nou. At the far end of that street, turn briefly right then left, picking up the sign for Castellnou de Seana and crossing a water channel to follow signs to the right on a tarmac road. Shortly after, your direction signs take you left and you continue straight ahead to cross a main road. Directly north of here, though a good 175km away, is the Pico Aneto (3,404m), which is the highest point in the Pyrenees; in between, the landscape is marked by a series of craggy *sierras* (or '*serras*' in Catalan) as the terrain builds in altitude towards the French border. After 1km or so, cross

217

STAGE 23

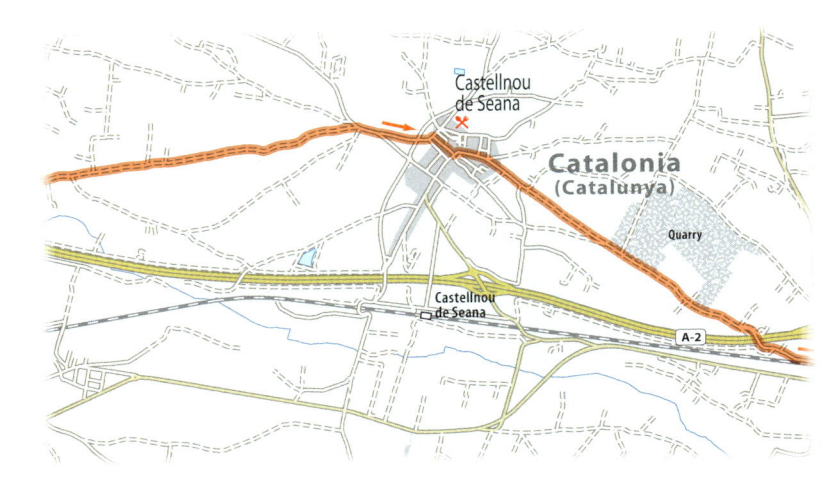

another main road, and on reaching a third one after around 1.5km, you cross diagonally to the left and traverse a water channel to take the second right and continue in the same direction as before, with a line of electricity pylons now parallel to you on your right. In less than 1km, you pick up the camino signs once more.

Soon the church tower of **Castellnou de Seana** comes into view. The path ends at a tarmac road, on to which you turn right towards town, then left, with the spire firmly in your sights. Take a right on to Carrer Major to reach the church square, just beyond which you turn left then right to find another square. If you fancy a drink, seek out the handsome **Café Modern** (Carrer Sant Blai; 973 32 08 43) off to your right. Its wavy roof-lines exhibit the Noucentisme architectural movement that reacted against Modernism. As a former centre of Republican youth, it was almost inevitably taken over by Francoists after the Civil War. To exit town, follow Carrer Calvari as it crosses a roundabout and turns to a dirt track with the A-2 highway ahead. Pass a huge quarry before taking the bridge across the highway.

Once across, you reach the railway tracks and now continue with these on your right, passing industrial buildings on the left. Beyond these, cross a bridge and 100m further double-back to find a roundabout where you pass beneath the bridge you have just crossed. Once under, turn left at a roundabout, and then right at a further one (the Hotel Bellpuig is on your left) to head into **Bellpuig**. On reaching the far end of a leafy square, with the town's brick-built theatre behind you to the left, find the Plaça Sant

Roc in front of you to the left with the Camino Ignaciano sun symbols to guide you. After 200m, turn right on to Carrer Major and, at its end, turn left on to Carrer Balmes. Follow this road, which turns sharp right before you reach the town's church, as it becomes a dirt track and leads into the countryside. Cross a main road and continue, now only 10km from Verdú.

Just under 2km from the main road, you rather unexpectedly pass the **Bellpuig Motocross Circuit** (see box, page 220). Shortly afterwards the path splits and you follow to the right, still signposted, soon crossing a wide irrigation channel and continuing ahead. At an old farmhouse, ignore a sign to the right for Peixana and continue straight ahead on the tarmac road. After a little over 1km, leave the tarmac to take a path signposted to your right and, after a further 100m, continue slightly uphill to the left. Ignore a curve to the right and carry straight on. From this plateau, there are great views over the flat cultivated countryside around you.

After less than 2km, Verdú comes into view, and you reach a road junction, with a shrine immediately on your right. Continue straight ahead on a dirt track as it descends and, at a five-way junction take the second left to reach the C-14 road. Crossing this, continue up towards **Verdú** and enter town on Carrer Sant Miquel, which then becomes Carrer Sant Pere Claver, named after Verdú's most famous son (see box, page 223). You will notice a few shops selling ceramics, something else for which Verdú is renowned (page 222). A little further along this street is the pilgrims' hostel, but if you are pressing on to Tàrrega today, go to page 224 for the beginning of Stage 24.

WHERE TO STAY AND EAT The pilgrims' hostel offers the only possibility for accommodation in Verdú, otherwise you'll need to continue for 4km to Tàrrega.

BELLPUIG MOTOCROSS CIRCUIT

Motorbikes are part of the fabric in Catalonia, but as you walk past the Bellpuig Motocross Circuit you might be prompted to ask – why? This modest-looking circuit has indeed hosted many national and world championship races in past years, but it is in Moto GP – motorbiking's equivalent to Formula 1, if you like – in which Spain, and in particular Catalonia, have found most global success in recent decades.

Listing Catalonia's GP champions will result in true bike aficionados nodding their heads in recognition and respect: Pol and Aleix Espargaró, Alex Crivillé, Sito Pons, Tito Rabat, Dani Pedrosa, Toni Elías, Emilio Alzamora and Albert Arenas. One name, however, stands out high and proud above all of these: Márquez. While Alex Márquez could also be added to the list above, it is his brother Marc who is the 'big beast' of Catalan GP racing.

But 'big' beast? Far from it. When Marc began his racing career, he was so small that over 20kg of weight had to be added to his bike to achieve the sport's minimum weight stipulations. Small in stature but a giant in his sport, he has six Moto GPs to his name and an additional two GP world championships in different classes. Marc Márquez and

located a bit off the camino route. Recently renovated, good-sized rooms. Restaurant; b/fast usually inc. *€50/70 sgl/dbl*

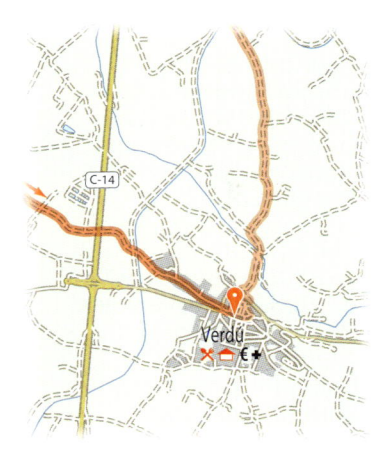

🏠 **Hotel Pintor Marsa** (24 rooms) Avinguda Catalonia 112, Tàrrega; 📞 973 50 15 16; **e** pintormarsa@hostaldelcarme.com; **w** hostaldelcarme.com (shared site with sister hotel). Good-quality hotel, a little off the camino route. Restaurant; b/fast usually inc. *€45/70 sgl/dbl*

🏠 **Refugi de Pelegrins San Pere Claver (Pilgrims' Hostel)** (32 beds) Carrer San Pere Claver 30, Verdú; **m** 616 89 36 02; **e** refugipelegrinsverdu@gmail.com; **w** pereclaver.jesuites.net. Run by the Jesuits, this pleasant hostel has a microwave & fridge but no other cooking facilities, although b/fast is available at a nearby bar. Reservations advisable, as no other options in town. *€12 pp, plus €2 for a blanket*

🏠 **Hotel Ciutat de Tàrrega** (26 rooms) Sant Pelegri 96, Tàrrega; 📞 973 31 47 37; **e** info@hotelciutattarrega.com; **w** www.hotelciutattarrega.com. In town, but also

---

his brother are both natives of Cervera, where the presence of his fan club and a special section of the town's museum are testament to the reverence in which he is held locally. Owing to his huge strength and determination, Marc is affectionately known worldwide as 'The Ant of Cervera' and the industrious insect's logo can be seen on his racing helmet. He has established himself as one of the sport's all-time greats. Locally, he is referred to as 'El Tro de Cervera' ('The Thunder of Cervera') and he is certainly a 'big noise' in this small Catalan town.

But we are left with the same question: why does Catalonia produce so many champions? When interviewed, one of them, Pol Espargaró, suggested that it was due to the number of facilities available at a young age and the preponderance of junior championships in Catalonia. These presented opportunities to many aspiring youngsters, often from the age of six! Not all of these made it to the heady heights of the Moto GP class, of course, but the list above shows that a disproportionate number of young Catalans did. And went on to become world champions.

STAGE 23

✕ **Bar Restaurant La Muralla** Carrer Firal Pere III 75, Verdú; ✆ 973 34 71 36. Food & service basic, open only at lunchtimes. *€10*
✕ **La Cava** Mestre Güell 5, Tàrrega; ✆ 973 31 13 80. A fairly new place, with a growing reputation for its inventive cuisine created under the expert supervision of chef Albert Marimón. A lively, buzzy atmosphere. Top tapas, great Catalan main dishes. *€13*
✕ **Restaurant El Terrisser** Carrer de Jesus 2, Verdú; ✆ 973 34 70 94; ⊕ daily. Next to the hostel. Greatly appreciated service & quality traditional food in good quantities. *€11*

TOURIST INFORMATION

ℹ **Tourist office** Plaça Bispe Comelles 13, Verdú; ✆ 973 34 72 16; ⊕ 09.00–14.00 Tue–Sun. If you ring in advance, they can organise visits to the castle or church. The Pere Claver sanctuary next to the refuge is always open, however.

WHAT TO SEE Wandering the narrow streets of compact Verdú is a pleasant enough activity and could be combined with a climb up the 11th-century **castle tower** – a slightly claustrophobic event, but one that rewards the brave with great views down over the countryside. Changing economics have seen almonds and pistachios replace more traditional crops in recent years, so the landscape has changed. Alternatively, you could poke your nose into one of the **ceramics shops** dotted around town, manly along Carrer Sant Miquel or Carrer de la Carrera, which runs parallel. Verdú is renowned for its black ceramics and although you will not want to buy a heavy water pitcher (*cantí*) for your onward journey, you could always just browse or get something shipped. You can also pop your head into the church or the Pere Claver sanctuary.

▼ Spectacular views await from the top of Verdú's castle tower *MS*

PERE CLAVER, THE 'SLAVE OF THE SLAVES'

'Slave of the slaves' might not sound like a great title, but that's the name Pere Claver chose for himself as he dedicated his adult life to the service of those less fortunate. In fact, to the service of those *much* less fortunate than Verdú's most celebrated man, who was born in 1580 into a wealthy family in this pretty Catalan town. After spending time at university in Barcelona, Pere Claver became a Jesuit in 1602 and a few years later was sent to what is now Colombia, in South America, to promote the Jesuit message.

Having decided that the native Amerindians were ill-suited to carrying out the hard work in their colonies, the Spanish imperialists had looked to Africa for slave labour to put into service in 'their' South American plantations and elsewhere. When Pere Claver reached Cartagena, the slaving 'industry' was already well established. By the time the ships arrived from Africa, many of the slaves had already perished and those who had survived the Atlantic crossing were delivered in truly appalling conditions. It was the time and place for Pere Claver to begin the work for which he would eventually be canonised. Ignoring the authorities' opposition, the young Jesuit insisted on boarding the ships as they arrived in port, bringing medicine and food to those suffering in the squalid holds. His work continued for nearly 40 years, during which time he is said to have baptised nearly 300,000 slaves. He also visited the plantations themselves and strove to encourage more humane conditions for the workers. He died in Colombia in 1654 and was canonised in 1888. As San Pere Claver, he is also one of the country's patron saints, as well as being the patron saint of slaves.

TRANSPORT Tàrrega is the nearest port-of-call if you need bus or train connections to Lleida in the west or Barcelona to the east. For times and prices, see **w** alsa.es and **w** renfe.es respectively.

Taxis

Taxis Bellpuig (Bellpuig) **m** 628 87 82 93
Taxis Font (Tàrrega) 973 31 15 67; **m** 636 98 58 50
Taxis Verdú (Verdú/Tàrrega) **m** 679 17 34 42

24 VERDÚ–CERVERA

Today is a short stage, and particularly so if you extended yesterday's walk and slept overnight in Tàrrega. If you are starting in Verdú, perhaps take the opportunity to wander the pretty streets and find out about its traditional ceramics, or start out early and spend time discovering the quirks of hilltop Cervera at the stage end. Believe it or not, despite having fewer than 10,000 residents, Cervera is a university town. Well, sort of (see box, page 227).

> **Start** Verdú (pilgrims' hostel) or Tàrrega (Església de Santa Maria de l'Alba)
> **Coordinates** 41.61095, 1.14225 (41.65651, 1.13945 if starting in Tàrrega)
> **Finish** Cervera
> **Difficulty** Easy
> **Distance** 17km (13km if starting in Tàrrega)
> **Duration** 4hrs 15mins (3hrs 15mins if starting in Tàrrega)

THE ROUTE Walk east along Carrer Sant Pere Claver to reach Plaça Bisbe Comelles, on which the town's castle and Santa Maria church stand. To the left of the church, find the Ignatian 'sun' emblem to exit the town through narrow streets adorned with beautiful stonework. You reach Plaça de l'Hospital and then the junction with the main road (LV-2101); cross over to find a rough path that descends through trees and vines diagonally for 50m to meet signs for Tàrrega, less than 4km away. Follow the signs until an unsigned junction, where you turn right as the road rises up a small brow, from where you can make out the buildings of Tàrrega. (The left fork, which you ignore, leads towards the elevated concrete water channel on the horizon.) Signage is a bit sporadic here, but you can see the traffic on the new Verdú–Tàrrega road running parallel to your route, off to your left.

Your path turns to tarmac around the halfway point and eventually you cross a wide water channel, from where the surprising size of **Tàrrega** – home to 17,000 people – fully reveals itself. Arriving in town, turn left on to Carrer Guardia Civil and follow it as it becomes Carrer l'1 d'Octubre de 2017, crosses the main C-14 road and continues to a footbridge where you cross the River Ondara. Continue on Carrer Sant Agusti and then turn right at Plaça Sant Antoni. You are now on the Carrer Major, and on reaching the main square (Plaça Major) you turn right on to Carrer d'Agoders and soon cross back over the C-14 to proceed on the Carrer de Jacint Verdaguer. This becomes the long Avinguda de la Generalitat, which carries you out into open agricultural land for around 1km and through the pretty, renovated village of **El Talladell**. The buildings here are made from the 'best stone in Catalonia' according to the claims of some residents – while I can't attest to whether this is true, they certainly look noble and handsome. A slight dog-leg in the road leads to a junction where you fork slightly right. You can relax now, as the path is

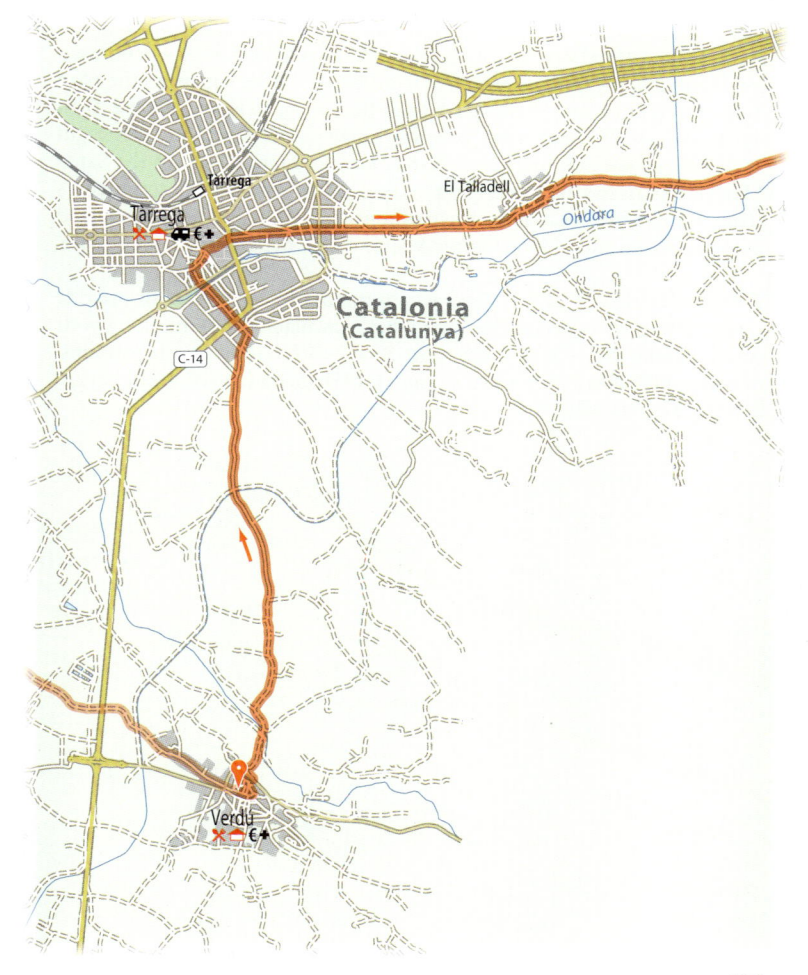

STAGE 24

straightforward and the signage is good. Cross the concrete water channel that joins from your right and soon, as the road turns right, carry straight on. In the distance, you now catch sight of the elevated city of Cervera.

At a junction, **Fonolleres** village with its castle is signed up to the left, but you carry straight on, leaving the tarmac and joining a wide dirt track. On your right, you pass a ruined, fortified tower-house, **Saportella**, which can trace its origins back to the 14th century. Another raised and be-castled village, **Granyanella**, peers down at you from the right but your route continues straight on. The path ends at a junction with the L-214 road with a ruined hermitage on your left; turn left on to this main road for around 700m until a sharp left-hand bend, where you cross the road and turn right up into the long Camí de Sant Magí to enter **Cervera**. Turn left on to Carrer Castell, past Cervera's ruined castle, to find and turn right at the Plaça Sant Domingo, into Carrer de Sant Domènec, past the Santa Maria church and into the Plaça Major, where you'll start tomorrow's stage. From here, most of the town's shops, bars and facilities are situated at the opposite end of long Carrer Major, which departs from the square.

WHERE TO STAY AND EAT The accommodations listed can all provide meals, though it is worth checking what is available when booking your room. Failing that, Cervera has more than a dozen other dining options, of which **El Ombu** (973 80 90 43) and **La Marinada** (m 627 42 20 11) are among the top picks.

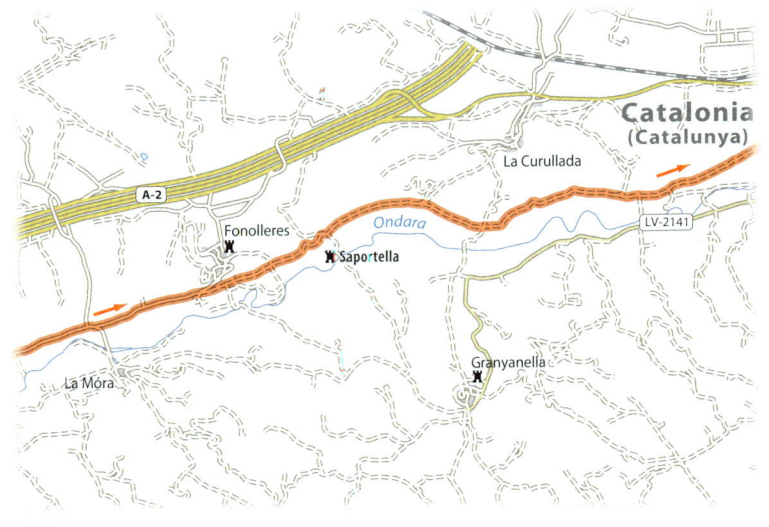

CERVERA, A TOWN WITH A UNIVERSITY

Entering the small Catalan town of Cervera, prepare yourself for a couple of surprises. The first of these is in the town centre, where you will find a grand old building that once housed the town's university. For all the world, you might expect a gaggle of students to emerge at any moment, laughing as they stroll across the capacious town square.

But here's the next surprise: the building actually ceased to function as a university in 1835. Those learning today within its confines will be much younger students, as it now serves as a school. But back in the early 18th century, Cervera's seat of learning briefly enjoyed a monopoly as the *only* university in Catalonia, as the town had supported King Philip V in the War of Spanish Succession. His punishment to those who had opposed him was to remove the rights of all Catalonia's other existing universities; his reward to loyal Cervera was to award the town exclusive rights to host the region's only university. But the foisting of such a privilege on a small town with no previous academic record was not a great success.

At one time in the late 18th century, there was an attempt to convert the institution into a Jesuit university, but this resulted only in the expulsion of two Jesuit professors. Meanwhile, those Catalans seeking to study medicine chose to do so in France, rather than succumb to the small-town charms of Cervera. The Chair of Mathematics, once created, was never even occupied, and overall the students' academic results were underwhelming. Now all that's left is this large building, looking beautiful if rather incongruous in the middle of compact Cervera.

▼ Although still standing today, Cervera's university ceased to function in 1835 *JB/S*

STAGE 24

🏠 **Hostal Bonavista** (20 rooms) Avinguda de Catalonia 14; ✆ 973 53 00 27; **e** hostalbonavista@hotmail.com; **w** hotelbonavistacervera.com. Close to the university, a stately establishment; stylish rooms have AC & heating. Restaurant/bar. *€60/68 sgl/dbl*

🏠 **Hostal Nobadis** (11 rooms) Avinguda del Mil·lenari Catalonia 49; ✆ 973 53 03 25; **e** info@nobadis.ct; **w** nobadis.cat. A little to the west of the town centre, with bright & pleasant rooms. Good-value daily menus available from its popular restaurant. *€52/65 sgl/dbl*

🏠 **Hostal Universitat** (10 rooms) Plaça Universitat 15; ✆ 661 78 64 77/661 78 64 83; **e** info@hostaluniversitat.com; **w** hostaluniversitat.com. Directly opposite the entrance to the former university, a nicely modernised & friendly place, with AC & Wi-Fi. B/fast & dinner available. *€40/60 sgl/dbl*

TOURIST INFORMATION

ℹ Tourist office (Centro de Acogida Turística) Avinguda Francesc Macià 78; ✆ 973 53 44 42; **w** turismecervera.cat. For Ignatian walkers, this is unhelpfully situated way out of the town centre, but the more conveniently situated museum will provide you with a map & enough information for a short stay.

WHAT TO SEE The **Museu Comarcal de Cervera** (Carrer Major 115; ✆ 973 53 39 17; **w** museudecervera.cat; see website for opening hours & prices) displays some medieval art and collections relating to the university. But the main attractions are the beautifully preserved rooms of the Duran I Sampere home, giving an insight into the lives of this 19th-century bourgeois family, and the large ground-floor section given to showcasing the career of Marc Márquez, the town's motorcycle hero (see box, page 220), complete with a number of his bikes. You can also enquire about availability of guided tours to the university (see box, page 227).

TRANSPORT Cervera is on the train line between Lleida and Barcelona. Buses leave two or three times per day for Manresa and Girona Airport in one direction, and for Tàrrega and Lleida in the other; see **w** teisa-bus.com for more.

Taxi
🚖 **Taxi Eduard** (Cervera) **m** 691 40 90 50

25 CERVERA–IGUALADA

A long, long stage today, and if time allows I recommend you split it over two days. When considering your options, remember that the next stage involves a bit of climbing, so you need to be on your best form. The first half of the stage is spent in a barely noticeable ascent up to La Panadella service area, where a cheap overnight stay can be had; the second half involves a downhill meander to Igualada. Another mid-stage option would be to stay at the Hostal Jorba, 5km beyond La Panadella. Along the way, your route travels along a combination of dirt track and largely unused tarmac. A very pleasant stroll if you choose to overnight at the halfway stage, but hard work if you don't.

Start Plaça Major, Cervera
Coordinates 41.665716, 1.270998
Finish Igualada (or La Panadella if dividing the stage in two)
Difficulty Difficult (if attempting the whole stage); easy (if splitting it across two days)
Distance 38.4km (16km to La Panadella then 22.4km to Igualada)
Duration 8hrs 15mins (3hrs 45mins to La Panadella then 4hrs 30mins to Igualada)

THE ROUTE Take the downward Carrer Sebolleria to the left of the police station as it becomes Carrer Santa Maria. At the bottom, turn right then immediately left to descend on Carrer de la Muralla and follow to the left along the top of the city walls with views out to your right over the

STAGE 25

flat-bottomed valley. At a break in the wall, turn right downhill with the church spire directly behind you and continue to reach the **Hostal La Savina** at the foot. Here, a helpful orange arrow opposite and on your right points towards the path to Vergós. Continue on a paved road and then a dirt track with the well-concealed River Ondara on your right.

The well-arrowed path is straight ahead. Cross the almost-invisible river and pass the 12th-century **Molí de Fiol** mill, turning left beyond it. After 1km you leave the riverside, turning left again with Vergós town now ahead of you. Signage for the Ignaciano here is poor, so head towards the very visible tunnel, but turn right before reaching it to enter **Vergós**. You will pass the pitch of Club Bitlles Vergós, the village skittles club,

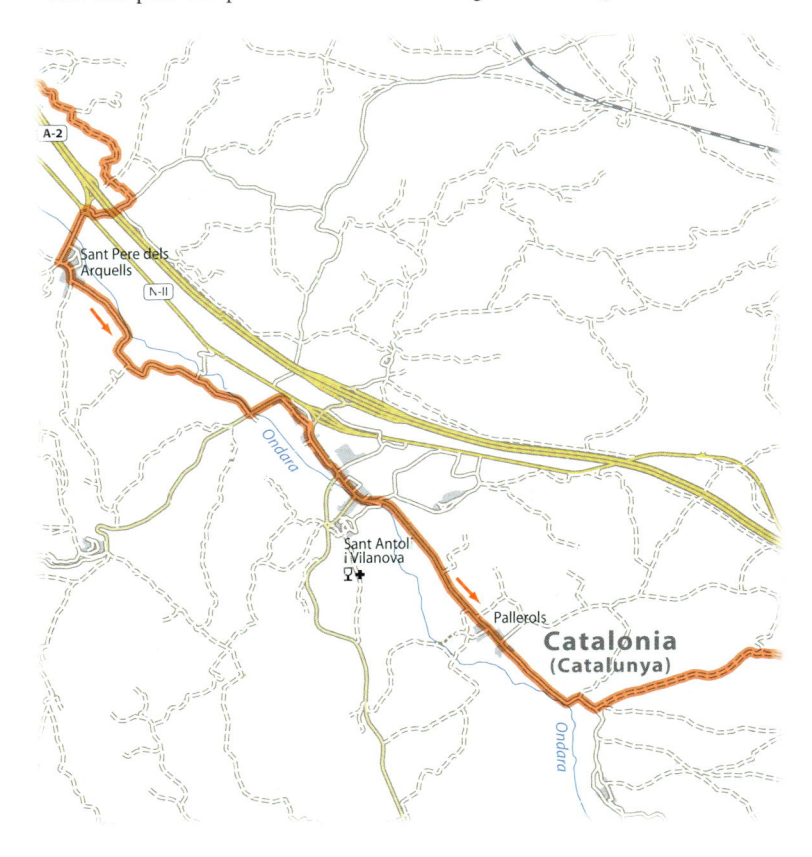

CERVERA–IGUALADA

▲ Look out for the abandoned military aircraft in Sant Pere dels Arquells *MS*

one of over 200 registered in Catalonia. Historical records document this game being played as far back as the 14th century. Note also the old communal clothes-washing facility (Safareig de Vergós) on your right and the church on your left as the road leads you out of town, staying parallel with the N-II. In less than 1km, cross this main road diagonally

STAGE 25

to reach a tunnel under the A-2 and, once through, follow the signs to the right for Igualada.

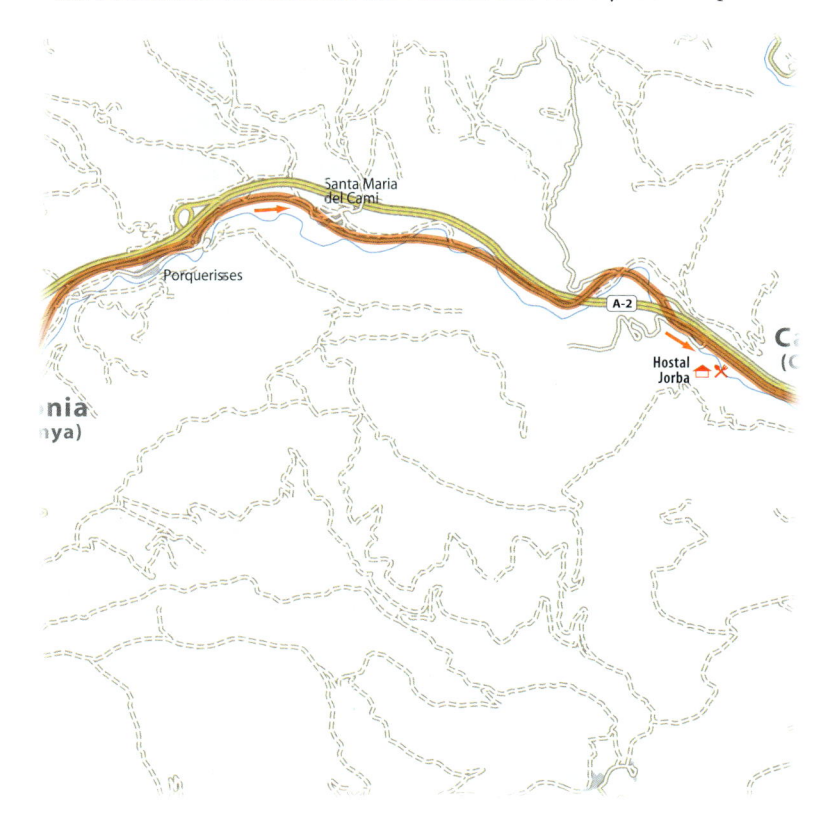

After a further 1km, your path leads to the left, away from the highway, and takes you on a loop that will then reconnect you with it after another 1km. On reaching a junction, you turn right by a quarry and again cross the A-2 via an underpass. Reaching a roundabout, continue into the village of **Sant Pere dels Arquells**. Look out to your left and prepare for a double take. Yes, there really *are* a few jet aircraft abandoned in a field, but you have not stumbled across a secret military plot: they are simply the property of a collector, awaiting restoration. A few metres beyond these curiosities, turn sharp left and, as you cross through and prepare to leave Sant Pere, take a left fork and continue into countryside on asphalt with fields on your right and low agricultural buildings on your left. The road ends after around 2km at a T-junction where you turn left, crossing the Ondara once more. On approach to the N-II once more, turn right in front of it and enter **Sant Antolí i Vilanova** village which you traverse without any deviation from the road. Cross a roundabout and continue on the same road, the LV-2302, to Pallerols just 1.5km further. Less than 1km beyond town, turn left on to a signposted path through a wooded area and continue uphill for 2km to reach **La Panadella** service area. A service area might not sound like a great choice for an overnight stay, but this quirky place is efficient and has some character (page 235). It's a welcome refreshment stop even if you're continuing your journey today.

When you're ready to continue, pass through all the services to reach a roundabout and carry on straight ahead, signed now for Sant Maria del Camí. Once over the roundabout, note the by-now-familiar Camino Ignaciano signpost indicating that Igualada is still a hefty 23.2km away. Although you are now walking on the main N-II road, it is almost devoid of traffic at this point thanks to the parallel A-2 highway that runs up above, taking all the heavy vehicles. After 5km of easy downhill walking, a sign directs you down to the right into the hamlet of **Porquerisses** (no

STAGE 25

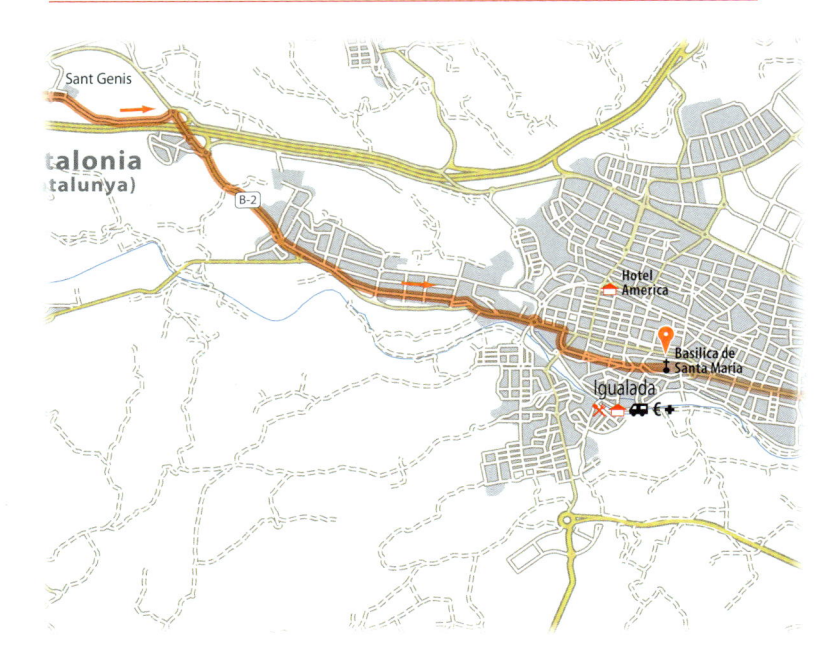

services); you can choose to follow it or simply stay on the main road and save a couple of hundred metres, as this little diversion serves little purpose and soon rejoins the N-II. Next you reach **Sant Maria del Camí** and, on exiting this 12th-century village, you can again continue straight down the quiet N-II, ignoring another unnecessary 'loop' which this time leaves on the left.

After KM marker 541, the N-II leads across the A-2 on a bridge, and 500m later you cross this busy road again, this time via an underpass to reach a petrol station and the **Hostal Jorba** (see opposite), with its rooms, bar and restaurant. Beyond this service area, continue as before to the right of the two highways, using the cycle path to avoid any traffic and reaching a roundabout where you turn right, continuing on the N-II. It is fortunate here that the heavy traffic prefers to use the A-2 and the cyclists spurn the cycle path in favour of the N-II, thus leaving the path for pilgrims. On reaching a roundabout over the A-2 and its slip roads, carefully cross it to take the exit opposite for **Jorba** village, passing another service area. The route now leads straight through town and, on exiting it, take an immediate turn-off to the right, signed for Sant Genís and Igualada.

After 1km or so, on a clear day, you will get your first sight of the stunning, jagged Montserrat mountain range that you will meet in close-up tomorrow. Shortly after, choose the bend in the road to the right, passing through **Sant Genís** village on Carrer Major and descending for 1km to a bridge across the A-2. Once over the bridge, proceed straight ahead at a roundabout, signed for Santa Margarida de Montbui. Continue downhill, eventually making use of a parallel road, the Carrer Felicia Matheu de Padró, to avoid the traffic, and on reaching a roundabout, continue ahead once more into **Igualada**. The road becomes the quiet, tree-lined Carrer de Jaume Serra i Iglesias and at its end, you dog-leg slightly right to continue on to Carrer de les Alzines, which merges back on to the main road. Descend to a busy roundabout, continuing straight ahead on Avinguda de Angel Guimerà. On reaching a petrol station, turn immediately right after it and cross a road junction to continue straight ahead on Carrer de Sant Ignaci as it becomes Carrer de Sant Domenech. At its end, this reaches Plaça de la Creu and the small Carrer de l'Argent, which leads off to the Santa Maria Basilica and the town centre.

WHERE TO STAY AND EAT Due to limited accommodation in Igualada, booking a few days in advance is advisable.

Hostal Bayona (40 rooms) On the A-2 highway, La Panadella; 938 09 20 11; e bayona@panadella.com. The best choice if you are splitting this stage into 2. A large friendly, lively hostel, with a restaurant much used by truckers. Good-sized rooms, some with bath, all with Wi-Fi. Basic but very acceptable with a real buzz & character about it. B/fast, lunch & dinner all available. Open 24/7; pilgrim discounts on request. €22/44 sgl/dbl

Hostal Jorba (20 rooms) On the N-II highway, KM 543; 938 09 00 52. Another option if you are splitting this stage into 2. Opens daily year-round for all meals. €20/40 sgl/dbl

Hotel America (34 rooms) Avinguda Mestre Montaner 44, Igualada; 938 03 10 00; e info@hotel-america.es; w www.hotel-america.es. A little way northwest of the centre, a big modern hotel with bar, restaurant & decent-sized, good-value AC rooms. €40/65 sgl/dbl

Refugi de Pelegrins (Pilgrims' Hostel) (12 beds) Carrer Prat de la Riba 47, Igualada; 938 04 55 15; e refugiigualada@aj-igualada.net. Reservations accepted, keys to be collected from Avinguda Gaudi 26, nearby. The refuge is located in the 'House of the Vigilartes of the Old Slaughterhouse'. The mind boggles. €10 pp

Somiatruites (7 rooms) Carrer del Sol 19, Igualada; 938 03 66 26; w somiatruites.eu. In the city's old tannery district, an upmarket, architect-designed choice. Bright, light-filled rooms all have a terrace & it has its own top-quality restaurant. Quality is reflected in the price. €85/105 sgl/dbl

✗ Exquisit Carrer Sant Josep 18, Igualada; 938 06 68 59; w restaurantexquisit.

STAGE 25

LANGUAGE AND IDENTITY: OILING THE WHEELS OR PUTTING A SPANNER IN THE WORKS?

We English speakers are very fortunate. Almost everywhere we venture, we will find someone who speaks our language. Speaking English does not automatically bestow any national identity on the speaker; to a non-English-speaking stranger, we could be English, American or Australian. Accents help, but a non-native English speaker may not be able to distinguish between them. Thanks to the influences of Hollywood pop music and the temporary supremacy of the British and American empires, English has become the default tongue of the world. The French would like it to be otherwise, but…

Protection of a language helps preserve the identity of its speakers, but it also inevitably puts up a barrier, often insurmountable, to the casual visitor. In many tourist destinations where a regional language is strong, it can be heartening to see that money has been spent in creating expensive information panels telling visitors about local history and culture. But those panels are sometimes only in the local language, meaning the knowledge that is imparted is lost to everyone except locals. A native Spaniard or competent Spanish speaker could make a

com. Generally accepted as one of the best restaurants in town & an opportunity to taste Catalan cuisine, combining the traditional with innovation. Vegetarians catered for. Weekday lunchtime menus are super value. A popular place, booking advisable. €16

TOURIST INFORMATION

Tourist office Carrer Garcia Fossas 2, Igualada; 938 01 91 16; w www.igualada.cat or anoiaturisme.cat; 19.00–21.00 Tue–Fri, 11.00–14.00 & 18.00–21.00 Sat–Sun

WHAT TO SEE Although there are only two stages left to walk, those who decide to pause here will discover that the city has a couple of quirky museums that are worth a visit. First up is the **Museu de Traginer Igualada** (Traginers 5; w museudeltraginer.com; 09.00–17.00 Tue–Sat, 10.00–17.00 Sun; €4.50), the city's Muleteer Museum dedicated to the role that four-legged beasts such as oxen, mules and horses have played in Catalonia's history. Secondly, those yearning for a swift return to their childhood might prefer a trip down memory lane with the **Railhome BCN Igualada** (Carrer d'Alemanya 43; w railhome.com; guided tours only, see website for details; €9), a private museum

fist of understanding Catalan text, for example, but others would have little chance. Few outsiders would understand Welsh or Basque.

As a Scot, I know that our Gaelic and old Scots languages are peripheral to our identity as perceived by the outside world. Instead, we have things that we can readily share. Any visitor to Edinburgh can listen to the bagpipes (and often they have no choice!) and anyone can enjoy watching *Braveheart* or sipping a whisky. Anyone can wear a kilt, if they really want to. Easily accessible to everyone, these are all globally recognised symbols, (usually) appreciated and require little interpretation.

If all your identity eggs are placed in the language basket, then connecting with the outside world becomes an issue. As a visitor, unless you speak the native language, you will derive very little from staring at Catalan-only information panels in quaint, historic Cervera, for example. But it's worth considering that it might be a price worth paying to preserve a language and a culture, which might otherwise disappear. And as a visitor, you can always visit the tourist office for more information.

which sports an impressive collection of model-size trains and life-sized railway-related accessories.

TRANSPORT Trains run eastwards from Igualada to Barcelona, with the rail service here being operated by the local Catalan company, FGC (**w** fgc.cat). There is no westbound option, so to backtrack to Lleida or beyond, you'll need a bus (**w** alsa.com).

Taxis
Taxi Juan Javier Montiel (Igualada) **m** 605 07 33 47
Taxi Marcial (Igualada) 938 04 55 03
Taxis Igualada (Igualada) **m** 609 47 82 19; **w** taxisigualada.com

26 IGUALADA–MONTSERRAT

A comparatively hard-ish stage that takes you to mighty Montserrat Monastery, a massive tourist draw that attracts 2 million visitors annually, cowering in its spectacular rocky environment. The setting is truly incredible and allowing time today or tomorrow to take a tour is thoroughly recommended. Although this stage demands more ascent and descent than anything since the Ignaciano crossed the Basque Mountains four weeks ago, it is much less arduous than those early stages and will carry no great challenge for the reasonably fit walker.

Start Igualada (Basilica de Santa Maria)
Coordinates 41.57866, 1.61843
Finish Montserrat Monastery
Difficulty Moderate/hard
Distance 27.5km
Duration 7hrs
Ascent 875m
Descent 460m

THE ROUTE The route starts out eastwards on Carrer del Roser which continues as Carrer de la Soledat and then Avinguda de Caresmar, before angling slightly left to become Avinguda de Montserrat. Cross the train tracks, with the station just off to your left, and after 400m take a right at traffic lights, picking up the familiar orange arrows. You climb to a roundabout, at which you continue straight ahead and stay on this road as it ploughs through a giant industrial estate, crossing two roundabouts and, at the third in front of the highway, you turn sharp left on to an old road heading away from the traffic. A sign for the Camí Ignasí (Catalan for Camino Ignaciano) now indicates you are on the way to Ca n'Alzina and Montserrat and you stay on this tarmac road to cross the A-2 highway via an underpass. Shortly after, you cross through another underpass, from where the tarmac leads upwards to cross the A-2 yet again, this time via a bridge. On the other side, turn left and reach a roundabout where you continue straight ahead, downhill. You merge into a larger road which joins from the right, then after only 50m take a right turn on to a narrower road leading into **Ca n'Alzina** village. This same road soon takes you into the larger adjacent village of **Castellolí**, with bars, restaurants and a pharmacy.

Your route leads you straight through and out again, as you climb with the A-2 road still to the left. After 500m, the road splits into three forks; choose the tarmacked middle option. Just as it appears that you are about

STAGE 26

to collide with the highway, veer right on a rougher, older road. Within 1km, you are directed left up a steep, narrow, short path to meet a bridge and yet again cross the A-2. Continue straight ahead, but after the first zig-zag in the road, leave it behind and take a signposted dirt path to the left through beautiful woods. After 1km of climbing through the trees, the path reaches a T-junction and turns left to join the main road a few metres later. Turn left on to this, but only briefly. Already you begin to get great panoramas over the heavily wooded landscapes of Catalonia. Having just rejoined the road, at the following bend you take a poorly signposted path off to your left to re-enter the forest. This narrow path continues to climb gently through the trees and, after 100m, reaches a clearing where the jagged peaks of Montserrat present themselves for inspection once again.

Follow a right-hand path, with the main road visible on your right, and at the next junction turn left. The path is now a wide dirt path parallel with the road below. At a cultivated area, you fork right towards some houses. Pass between them on tarmac for 100m on Carrer

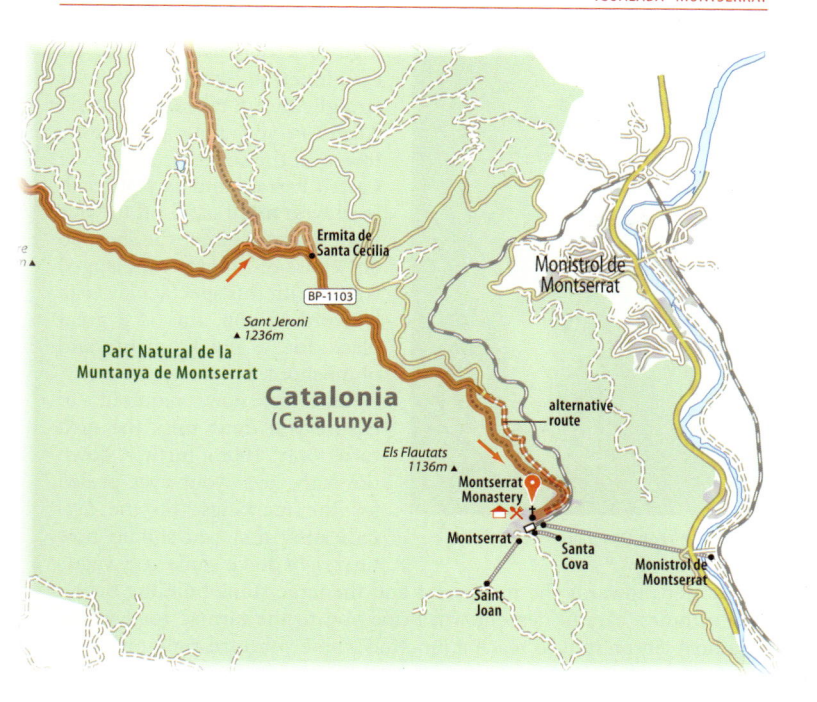

Castellolí then turn left on to Carrer Verge de Montserrat and follow this long residential road for some time, as it rises, dips, bends and rises again. This is the **Montserrat Park** settlement, still some distance from our destination. Reaching a junction, turn left to find you are still on the Verge de Montserrat; after 500m the road ends at a crossroads where you continue straight ahead, now signposted for Can Masana. Pass through the pretty settlement of **Sant Pau de la Guàrdia**, home to two restaurants; at the second one veer left to join a dirt path. Enjoy the fantastic mountain vistas from here before forking left again, with an equestrian centre down below to your right, then fork immediately left once more. This wide path rises and this time you ignore a left fork, still enjoying panoramic views to the right. You pass the village **cemetery** to your left and after more views – off to the left this time – the path climbs more steeply as you share your camino with many other local and national paths, evidenced by multitudinous, multicoloured waymarking to complement the natural hues of the wild thyme and heathers. Pine scents fill your nostrils, helping you to forget the busy

STAGE 26

▲ The Camí dels Degotalls *MS*

highways of earlier stages. At a T-junction with views now straight ahead, take the left fork. Ahead of you, note a tall stone tower on the summit. This is the **Castell Ferran**, and as you reach level with it – it's still off to your right – you will get the 'best so far' views of Montserrat's jagged teeth. With this spectacular vista in front of you, this is a great place for a break, drink and photoshoot.

Care is now required to ensure you don't miss the next turn: only 100m further down the path, keep your eyes peeled for the markings (on the *left*) indicating that you should now turn *right* down some very vague rocky steps towards the main road and the large stone building below. Ten minutes' careful descent will bring you to the tarmac road where you turn left on to it to reach a junction where you turn right on to the BP-1103 road, signed for Montserrat. At this point, don't get distracted by other signs for Montserrat, as these will take you on longer, steeper mountain paths which are outside the scope of this book, as they are not recommended for pilgrims. Your route to the end of this stage is now along this road, with 9km to walk to the monastery. Depending on the time of year, it could be deathly quiet or nose-to-tail vehicles.

After passing through a tunnel, you soon see a monastery down to your left... but this is not Montserrat! Later on you pass close to the **Ermita de Santa Cecilia**, on your left and then, after the 6km road marker, you approach a second tunnel, but can avoid walking through it by taking a path to the left that skirts around it. Beyond the 7km marker, look out for **Camí dels Degotalls** signed off to your right; despite it being a longer route, this path is recommended for pilgrims, certainly in periods of high vehicle traffic, and will bring you out by the Montserrat cafeteria. It runs along parallel with the road below, offers some shade, better views and is decorated with ceramic commemorations of people's pilgrimages from across Spain. If you choose to continue by the road, you will reach the monastery a bit quicker, but will have to traverse the enormous visitor car parks.

🏠 **WHERE TO STAY AND EAT** Given the relative isolation of the monastery and the high numbers of visitors in peak periods, it is best to book your accommodation well in advance. The site has a restaurant, bar, café and self-service cafeteria. Note that neither accommodation has any air conditioning, but the altitude means that this is rarely a problem.

🏠 **Pilgrim Refuge** (14 beds) Centre de Coordinació, at the monastery site; ↘938 77 77 77; **e** ccpastoral@santuari-montserrat.com. The pilgrims' refuge has now closed. Pilgrims are now accommodated in dormitory accommodation at the Abat Oliba (below) but need to present themselves at this centre first. Sheets, but no blankets. Free Wi-Fi; b/fast inc, pilgrim's menu (€10) in evening. Cooking facilities. *€8pp, reservations advisable*

🏠 **Alberg Abat Oliba** (60 rooms) Plaça Abat Oliba, Montserrat Monestir; ↘938 77 77 01; **e** reserves@larsa-montserrat.com. On the monastery site, cheaper & more basic than its sister hotel (below), but with everything you need. A slightly institutional feel. Large rooms with bunk beds, plus private rooms. B/fast inc. Restaurant nearby. *€58 sgl or dbl*

🏠 **Hotel Abat Cisneros Montserrat** (82 rooms) Montserrat Monastery; ↘938 77 77 01; **e** reserves@larsa-montserrat.com. A 3-star hotel, right on site next to the monastery. Rooms have heating; Wi-Fi in public areas. B/fast inc; bar & restaurant. *€75/110 sgl/dbl*

TOURIST INFORMATION

ℹ️ **Information office** (Monastery) ↘938 77 77 77; **e** informacio@larsa-montserrat.com; **w** montserratvisita.com. Tickets for visiting the site can be purchased at **w** tickets.montserratvisita.com/en.

WHAT TO SEE Arriving here late in the afternoon and leaving early the following morning will give you little time to experience all that Montserrat has to offer, so two nights here are recommended if your timetable and budget allow. After all, this is one of Spain's top tourist attractions.

Montserrat has suffered like many Spanish religious sites, with its destruction by Napoleon's invading army in the Peninsular War, the confiscation of monastic properties following legislation in 1835 (only one monk remained after that!) and more woe during the Spanish Civil War. But each time it has bounced back, with reconstruction and renewal.

A good place to start your visit to Montserrat is the **Espai Audiovisual (Audiovisual Space),** located opposite the funicular railway station, where an English-language video sets you up with a great introduction to the mountain, the monastery and the UNESCO Global Geopark of Central Catalonia. Today around 80 monks from the Benedictine order occupy the monastery. An iron sculpture of St Benedict stands guard over the entrance to the part of the monastery barred to visitors.

Montserrat's **basilica** is a mainly Gothic structure, with Renaissance touches and influences of traditional Catalan architecture. One of its many chapels is dedicated to Ignatius of Loyola, while a history of Montserrat is depicted on one of the walls of the basilica's atrium. As you enter the basilica, you'll see queues on the right-hand side to see *The Black Madonna*, a wooden sculpture known as *La Moreneta* that is said to have been carved in Jerusalem. Revered by the many pilgrims who visit, it sits behind glass, but one hand holding a symbol of the globe protrudes, inviting you to touch or kiss it. Visiting in the afternoon is advised, otherwise you could wait up to 45 minutes.

The **Escolanía choirboys** (**w** www.escolania.cat) sing in the basilica twice a day (at 13.00 and at vespers) on weekdays and at various times at weekends, but they are absent in July. The Sunday mass is the best time to listen, but pre-booking through the tourist office or online is required, due to their popularity. Documentary evidence shows that this liturgical choir dates back at least as far as 1307. An on-site school provides them with general education as well as musical formation. It is worth checking their website, as their reputation means they are often in demand to perform abroad.

▼ *La Moreneta – The Black Madonna* C/S

If you want to stretch your legs (!), there are plenty of opportunities to follow short walking trails around the site. The mountains are dotted with hermitages, and a funicular railway leads higher up to within easy walking distance of **Sant Joan**. Another leads to **Santa Cova (Holy Grotto)**, where legend states *La Moreneta* was concealed from the Moors during the time of Islamic dominance of the Iberian Peninsula – and where it was then rediscovered by shepherds towards the end of the 9th century. Montserrat's current status as a site of pilgrimage is down to this rediscovery.

Art lovers won't want to miss the **Museu de Montserrat** (✆ 938 77 77 45), home to works by luminaries such as Caravaggio

▲ Looking out over Montserrat's monastery CF/CCDB

through to avant-gardes like Dalí and modern artists such as Sisley. Picasso also features strongly: when you see the two phenomenal paintings he did as a young teenager, you see 'genius' defined. Catalan artists are also prominent.

TRANSPORT From the monastery site, there is a cable car (Funicular Aeri de Montserrat) and a rack railway, both of which descend to the town of Monistrol de Montserrat, from where there are frequent trains to Manresa or all stops to Barcelona (Plaça d'Espanya).

Taxis

Marceli de Claret (Monistrol de Montserrat) 938 35 03 84; **m** 607 32 99 46. Probably the closest taxi service for Montserrat Monastery.

Taxi Castelloli (Castellolí) **m** 686 22 93 84

27 MONTSERRAT–MANRESA

Hopefully you will not have over-celebrated on reaching Montserrat (a monastery setting is perhaps not ideal for partying) and remembered that you still have a reasonably hard stage remaining to reach the real objective: Manresa. Once you have partially retraced your steps of yesterday along the tarmac road, you can look forward to a scenic end to your pilgrimage with little interference from traffic on pleasant paths surrounded by pine and, at times, bamboo. Don't let any over-eagerness force your pace, as a fairly significant ascent lies in wait only 7km or so from the stage end. Manresa also awaits, full of Ignatian reference points and replete with plenty of attractions and perhaps a surprise or two. The tourist board have invested heavily to make their Ignatian city visitor-friendly, so if you can treat yourself to a day or two here as reward for your sterling efforts on the camino, then do so. Afterwards, getting to Barcelona and its airport is a very straightforward matter.

Start Montserrat Monastery
Coordinates 41.59331, 1.83768
Finish Manresa (Centre d'Acollida de Pelegrins (Pilgrim Welcome Centre))
Difficulty Moderate/hard
Distance 24.7km
Duration 6hrs 15mins
Ascent 480m
Descent 980m

THE ROUTE Orientation at the start of today's stage is simple, as initially you retrace your steps from the previous stage, either by going straight back along the BP-1103 road or – as is advised for walkers – choosing the Camí dels Degotalls (page 242). This path soon joins the BP-1103 anyway and, just before reaching the Ermita Santa Cecilia hermitage, look out for a concrete road that leads off to the right, signposted GR-4. You pass with the hermitage on your left and descend on a wide dirt track with the BP-1103 road now up above. Today you will see a variety of waymarkings: red and white, yellow and white and blue and white, to accompany the familiar Camino Ignaciano signs and symbols, but the Ignatian route is always clear.

At a left-hand bend, continue straight ahead on a narrower, downward path signposted for Sant Cristòfol, and then soon take a sharp left, again signposted. The path turns to a roughish road among some sizeable

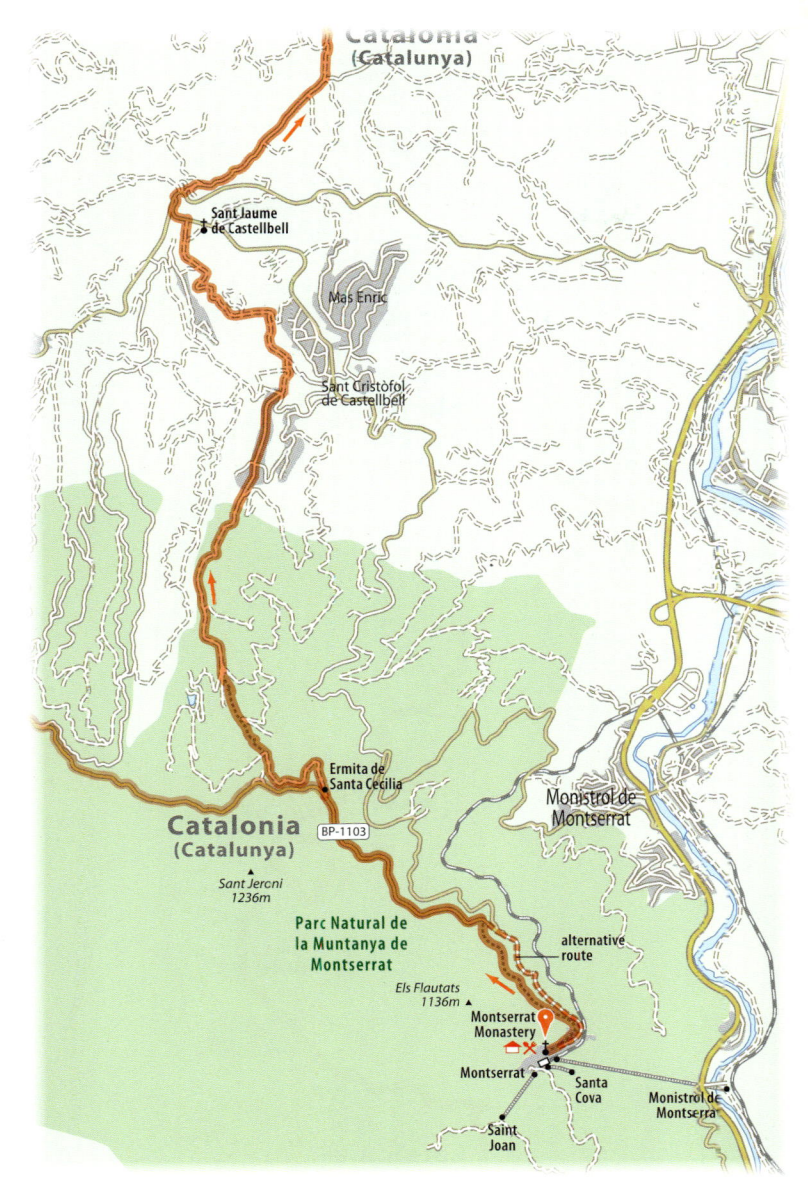

MONTSERRAT–MANRESA

247

STAGE 27

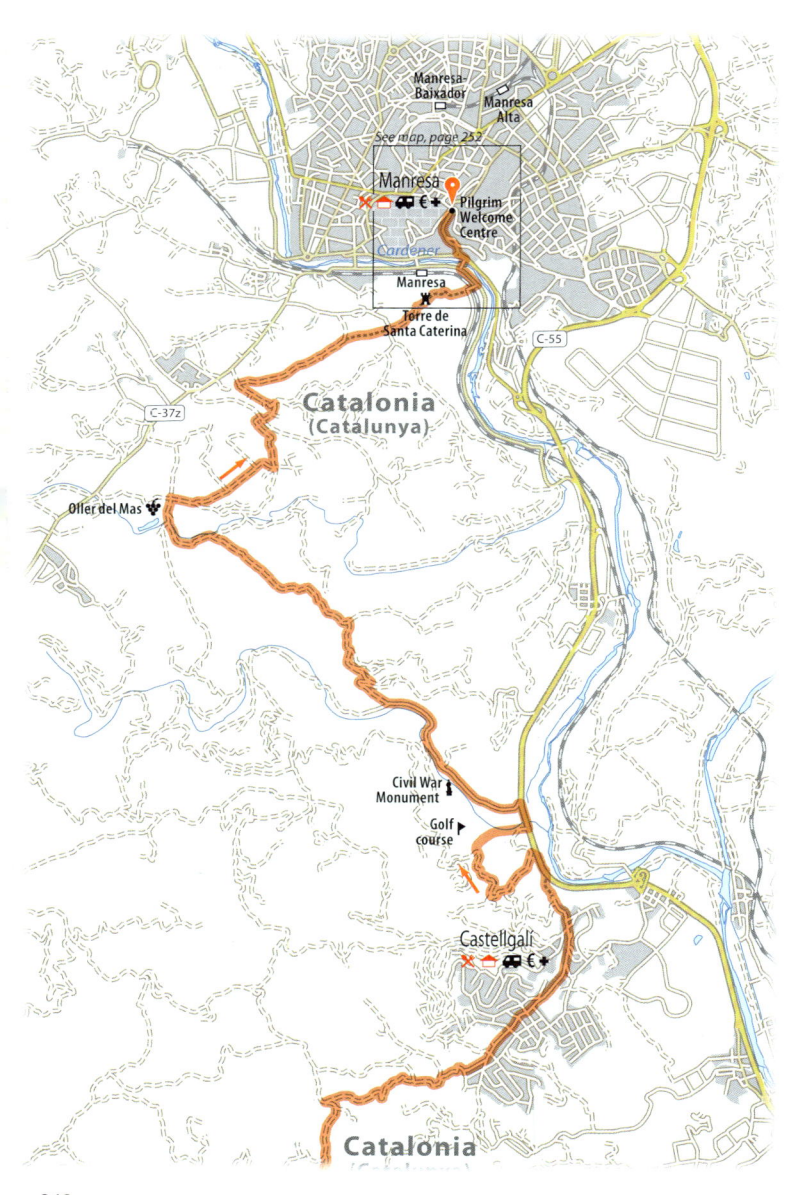

▲ En route to Sant Jaume de Castelbell *MR/MT*

residential properties and you continue on Carrer de les Agulles, still 20 minutes from Sant Cristòfol. At the end of this lengthy road, as it curves right, choose the path signed for Castellgalí and Manresa. Cross with open fields to your left and, reaching a T-junction, ignore the sign for Sant Cristòfol and instead turn left for **Sant Jaume de Castellbell**. Note the peculiar orientation table that soon appears incongruously on your right, set out like a desk with a chair: on a clear day, you can use it to identify each of the jagged peaks of Montserrat, now in front of you. Ignore the wide path to the right – your direction is as before, enjoying the diversity of the vegetation which varies from pine and heather through to wild thyme and even bamboo. Cross a stream bed at a house and ignore the blue-and-white waymarking to the right for the Ermita de Sant Jaume. The path soon meets a road joining from the right and you proceed downhill to a T-junction where you turn right at the El Raco restaurant (usually closed). Immediately beyond the restaurant, turn left for Castellgalí and Manresa.

Your brief flirtation with tarmac today is now over, and the path rises to pass a farm on your left. At a junction of paths, the orange arrows steer you left. Cross a stream and turn sharp right beneath the gaze of an imposing

STAGE 27

Catalan farmhouse. Shortly beyond, on a right-hand curve, leave the wide track to briefly enter woods, following blue-and-white signage, then turn left on to a new wide track. You rise to a T-junction and turn right on to another wide track that soon veers left, where the first buildings of **Castellgalí** make their appearance. There is a refugi here (page 253), and its adjacent swimming pool might tempt you to stay the night and prolong your camino for an extra day. Your route enters town, and you turn left

A MODEST MONUMENT

Much has been written about the Spanish Civil War, fact and fiction. As with many events in history, separating the two can be difficult. Spain still bears the scars of the conflict, and the tension that has simmered away over the decades can occasionally erupt to confirm that the country has not quite come to terms with the brutal struggle that decimated and divided it in the late 1930s. Witness the national debate that was reignited only a few years ago over whether General Franco's bones should be moved from his tomb at the wistfully named Valle de los Caídos ('Valley of the Fallen') north of Madrid. That huge site boasts the world's tallest stone cross, a Benedictine abbey, hospice and a religious school.

In 2019, over 40 years after the dictator's death, his coffin was indeed eventually unearthed and taken by helicopter to be reburied in the El Pardo cemetery near Madrid. But only a fraction over half of Spain's members of parliament had voted to have Franco's body dug up; nearly half of them abstained. One body may have now gone from the Valle, but over 33,000 still remain there, all victims of the conflict. They are the silent witnesses to a dark, dark period in Spain's recent history.

Elsewhere in the country, bodies are occasionally still being tracked down, and dug from ditches or unearthed from the depths of forests before being reburied. Now, as you pause a couple of kilometres beyond Castellgalí, you are standing before a much more modest monument to victims of the war. On 27 July 1936, two nuns by the names of Rosa Josefa Jutglar i Gallach and Regina Pilar Pica i Planas were taken by militiamen from a nearby house and executed. Compared with the imposing edifices at the Valle de los Caídos, this monument erected by the side of a Catalan walking trail is insubstantial. But it is sobering, and at least these two innocents have not been forgotten. Spain's slow healing process continues.

▲ Manresa's Santuari de la Cova and Basilica de la Seu *TG/MT*

on to tarmac where clear pavement signing leads you through. Castellgalí has a few bars and restaurants for those in need. Your next waypoint is the town's handsome church, which you soon pass on your right, before continuing straight downhill to the end of town to find a narrow path that descends beside a row of electricity pylons. This is in fact an old pilgrim route from the 12th century, long pre-dating Ignatius. At the foot of this, turn left on to the busy C-55 and, after a few hundred metres, turn left again on to a path that leads into the adjacent woods on a loop that passes one side of a golf course before returning to the main road. Having reached the road, after only 200m beside the traffic turn left again to thankfully leave it behind. Walk along the other side of the golf course and then above the waters of the river below. Perhaps this is a surprising place to find a reminder to the Spanish Civil War, but the monument you see here gives cause for thought and reflection (see box, opposite).

The road soon forks right towards some cliffs (beware rockfalls after rain) and you walk directly beneath them to soon pass a huge house on your left as the path begins to ascend. Now your pilgrim's resolve will be tested as the route zig-zags up until you reach a cultivated area and eventually the summit at a junction, where you turn left to continue. After only 400m, your climbing is rewarded by the sight of still-distant Manresa off to the right. Descend through pine and mixed forest; the route appears to be heading in the wrong direction, but soon curves right to orientate you towards your goal. Immediately past the **Oller del Mas** vineyard and castle

STAGE 27

(see box, page 254), turn sharp right along a wide dirt track with Manresa (at last) straight ahead and reassuringly in your sights.

Continue ahead, leaving a large stone house to your left and descending on concrete before turning sharp left on a tree-lined dirt and stone path that takes you downhill as it twists and turns. On exiting this tree-covered path, turn right to cross a stream on a concrete bridge and turn right again at the bridge end to follow the sign up to the left for **Manresa**. Follow a wide dirt road to the left, and left again, as you pass another grand, stone house. After 200m, turn sharp right, crossing between fields, continuing ahead as your path becomes rougher and narrower. It narrows again as a dry-stone wall flanks you to the left and you cross a road with now only 3km to go.

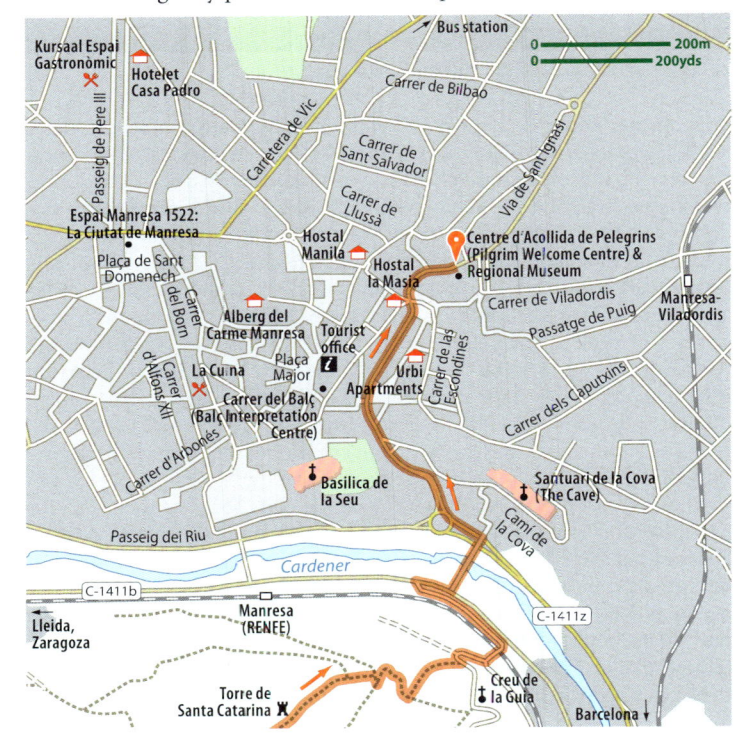

Follow the first sign for the **Torre de Santa Caterina** – often proudly flying the Catalan flag – 300m ahead, and pass with it on your left to descend on a grassy path that becomes steps. At the foot of the descent, turn left and then right to cross the railway on the road bridge. With the railway on your left and the river to your right, you now cross the latter on the old arched bridge. At the end of the bridge, follow the signpost for the Centre d'Acollida de Pelegrins (Pilgrim Welcome Centre) and take the short uphill road to turn left and then right on to Carrer de Montserrat to carry on uphill for a few hundred metres to reach the centre and get your certificate. Congratulations – you have made it!

WHERE TO STAY AND EAT

Alberg del Carme Manresa (85 beds) Plaça Milcentenari; 938 75 03 96; e alberg.manresa@gencat.cat; w xanascat.gencat.cat. Dorm beds & rooms, sheets & blankets, but not towels provided. B/fast available at extra cost, but no cooking facilities. Reservations advisable. *€13–17 dorm, €30/45 sgl/dbl*

Hostal la Masia (6 rooms) Plaça Sant Ignasi 21; 938 72 42 37; m 633 84 80 04; e info@lamasiamanresa.com. Close to the city centre, very close to the Pilgrim Welcome Centre. Basic but acceptable. *€35/40 sgl/dbl*

Hostal Manila (8 rooms) Carrer Sant Andreu 9; 938 72 59 98; e reservasmanila.gmail.com. Very central, though in a slightly rough-&-ready neighbourhood. *€35/45 sgl/dbl*

Hotelet Casa Padro Passeig de Pere III 38; 938 72 37 51; w hoteletmanresa.com. Housed in a beautifully renovated Catalan Art Nouveau-style building, retaining many period touches, this is the city's boutique/upmarket choice. Relaxing roof terrace bar, spacious rooms. B/fast inc. *€115–150*

Oller del Mas (22 cabins) Carretera d'Igualada (C-37z) KM91; 938 76 83 15; e enoturisme@ollerdelmas.com; w ollerdelmas.com. A couple of relaxing nights here & you would soon forget about your 675km journey. An upmarket place, a short taxi ride from Manresa, surrounded by vineyards & forest, steeped in history. Accommodation in luxury detached cabins in the woods. Winery, restaurant, pitch & putt, horseriding, gym & seasonal pool on site. See box, page 254. 2-night min stay. *€230 sgl or dbl*

Refugi Castellgallí (18 beds) In Castellgalí, signposted off the route, 10km before Manresa; m 628 99 64 00; e todolimr@diba.cat or casalculturaldecastellgali@gmail.com; w refugipelegrinscastellgali.com/inicic. Run by the enthusiastic municipality, a recent creation in a chunky, rustic building. Microwaves, fridge & blankets all available. Public swimming pool next door (Jun–end Aug). *€10*

Urbi Apartments (47 apts) Carrer de la Codinella 9; m 608 56 61 26; e reservas@urbigrup.com; w urbi-apartments.com/ca. Fully renovated & spacious apartments in an 18th-century building. Very central. Apartments have washing machines/dryers. *€70 sgl or dbl*

✕ Kursaal Espai Gastronòmic Passeig de Pere III 35; 938 72 21 88. In the elegant, Modernist theatre building, a popular choice among locals. Occasional wine-themed evenings with tasting menus. Paella is a favourite, but the set menus at lunch (€16) & dinner (€22) are best value. Outdoor terrace or AC interior. *€15*

THE WINES OF CATALONIA

While Rioja and Ribera del Duero reds and Galician whites such as Alberino are probably Spain's internationally best-known still wines, it is left to Catalonia to provide the celebratory bubbles with its famous, good-time Cava. Admittedly, it is also produced in Aragón, La Rioja and elsewhere in Spain, but Catalonia is the sparkling wine's undisputed heartland. And despite 150 years of history, and the strict adherence to the traditional processes of the *méthode champenoise* (second fermentation), Cava producers are far from stuck in the past. Much of the growth is already organic, and there is a commitment that by 2025 all Reserva, Gran Reserva and Paraje Calificado categories of Cava will be of certified organic production.

The Camino Ignaciano happily ends its route in the wine region of Pla de Bages, one of the 12 appellations or designated wine regions of Catalonia. Here in this central area surrounding Manresa, the privilege of a DO (Designation of Origin) was only regained as recently as 1995. Over a century ago, the phylloxera plague destroyed most of the vines in this area, but a painstaking and determined plan to replant much of the vine growth has thankfully resulted in restoring and then maintaining a small but high-quality industry. Pla de Bages is indeed small, hosting only 15 of Catalonia's 600 wineries.

One peculiarity of the area's wine history is the lasting presence of distinctive dry-stone huts, used in times gone by for the barefoot crushing of grapes. As an experiment, this traditional method has even been revived in recent years by one Catalan wine producer.

One winery worth stopping in en route to Manresa is the award-winning **Oller del Mas** (968 73 83 15; **w** ollerdelmas.com). Its vineyards surround a rather grand, stately looking, beautifully restored medieval castle, well worthy of a visit. Oller del Mas perfectly embraces the happy marriage between the old and new, claiming a thousand years of history, while embracing modernity with an on-trend, all-organic production for its reds and whites. And in terms of wine tourism, Oller de Mas offers the full package with winery tours, hotel packages (page 253), pitch and putt, horseriding, pool and a top-quality restaurant. Wine-loving walkers looking to reward themselves at the end of the Ignaciano: take note.

✕ **La Cuina** Carrer d'Alfons XII 18; 938 72 89 69. One of the city's best restaurants, with a semi-formal dining room & classic cuisine. *Menu del diá* is a bargain, à la carte will hike the cost, but rarely disappoints. €18

TOURIST INFORMATION

Centre d'Acollida de Pelegrins (Pilgrim Welcome Centre) Via Sant Ignasi 40; 938 74 11 55; 10.00–18.00 daily. This is where you get the final stamp in your pilgrim's passport & pick up your certificate of completion, available in various languages.

Tourist office Plaça Major 10; 938 78 40 90; w manresaturisme.cat; mid-Sep–end Mar 10.00–14.00 daily & 17.00–19.00 Fri–Sat, Apr–mid-Sep 10.00–14.00 & 17.00–19.00 Tue–Sat, 10.00–14.00 Sun, Mon & hols. Dispenses the usual maps, good information in English & employs some English speakers. Make it your first port of call.

WHAT TO SEE At journey's end, whether you are a Jesuit or not, take a day or two in Gothically splendid Manresa to discover its attractions. There is, of course, always the temptation to rush off to Barcelona, just down the road, but save that for a separate occasion. For those who are interested in furthering their knowledge of Ignatius and the Jesuits, there are no fewer than 22 Ignatian sites detailed in the tourist office's publications and map. A few of these are listed on the following pages.

▼ The Santuari de la Cova is an undoubted highlight of the route CF/CCDB

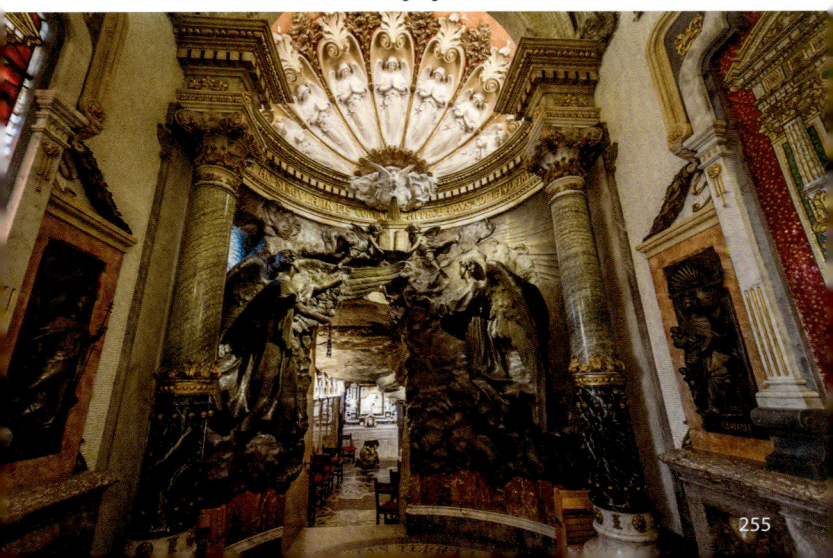

STAGE 27

Aside from those, a wander around the **Passeig de Pere III** area with its impressive Modernist architecture is also recommended. This beautiful, tree-lined avenue is where locals gather to drink and chat – a hugely civilised place with all the vibrant life of Manresa out on display.

Manresa pulls its weight when it comes to festivals, with the principal ones being the **Festa de la Llum** (Feast of Light) on 21 February, and the **Festa Major** ('Big' Festival), which takes place in late August or early September. Full details of these and others are on the tourist board website (**w** manresaturisme.cat). **St Ignatius Day** is 31 July, the day of his death in 1556.

Santuari de la Cova (Sanctuary of the Cave)

(Camí de la Cova 17; **w** covamanresa.cat) Together on the same site as the 19th-century Centre of Ignatian Spirituality, this has expanded in stages over the years, and the current building now energises and fills the line of sight of the weary Ignatian pilgrims as they prepare to enter the city. From the exterior, visitors can admire the building's Baroque façade and Catalan Baroque/Jesuit architecture. Once inside, arguably the church's main attraction is now the stunning display of mosaics (see photo, below), created as recently as 2020 by Slovenian artist and Jesuit, Marko Rupnik. The beauty of his work here is enough on its own to make a visit to the sanctuary a 'must'. Once through the church, the antechamber was once the place of worship, but now serves as the entrance hall to the cave. Notable here is the early 20th-century decoration, courtesy of another Jesuit, Martin Coronas. The cave itself can be found beyond the antechamber: it is small and features Joan Grau's alabaster altarpiece, which shows Saint Ignatius writing his *Spiritual Exercises*.

▼ One of Marko Rupnik's impressive mosaics MS

Basilica de la Seu

(Baixada de la Seu 1; **w** seudemanresa.cat) Sharing the skyline with the cave as you descend into Manresa, this Catalan Gothic church is the work of architect Berenguer de Montagut. Building work began in 1322, some 21 years after the council

IGNATIUS AND MANRESA

Although he was a Basque and his roots were in Loyola, now a distant 675km away, it is with the Catalan city of Manresa that Ignatius will surely be linked in perpetuity. For Jesuits across the world, this is a very special place. And for those pilgrims and other walkers who decide to linger in this historic city of some 80,000 inhabitants, there are plenty of spiritual reference points with which to connect. In the words of the Argentinian Nobel Laureate, Adolfo Pérez Esquivel, 'Manresa has a treasure in its hands: the stay of San Ignacio in the city.'

Over many centuries, the ravaging effects of the elements on the soft-cliff surroundings of the River Cardener had resulted in a collection of caves, put to good use in the 16th century by hermits who lived in them to pray and contemplate. Ignatian legend has it that the man himself began to write his *Spiritual Exercises* in one of them during his time in the city, though the exact venue is rather uncertain (page 256). Ignatius's time in Manresa was enforced, as his plan to reach Barcelona was thwarted by an outbreak of plague in the city. While his 11 months of waiting were fundamental to the writing of the *Spiritual Exercises* and therefore productive, it was not always a happy time for a man still struggling to come to terms with his conversion. He was ill several times, having punished himself with periods of severe fasting and self-harm. As a result, he suffered from depression and even considered suicide. Thankfully, he was taken care of by a number of Manresan families who helped him on his recovery. On a more positive note, the future saint spent much time looking after the sick and feeding the poor. His Manresan legacy is assured.

had approved its construction and, like many churches, it has been added to across the centuries: the belfry dates from the 16th century, the Capella del Santíssim (Chapel of the Blessed) from the latter half of the 17th. A local architect, Alexander Soler I March, designed the baptistery in the 20th century. Ignatius frequently visited La Seu for confession and spiritual advice.

Carrer del Balç (Balç Street Interpretation Centre) (Baixada del Pòpul)

This is a preserved medieval period street, with poorly lit narrow streets, porched galleries and even a well conspiring to recreate the atmosphere of Manresa in the time of Peter IV 'The Ceremonious' (1319–87). The interpretation centre has an excellent English-language audiovisual display, with various 'talking heads' describing everyday life, and a visit here is highly recommended to all.

Espai Manresa 1522: La Ciutat de Manresa (Manresa 1522 Exhibition: the City of Ignatius) (Carrer Mestre Blanch 4) This exhibition space makes use of the former cloister, which has a subtitled film and shows the city as it was in the early 16th century, the time of Ignatius.

TRANSPORT When you're ready to head home, the airport at Barcelona El Prat is just 65km away and with excellent train connections from Manresa. Make good use of the regional FGC (Ferrocarrils de la Generalitat de Catalonia) network, which operates trains on Line R5 every 20 minutes from 06.00 to 23.00 daily and departs from three stations in town, but *not* from the main train station. The most central of the city's stations is Manresa-Viladordis. If you are visiting Barcelona city, the train will take you all the way to the Plaça Espanya (90 minutes); if you are airport-bound, then take the train as far as Europa I Fira and change on to the metro to reach the airport (allow 2 hours travel time). All details are on **w** fgc.cat. Use the main Manresa station down by the river to travel on Line R12 to Cervera, Lleida and other westwards destinations, and you can also travel to Barcelona city from here on Line R4, but this station does not offer such easy airport connections (**w** rodalies.gencat.cat).

For those returning home by air, you could also consider **Girona Airport** which can be reached by bus from Manresa. There are half-a-dozen services per day, fewer at weekends, with a journey time of 95 minutes. Services are provided by Teisa (**w** teisa-bus.com).

Taxis

Radio Taxi Manresa (Manresa) ☎938 74 40 00

Taxis Manresa (Manresa) ☎938 77 08 77; **w** taxismanresa.cat

Appendix 1

LANGUAGE

It's impossible in the space available to teach you to speak Basque or Catalan, and in truth you are unlikely to be in a situation where you will actually *need* to speak it to get by. A few useful phrases in these two languages are provided on pages 23 and 27 respectively, and you will delight and surprise Basques and Catalans if you use these. Spanish is spoken across all five Autonomous Communities through which the Camino Ignaciano passes, and in some towns and villages you will struggle to find anyone who speaks English. The words and phrases here are chosen as being those that might be of most use to walkers.

SPANISH (CASTILIAN) For the most part, Spanish is pronounced as it is written, which makes it a relatively easy language to learn. Anyone who has watched a Spanish TV chat show will know that Spanish is spoken very quickly and often by two (or more) people at once: understanding what is being said is usually the biggest challenge for non-natives.

VOCABULARY AND PHRASES
Essentials

English	Spanish
Good morning	*Buenos días*
Good afternoon/evening	*Buenas tardes*
Hello	*Hola*
Goodbye	*Adiós*
My name is …	*Me llamo …*
What is your name?	*¿Cómo te llamas?*
I am …	*Yo soy …*
… from England	*… de Inglaterra*
… from Scotland	*… de Escocia*
… from Wales	*… de Gales*
… from Ireland	*… de Irlanda*
… from the United States	*… de los Estados Unidos*
… from Canada	*… de Canada*

APPENDIX 1

… from Australia	… *de Australia*
… from New Zealand	… *de Nueva Zelanda*
How are you?	*¿Cómo estás?*
Pleased to meet you (m/f)	*Encantado/encantada*
Thank you	*Gracias*
Please	*Por favor*
Sorry!	*¡Disculpe!*
You're welcome (don't mention it)	*De nada*
Cheers!	*¡Salud!*
Yes	*Sí*
No	*No*
I don't understand	*No entiendo*
Could you speak slower?	*¿Podría hablar más despacio?*
Have a good trip! (specific to pilgrims)	*¡Buen camino!*

Questions

How?	*¿Cómo?*
What?	*¿Qué?*
Where?	*¿Dónde?*
What is it?	*¿Qué es?*
Which?	*¿Cuál?*
When?	*¿Cuándo?*
Why?	*¿Por qué?*
Who?	*¿Quién?*
How much?	*¿Cuánto?*

Numbers

1	*uno*
2	*dos*
3	*tres*
4	*cuatro*
5	*cinco*
6	*seis*
7	*siete*
8	*ocho*
9	*nueve*
10	*diez*
11	*once*
12	*doce*
13	*trece*
14	*catorce*
15	*quince*
16	*dieciséis*

17	*diecisiete*
18	*dieciocho*
19	*diecinueve*
20	*veinte*
21	*veintiuno*
30	*treinta*
40	*cuarenta*
50	*cincuenta*
60	*sesenta*
70	*setenta*
80	*ochenta*
90	*noventa*
100	*cien*

Time

What time is it?	*¿Qué hora es?*
It's … in the morning/afternoon/at night	*Son las … de la mañana/de la tarde/de la noche*
today	*hoy*
tonight	*esta noche*
tomorrow	*mañana*
yesterday	*ayer*
morning	*mañana*
afternoon	*tarde*
evening	*anochecer*

Days

Monday	*lunes*
Tuesday	*martes*
Wednesday	*miércoles*
Thursday	*jueves*
Friday	*viernes*
Saturday	*sábado*
Sunday	*domingo*

Months

January	*enero*
February	*febrero*
March	*mars*
April	*abril*
May	*mayo*
June	*junio*
July	*julio*
August	*agosto*
September	*septiembre*

October	*octubre*
November	*noviembre*
December	*diciembre*

Getting around – public transport

A (return) ticket to … please	*Un ticket de ida y … vuelta, por favor*
I want to go to …	*Quiero ir a …*
How much is it?	*¿Cuánto cuesta?*
What time is the train/bus to …?	*¿A qué hora es el tren/ autobús para ir a …?*
ticket office	*Taquilla*
timetable	*Horario*
from	*desde*
to	*hasta*
airport	*aeropuerto*
bus	*autobús*
bus station	*estación de autobuses*
plane	*avión*
train	*tren*
train station	*estación de tren*
ferry	*ferry*
car	*coche*
taxi	*taxi*
here	*aquí*
there	*ahí*

Directions

Where is it?	*¿Dónde está?*
go straight ahead	*siga adelante, todo recto*
turn left	*gire a la izquierda*
turn right	*gire a la derecha*
… at the traffic lights	*… en el semáforo*
… at the roundabout	*… en la rotonda*
north	*norte*
south	*sur*
east	*este*
west	*oeste*
behind	*atrás*
in front of	*delante*
near	*cerca*
opposite	*enfrente*

Accommodation

Where is a cheap/ good hotel?	*¿Dónde puedo encontrar un hotel*

LANGUAGE

Do you have any rooms available?	*¿Tiene habitaciones disponibles?*
How much is it per night?	*¿Cuánto es por noche?*
I'd like …	*querría …*
… a single room	*… una habitación individual*
… a double room	*… una habitación doble*
… a room with two beds	*… una habitación con dos camas*
… a dormitory bed	*… una habitación con literas*
What is the Wi-Fi password?	*¿Cuál es la contraseña para el Wi-Fi?*
Is breakfast included?	*¿Está incluido el desayuno?*
How much is breakfast?	*¿Cuánto cuesta el desayuno?*
Are there discounts for pilgrims?	*¿Hay descuentos por peregrinos?*

Food

Do you have a table for … people?	*¿Tiene mesa para … personas?*
I am a vegetarian	*Soy vegetariano*
Please may I have the bill	*La cuenta, por favor*

Basics

bread	*pan*
butter	*mantequilla*
cheese	*queso*
oil	*aceite*
sugar	*azúcar*

Fruit

apples	*manzanas*
bananas	*plátanos*
grapes	*uvas*
lemon	*limón*
melon	*melón*
nectarine	*nectarina*
orange	*naranja*
peach	*melocotón*
pear	*pera*

APPENDIX 1

Vegetables
carrot	*zanahoria*
garlic	*ajo*
onion	*cebolla*
pepper	*pimiento*
potatoes	*patatas*

Fish
anchovies	*anchoas*
cod	*becalao*
hake	*merluza*
monkfish	*rape*
squid	*calamar*

Meat
beef	*carne de vaca*
chicken	*pollo*
lamb	*cordero*
pork	*cerdo*

Drinks
beer	*cerveza*
coffee	*café*
fruit juice	*zumo*
milk	*leche*
tea	*té*
water	*agua*
wine (red)	*vino tinto*
wine (white)	*vino blanco*

Shopping
I'd like to buy …	*Me gustaría comprar …*
How much is it?	*¿Cuánto es?*
I don't like it	*No me gusta*
I'll take it	*Me lo llevo*
Do you accept …?	*¿Acepta usted …?*
credit card	*tarjeta*
more	*más*
less	*menos*
smaller	*más pequeño*
bigger	*más grande*

Communications
I'm looking for …	*Estoy buscando …*
bank	*banco*
post office	*correos*

tourist office / *oficina de turismo*

Health

diarrhoea	*diarrea*
doctor	*médico*
prescription	*prescripción*
pharmacy	*farmacia*
painkiller	*analgésico*
antibiotic	*antibiótico*
antiseptic	*antiséptico*
tampon	*tampón*
condom	*preservativo*
sunblock	*protector solar*
I am asthmatic	*Soy asmático*
I am epileptic	*Soy epiléptico*
I am diabetic	*Soy diabético*
I'm allergic to …	*Soy alérgico a …*
penicillin	* penicilina*
nuts	* frutos secos*
bees	* abejas*

Other

my/mine	*mío*
ours/yours	*nuestro/vuestro*
and/some/but	*y/algunos/pero*
this/that	*esto/aquello*
cheap	*barato*
expensive	*caro*
beautiful/ugly	*bonito/feo*
old/new	*viejo/nuevo*
good/bad	*bien, bueno/malo*
early/late	*pronto/tarde*
hot/cold	*caliente/frío*
difficult/easy	*difícil/fácil*

Emergency

Help!	*¡Socorro!*
Call a doctor!	*¡Llamad a un médico!*
I'm lost	*Me he perdido*
Go away!	*¡Vete!*
police	*policía*
fire	*fuego*
ambulance	*ambulancia*
hospital	*hospital*
I'm not feeling well	*No me encuentro bien*
I'm injured	*Estoy herido*
I have a blister	*Me ha salido una ampolla*

Nature and surroundings

river	*río*
stream	*arroyo, corriente*
lake	*lago*
reservoir	*embalse*
mountain	*montaña*
mountain pass	*puerto*
trail	*camino, sendero*
asphalt, tarmac	*asfalto*
forest	*bosque*

Directions

descent	*descenso*
ascent	*ascenso*
east	*este*
west	*oeste*
north	*norte*
south	*sur*

THE JESUITS IN THE MODERN WORLD — *Padre Josep Lluis Iriberri, sj*

Even in Ignatius's time, the Jesuits extended their influence across all continents and their presence today remains in the apostleships that were accepted from the outset in colleges, parishes and universities. To these institutions can be added some new ones, such as the Jesuit Service for Refugees, the Faith and Culture Centres and 'pilgrimage tourism' through the obvious example of the Camino Ignaciano.

As of 2021, 14,839 Jesuits continue to serve, advancing the mission that Ignatius established in the 16th century. Their presence can be found on every continent, albeit in disparate and declining numbers. The largest group is in Asia (5,492), followed by Europe (3,573) and the United States/Canada (2,183). The Jesuits have always sought to adapt in each moment to historical circumstances, since in their DNA is the desire to provide a more extensive and better service to specific local communities, as well as to humanity in general. The unique characteristic of the Jesuits, therefore, has been the inculturation of the Gospel into the various cultures to which they have been sent. Confronted with the challenge with which global humanity finds itself currently facing, namely having to struggle for its survival on the planet, the Jesuits have defined four mission statements for the future, which constitute a 'horizon' towards which they wish to direct their priorities for action:

Equipment

shoelaces	*cordones*
sunscreen	*crema solar*
map	*mapa*
mobile signal	*señal móvil*
campground	*camping*
tent	*tienda (note this also means 'shop')*
hiking boots	*botas*
walking stick	*baston*
hat	*sombrero*
backpack	*mochila*
water bottle	*botella de agua*

1. To show the path towards God. This is a matter of applying to the 21st century the *Spiritual Exercises* which Ignatius experienced from his time in Manresa in 1522. The Camino Ignaciano is an ideal tool through which to live, through the experience of pilgrimage, in the manner shown to us by the Gospels and the autobiography of Ignatius of Loyola, and to allow us to meet God.
2. To walk with the 'excluded'. This is a question of recreating in our world the style of Ignatius, who assumed a burden for social action in favour of the prostitutes and the poor people of Rome. Ignatius the pilgrim always very much took into account the needs of the poor, remembering that he himself was one of them during his time in Manresa and Barcelona. In the 21st century, the Jesuits do not want to stray from the original inspiration of their founder.
3. To accompany young people on the Camino. Youth is the future. To accompany them on their own journey to maturity is a priority. The Camino Ignaciano is an instrument for this development, which one would hope to be a personal and profound maturity, in harmony with the world of justice and peace for all.
4. To take care of our 'Communal House'. The Jesuits recognise the urgency for direct actions which help to alleviate, if not actually solve, the many ecological problems which we have created. To collaborate in the social initiatives which orientate towards this goal and which promote love towards Creation is a priority of the Company of Jesus.

Appendix 2

FURTHER INFORMATION
BOOKS
The Jesuits
O'Malley, John W *The Jesuits, A History from Ignatius to the Present* Rowman and Littlefield, 2014. Concise and well-balanced history.

General
Buck, Tobias *After the Fall* Weidenfeld & Nicholson, 2019. For those interested in modern Spanish history, this excellent book looks at Spanish issues through a series of essays, ranging from Catalan Nationalism, the rise of populist parties, the Franco legacy, unemployment, the banking crash and more. Recommended.
Chislett, William *Spain: What Everyone Needs to Know* Oxford University Press, 2013. A compact history of Spain from the period of Muslim conquest in 711 to beyond the Franco period.
Tremlett, Giles *Ghosts of Spain* Faber and Faber, 2006. A number of insightful and thought-provoking chapters take the reader through a journey across Spanish modern history and everyday life. Recommended.

Travel guides
Stewart, Murray *The Basque Country & Navarre* Bradt, 2019
Symington, Andy *Bilbao & Basque Region* Footprint, 2017
Symington, Andy *Northern Spain* Footprint, 2017

WEBSITES
w caminoignaciano.org The official website of the route, administered by the Jesuits. Useful content for those who want to follow a spiritual journey, as well as a physical one.
w caminoignaciano.co.uk The author's own website, covering the Camino Ignaciano.
w Catalonia.com Official tourism website for Catalonia; see ad, page 210
w lariojaturismo.com/en Official tourism website for La Rioja; see ad, page 104
w tourism.euskadi.eus/en Official tourism website for the Basque Country; see ad, page 64
w turismodearagon.com/en Official tourism website for Áragon
w visitnavarra.es Official tourism website for Navarre; see ad, page 142

Index

Main entries are in **bold**, maps are in *italics*.

accommodation 36–8
   camping 36–7
   hostales and *pensiones* 37–8
   hotels 38
   pilgrims' hostels 37
Agoncillo 116, 120
Aguas Mansas (castle) 116
Aizkorri–Aratz 2, 67–8
Alagón 158, 159
Alcalá de Ebro 154–5
Alcanadre 119–20
Alcarrás 202, 206
Alda 82, 83–4
Alfaro 30, 128–9, **130–3**
Amics del Camí ('Friends of the Way') 214
amphibians 11
Aragón 25–6
Araia 76–7
Arantzazu 29, 70–1, 72
Arrúbal 117, 120
Azkoitia 58, 63
Azpeitia, railway museum 57

backpack 45
Basque Country, The 20–3
Bell-lloc d'Urgell 214–15
Bellpuig 218, 219
   Motocross Circuit 220–1
Bilbao 21, 44
birds **8–10**, 128–9, 138
boots, hiking 45–6
budgeting 41
Bujaraloz 183, **187**, **188**

Butsènit 204

Calahorra 124–6
Calle del Laurel (Logroño) 111
Camí dels Degotalls 242
Camino de Santiago viii, 16, 19, 24, 98
Canal Imperial 150
Candasnos 192
car, touring the camino by 20–1
Cartuja Baja 171, **173**
Castejón 135
Castellgalí 250–1, 254
Castellnau de Seana 218
Castillo de Cortes 146
Castillo Maitierra (winery) 124
Catalonia 26–7
Catherine of Aragón 151
certificate of completion 33
Cervera 224, 226–8
cheese **59**, 75
children, travelling with 42
climate **4–5**
clothing 44–7
conservation 7
credenciál 32–3
currency 40

Desert Festival, Los Monegros 195
Don Quixote 151, 155
donkey trekking 31

drinks 40

eating and drinking 38–40
eating out 39–40
Ebro, River 2, 3, **114**, 171
El Palau d'Anglesola 214, 215–16
Embalse de la Grajera 105
emergencies 49
enclaves 161
equipment 44–9

Ferdinand II 150
flag, Catalan 203
flora and fauna 5–12
food 38–40
footwear 45–6
Fraga 194, **197–9**
Francis Xavier 141
Franco, General 7, 250
Fuenmayor, 100, 102
Fuentes de Ebro 175, 177

Gallur 151
Genevilla 88, 89
geography 2
geology 2
getting around 35–6
getting there and away 34–5
Goya, Francisco 169
grading (stages) ii

Hemingway, Ernest 25
highlights 29–31
Ignatius **12–13**, 154, 257
Igualada 235, **236–7**

269

Jesuits **12–18**, 266–7
Jorba 234

kids, travelling with 42
Kripan 94, 95

La Panadella 233
La Rioja 23–4
Laguardia 29, **96–7**, 98
language **18**, 23, 27, 199, 236–7, 259–67
Lapuebla de Labarca 99
Legazpi 66
Lleida 27, 30, **206–9**, *208*, 211
Logroño **107–11**, *110*
Los Llanos (dolmen) 95
Los Monegros 3, 4, 6, 30, 78, **179**, 182, 186, 195
Loyola 53–7
 casa natal or *casa torre* 55
 sanctuary 55–7
Luceni 153

Mallén 143, 149
mammals 10–11
Manresa 31, 248, **252–8**
 Pilgrim Welcome Centre 253, **254**
 1522 Exhibition 258
 Balç Street Interpretation Centre 257–8
 Basilica de la Seu 256–7
 Santuari de la Cova (The Cave) 256
maps and apps 42–3
Marqués de Montecierzo 136
Márquez, Marc 220–1, 228
Meano 91, 92

mobile phones 41
money 40–1
Montserrat 242–5
 monastery 31, 238, 243–5
Morris, Jan 151
motorbike racing 220–1, 228
mountain rescue services 49
mudéjar architecture 158

Navarre 24–5
Navarrete 101–2
Navas de Tolosa (battle) 137

Oller del Mas **253**, 254
Orbiso 87
Osborne bull 109

packing 44–9
passport, pilgrim's 32–3
pelota 63
Pere Claver 223
Pignatelli, Ramón 145
pilgrimage 16–17
Prao de la Paúl 96, 98
protected areas 7
public holidays 42
public transport 35–6

Ramón y Cajal, Santiago 161
red tape 32
reptiles 11
rucksacks 45

safety 49
San Martín de Berberana 118
San Román de Millán 77, 79
San Vicente de Arana 84, 85

Sancho Panza 151, 155
Sant Pere dels Arquells 232
Santa Cruz de Campezo 88
Segre, River 204
snails 207
Society of Jesus *see* Jesuits
sotos **134**, 137
Spanish Civil War 250
storks **128–9**, 132

Tàrrega 217, 220, 221, 224–5
taxis 36
telephones 41
tour operators 32
tourist information 31, 268
trail markings 43–4
Tudela (de Navarra) 139–42

Urola, River 2
Utebo 162–3

Valle de Arana 78, 82
Venta de Santa Lucia 183–4
Verdú 220–3
Vergós 230–1

walking distances/times ii
waymarking 43–4
when to walk 20–1
Wi-Fi 41
wildlife 8–12
wind power 162
wine, Catalonian 254
wine, Rioja 112

Zaragoza 26, 30, 160, **164–70**, *168*
Zumarraga 61–3